The Genesis of Somalia's Anarchy
A Footprint in the Past

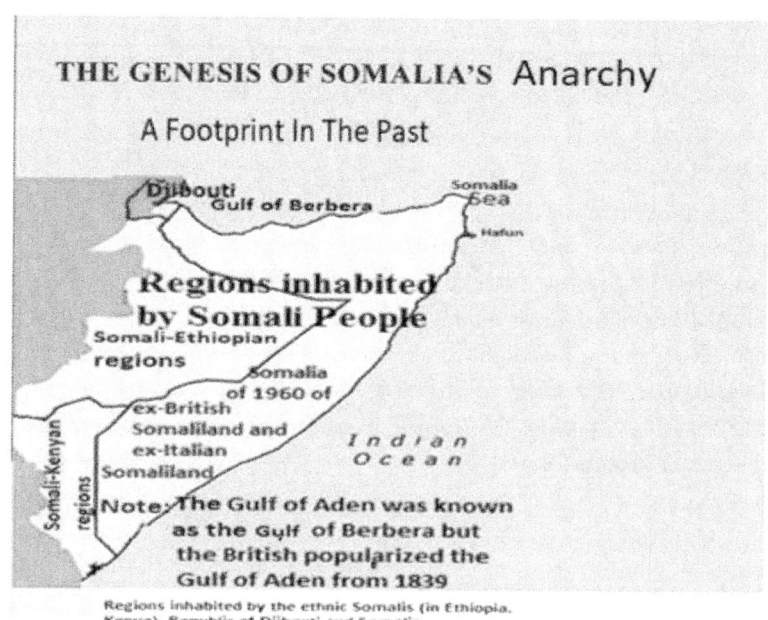

Ali Abdigir authored more than 20 books, fiction and nonfiction

The Genesis of Somalia's Anarchy is a chronological approach of telling the history of the Somalis of over 5000 years.

Copyright@ Ali Mohamed Abdigir (Aliganay) Second Edition, 2020, USA   The Genesis of Somalia's Anarchy: A Footprint in the past
All the rights for Ali Mohamed Abdigir
 (caliganay54@hotmail.com/abdigir54@gmail. com).
Copyright@ Ali Mohamed Abdigir
First Edition, 2019, KPD.amazon.com, USA
Genesis of Somalia's Anarchy (Sequential events of the Somalis), ISBN: 9781091869363

Spelling of Somali cities and other names

Almost all the Somali cities and places are spelled in Somali, with long vowels. You will see Hiiraan, Gaalkacyo, Burco, Sheekh, Hargeysa, Boorama, Kismaayo, Ceerigaabo, Laas-Caanood, Laas-geel Dhuusamareeb, Majeerteen, Isaaq, Hawiye, raxanweyn (Rahanweyn), Daarood and so many.

Contents

Acknowledgements 8
Preface 11
Chapter One
  Ancient Footprints 15
CHAPTER TWO
  Ancient Egyptians and Puntites 17
CHAPTER THREE
  Modern Footprints 1 31
CHAPTER FOUR
  Modern Footprints 2 43
Chapter FIVE
  Betrayal of Treaties 60
CHAPTER SIX
  The Exile Government of Sayid Hassan 77
Chapter SEVEN
  The fall of Exile Government 97
CHAPTER EIGHT
  Geoffrey Archer V Sayid Mohamed 107
CHAPTER NINE (1969-1977)
  WW2 and the Somali Nationalism 114
Chapter TEN
  The New Republic 125
Chapter ELEVEN
  Military Government 149
Chapter Twelve
  Clan Exploitation 161
Chapter Thirteen
  Wide Spread Revolts 171
Chapter Fourteen
  The major Turmoil 182

Chapter Fifteen
   Last Day of Barre's President   188
Chapter Sixteen
   Further Disintegration   201
   Chapter Seventeen
   The Intervention of Southern Somalia   217
   Chapter Eighteen
   Consequences of Undefined Objectives   228
   Chapter Nineteen
   Canadian Arms Role of Restore Hope   241
   Chapter Twenty
   What it takes to Negotiate   251
   Sequential Dates (Appendix A)   268
   Index   273

Acknowledgements

After all the thanks for Almighty, I thank my wife, Ms. Hidigo G. Ahmed who does make sure I have a quiet time in the house.

There is a statement I learned in my early schooling years which never slips from the mind. If you understand the problem, you have taken the first step toward a solution. If you know an honest scholar to call about your subject when you need help is a blessing. Farah Mohamud Mohamed, the author of The *Timelines of Somali History: 1400-2000 (a guide for Somali historians), Saxarla (novel), Queen Arraweelo* and many more always answer my calls. He advised me so many times to rewrite a sentence in terms of appropriateness, clarity and a point of history or a fact. It has been my pleasure and luck to have Farah as a friend, scholar and as an adviser.

I convey my appreciation to Abdullahi M. Abdi, Dr. Yusuf M. Abdi, Ahmed Ibrahim Awale (author of many books like Dirkii Sacmaallada, Mystery of land of
Punt Unraveled), Abdisaid Abdi Ismail (Author of Xadka Riddada Maxaa ka run ah? Halgankii tukeyaasha) and Dr. Ibrahim Abikar Noor (Somali airlines ex-pilot) who all gave me valuable advice about the manuscript.

I would also like to express my gratitude to Abdullahi Ahmed Abdulle (Azhari), an Ex-pilot and the author of *Burburkii Bulshada iyo Barakicii Duuliyeyaasha* who always reads my manuscripts with keen interests and does not hesitate to give an honest critique.

To my wife Hidigo G. Ahmed and my children Safiyo, Ebyan, Sharmaarke, Dalmar, Bilan, Bashir, Sagal, Bashi and Basro, and to my mom who could not witness the success of her boys. I also dedicate this draft to the Somalis in all over the world.

Preface

A people without the knowledge of their past history, origin and culture is like a tree without roots. __Marcus Garvey

It is hard to be impartial in a society that authorship and reading have no strong roots in its culture. At the same time, as a writer, you are legally bound to mention the source of quotations in your writings instead of passing them as your own. Most of the time, the Somalis prejudge their authors with such quotations. However, that shall not discourage them from writing. This book examines how some pieces of Somalis' history were documented

Many entries in this book may shock and surprise some readers. We pieced together fragments of Somali stories which will raise the eyebrows of many. Laas geel rock arts near Hargeysa contain some of the earliest known rock art on the African continent and features many elaborate pastoralist sketches of animal and human figures. Café drawings, and archaeological findings also hint that the Ancient Somalis are the first people who domesticated the camel during the 3rd and 2nd Millennium BC and developed a profitable trade system.

The Genesis of Somalia's Anarchy is a footprint of Somali history to the present (2020). *"Intii qar jirey, quruurux isna waa jirey (roughly: As long as rocks existed, fragments existed)."* This is another way of saying "People have inhabited the Somali peninsula for practically as long as anywhere on earth. And there is no reason to assume that those inhabitants were other than the ancestors of the Somalis."

The history of the Somali is much older than the one of the Egyptian Pharaohs. Historians and archeologists are almost concluding that Pharaohs originated from Eastern Africa—closely from the eastern-most of Africa, presently Somalia. Egyptian Dynasties always dreamed of getting to The Land of Gods, Land of Exotic Smells, The Paradisal Land, The Sacred Land, The Land of Punt. They used all those names for a single geographical location, The Land of Punt.

But the Somali history should be rewritten by honest historians. Mainly for lack of funds and public enthusiasm, Somali scholars and the general educators as well do not put much effort into the researches of their history and make their conclusions from their findings. Such misfortunes place the Somalis and the Africans in general in a disadvantaged situation of screening out the narrations of dishonest Western and Arabian scholars about the history of Africa. The *Genesis of Somalia's Anarchy: A footprint in the Past* consists of 20 chapters. At least four of them speak of the people's history before the European dismemberment.

Ifat Sultanate in the northwest which overthrew Showa kingdom in 1285 and Ajuuraan Sultanate around Banaadir region flourished during the Middle Ages. Their successor states continued to thrive through the 16th and 19th centuries respectively. We have to remind the reader one thing. Some historians push the date of born of Ifat to 9th century, but 13th century is the most common.

The Warsangeli Sultanate also born in 1298 did not rule a large area and not as famous as Adal-Ifat. We can think of a couple of reasons why it expanded not enough. It had no adversaries since Ifat-Adal Sultanate was in between itself and the Abyssinians. Also, both Berbera and Saylac had far better commercial importance than Laas Qoray, the base of the Warsangeli Sultanate. Much is not known also if the Sultanate had expanded its influence to the northeastern regions, which mid—eighteenth century got a new kingdom, the Omaniyah—and later Sultanate of Yusuf Ali of Hobyo branched from it. There were two Sultanates around the southern Somalia.

Gelledi sultanate which overthrew Ajuuraan Sultanate late-17th century existed until it succumbed to the Italians in 1908. Ifat/Adal, Warsangeli, and Ajuuraan Sultanates, all came into life during the 13th century. We can say therefore, a wind of the Sultanate was blowing on the Somali peninsula in that century. *Sultan Abdullahi Deria, Sultan Abdullahi Sultan and Sultan Mohamud Ali signed treaties with the British, Sultan Yusuf Ali (cousin of Boqor Osman Mohamud), and Boqor Osman Mohamoud, signed treaties with the Italians.*

The rest of the country which later became Somalia in 1960, various local Somali authorities, Sultan Osman Ahmed of the Gelledi Sultanate and Zanzibari Sultanate, which controlled an area including Warsheekh (now part of the middle Shabeelle region) with horror oo slavery, signed with the Italians. The traditional leaders of the Issas and the Afars of the Jabuuti peninsula had signed off their land to France as well.

With or without the signatures of the traditional leaders, the Europeans had the will and the resources to occupy. But those Somali leaders mentioned had the same choices as Sayid Mohamed Abdulle Hassan (1856—1920). Therefore, that is why Tom J. Farer, the author of *War Clouds on The Horn of Africa: A Crisis for Détente wrote*, "No account of Somali modern history would be complete without some reference to the unsuccessful war of independence organized and led by Sayid Mohamed Abdulle Hassan." Further researches are deemed necessary of what disease, Malaria or influenza that killed Sayid M. A. Hassan and many of his diehards. <u>Was that the Spanish Flu (A strain of H1N1 Flu, A Promised Land, Obama, 2020, page 385) of 1918—1920, other flu or Malaria?</u>

During World War Two, African nationalism escalated, and that did not only rekindle the Somali nationalism, but the Italian-Somaliland became one of those colonies which the Potsdam (German city, July 17-August 2, 1945 of Russia, Great Britain and USA) Conference decided not to return them to Italy as a colony. Since it was defeated, the Italian colonies before the war were taken over by France and UK colonies.

The Somalis were a nation of a clan and used to fight among themselves for water and pasture, and used to defend against intruders as well. That is what a nation is all about, but the bad part of that is that the Somalis did not document the history, somebody else did in their own world view.

In 1947, with a new name, Somali Youth League (SYL) with an anti-Italian attitude, and by a dynamic leadership of Abdullahi Isse (1922—1988), a real Somali nationalist, the movement took an independence agenda to the United Nations. There is no way of going back from that British Somaliland and Italian Somaliland made Somalia, but that was an emotional and circumstantial, built on weak foundations. Reevaluating the footprint and analyzing that, both financially and educationally, the nation was not in a position to govern itself. You will see some quotations by the Somali intellectuals of the time. The Somali National League (SNL, formed 1935 or

1936) of British Somaliland and the Somali Youth League (SYL, formed 1943) led the nation into a statehood but stumbled into mismanagement and corruption. What made worse was the military administration of 1969, which is credited to the current (2020) chaos running in its 32nd year.

The year 1974 was unique in Somalia. More than four main events that each came with its circumstances took place. Somalia became a member of the Arab league. It became the only non-Arabic speaking member. The linkage of Puntland to the Arabs is not by blood. It is rather of the proximity, religion and a matter of economic interests. Some non-Arab African nations further distanced themselves from Somalia. The alliance created a confusion of whether the Somalis see themselves as Arabs or black Africans.

There was an African Union Meeting which did not help the economy though with just a temporary face-lifting for the administration. The Supreme Revolutionary Council (SRC) Council went further than the introduction of the Somali script. The literacy campaign of 1974 was one of the best remembered of the military regime. When the military toppled the democratic administration in October of 1969, more than eighty percent (not many disputes this number, or not controversial to say) of the population were nomads and could not read and write any script. *The Road to Zero by Mohamed Osman Omar, p67, "In the first years of independence, the issue of the introduction of a script for the Somali language was debated…. When rumors spread that the Government intended to adopt the Latin script, there was a huge demonstration after the Friday prayers, with the crowd chanting the slogan: Latin, Ladin," the latter word is Arabic for atheism or without religio."*

There has never been any proper census taken, not even in the towns. The figures that the Government and the international organization used were estimations. As I was one of the students, literacy campaign was a challenging and testing job to have undertaken. During the last two months of the campaign, while performing our duties, we were trained to learn how to take a census—the fourth main event of 1974. More than 20,000 of intermediate, high school students and teachers participated in the operation.

According to (Aadan Maxamed Cali (Maalmihii Noloshayda (Days of my Life, 64))), the minister of education of the time, "more than 28,000 personnel including the students and the teachers took part in the overall operation." The census which was the most difficult and the second part of the campaign was done in 1975. But was not smooth operation.

Characteristically, the Somalis are curious, questioning and independent people by nature. Therefore, it was hard to convince them of why their number and the number of their animals were being investigated. Those events and more created a new political atmosphere in the Horn. Sometime in WORLD WAR TWO, a British officer said to an old Somali man, "What do you want most?" "To be well governed, but to be left alone," the old man. The officer wrote, "I often thought of that and found that I agreed with it, but how to get it?"

The real Somali civil war started in 1988. Any administration of Somalia before that was better off of whatever came after 1991. The military administration killed less than 60, 000 (50,000+ in the north (Somalia: The Untold Story, page 5, Making Sense of Somali History, by Abdurahman Abdullahi (Baadiyow), 154)), but in Mogadishu (believed to be built in 908, Sir Charles Eliot, 1905, 11) alone, in 1991, 200,000 were killed.   [Twentieth Century Atlas __Death tolls and Casualty Statistics for Wars, Dictatorships and Genocides (www.users.erols.com, Conflict Trends (no. 23)), Real-Time Analysis of African Political Violence, February 2014), from 1991 to 2013, the people killed in Somalia are 510,000. Add that to 50,000 killed in the north in 1988-1990, more than 5000 persons in Gaalkacyo and the surroundings including clan-war fares]. The Civil War caused the deaths of more than 600,000 people, and unfortunately, it is not something only in the past. We will cover appropriately.

Without the massive airlifts of relief supplies, especially the most needed food and medicine to remote areas by the U.S. Air Force, the German Air Force, the Royal Canadian, and many others, the number of people died for starvation would have been much higher than it was when the operation ended in 1994. About the Operation Restore Hope of 1992, America lost 44 servicemen in Somalia. The original justification for sending foreign troops to Somalia was easy and appropriate, and the exit was quick with disappointment. The UN failed Somalia politically when it took sides in the internal power struggles.

In a time of uncertainty and crisis, people look for leaders who stand up for the challenge to solve problems, and take the necessary steps to save the people. Those who stood for that challenge and that the people lined behind them, could not go above clan mentality and egoism. After that, the road is the present (2020) Tiih (loop of chaos, maybe Meehanaw or Jaahwareer in Somali).

The Genesis of Somalia's Anarchy takes you on a path of chronological approach of telling the history of the Somalis of over 5000 years. The current writers and researchers plus the coming generations have a chance to choose topics to expand. The language used in this book is very simple with short sentences.

Before moving to the other 20 chapters of the book, we pre-mention some footprints that need in-depth researches of the systems of those who occupied the Somali peninsula. The Somali people in pre-Islamic times are believed to have adhered to a complex henotheistic system (religious system), with a set of deities superseded by a single all-powerful figure called "Eebbe (God, as known as Waaq). Even the Somali scholars are not comfortable to find the religious backgrounds of this nation on the eastern horn of Africa. Religious temples dating from Antiquity known as Taallo (coming figure) by the Somalis were the centers where important ceremonies were held by a Wadaad priest.

The questions which the generations ask: If the scientists are allowed to dig those unique and ancient graves, will we know more of the Somali religions, cultures and civilizations?

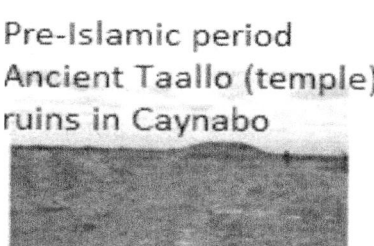

Pre-Islamic period
Ancient Taallo (temple) ruins in Caynabo

The Omani slave traders in southern Somalia who were nothing but horror, the Turks and the Egyptians inserted their influences only at the coasts. The only thing learned from them is the Islamic religion, which even the Somalis neither flowed its principles. Italy colonized southern Somalia for over 60 years, Britain over 80 years on northern Somalia and North Eastern region of Kenya and France more than 110 years over Djibouti.

"Justice delayed is a justice denied," Martin Luther King. Though the Europeans colonialists violated their treaties with the Somali clans, they had installed two very important policies—the introduction of schooling and the abolition of slavery. The events that have helped the collapse of Somalia and anarchism afterward will enlighten the young generations to pursue further researches.

Preface referenced notes
__The East Africa Protectorate, 1905 by Charles Eliot
__Archaeological expedition of a British-Somali in the northern half of Somalia lead by Dr. Neville H. Chittick of Britain (1924 –1984)
__Aksum and Nubia   11
__Periplus of Erytharean Sea
__War Clouds on The Horn of Africa: A Crisis for Détente
__Oxford Atlas of the World, 1490 BCE:284
__Modern Middle East Nations and Their Strategic Place in the __World: Somalia by LeeAnne Gellettly, 2004, Mason
__Maalmihii Noloshayda (Days of my Life, 64)
_Conquest of Abyssinia

Chapter One

Ancient Footprints

   Somalis are always on the move, always seeking fresh pastures. We the Somali writers and others as well are also on the move to dig the other untold chapters of the Somali history. We cannot just be happy with what others wrote about the Somalis. In the pursuit of the unknown, the researches, writings, and rewritings of the Somali history should be a never-ending drive. We will cover many types of Somali nationalism in various forms and stages.
   It is hard to swallow that 1415 AD is the first time that the name "Somali" came into writing. One of the worst battles between Abyssinian Emperors and Somali/Islamic Sultans took place more than a century later.
   As far as humans lived on earth, Somalis lived in the Horn of Africa. Phillip Briggs said on page 3 of his book 'Somaliland with Addis Ababa and Eastern Ethiopia,' "People have inhabited the Somali region for practically as long as anywhere on earth." And there is no reason to assume that those inhabitants were other than the ancestors of the Somalis. There is another important possibility we put in here.

Humans have not come up yet anything different that Africa is the continent of the human origins. Somalia is the most eastern country of Africa having access to very important straights, the Red Sea, to Bab-Al-Mandab connecting to the Gulf of Berbera to the Somali Sea (Cape Guardafui below the Arabian Sea) and then south-westward along the Indian ocean to Raas Kaambooni at the so-called border with Kenya.

Hence, perhaps, the Horn of Africans are one or one of the first candidates who populated the rest of the world around 200,000 years ago. The narrowest non-man-made straits that probably Africans crossed to the rest of the world are between Africa and Arabia, and Africa and Europe. They are the *Strait of Bab Al Mendab* (gate of tears) between Yemen on the Arabian Peninsula and Djibouti in the Horn of Africa (32 KM), and the *strait of Gibraltar* between Morocco and Spain (15 KM).

Ancient Egyptian Kingdoms had close relationships with the inhabitants of the Eastern Horn of Africa, the Puntites. Records show that Pharaoh Sahure (2500 BC, Somaliland with Addis Ababa and Eastern Ethiopia, 4) and Pharaoh Hatshepsut, the first female Pharaoh traveled to the waters of Puntites, the Gulf of Berbera while some other expeditions are not known yet. It is less than 200 years from 1839 AD, when the British captured the harbor of Aden, present-day Yemen and campaigned to call the water between Yemen and Somalia "the Gulf of Aden."

The waters were the Gulf of Berbera and the Somalian Sea (Cover) even before the Julian and Gregorian Calendars (from 45 BC up to 1582 AD is known as Julian Calendar and the whole AD (after death) which runs now 2020 is called Gregorian calendar).

King Mernera, a pharaoh of the sixth Dynasty ordered Harkhuf, a nobleman of the kingdom to make expeditions into Nubia and further to the Land of Punt (The Horizon History of Africa, volume 1, 55). Pharaoh Hatshepsut made a reality about less than 3,514 years ago from today, 2020. The exact dates of the expedition are not exactly in agreement but very close in times. Oxford Atlas of the World, 1490 BCE:284 and Modern Middle East Nations and Their Strategic Place in the World: Somalia by LeeAnne Gellettly, 2004, Mason Crest Publishers, Making Sense of Somali History by Dr. Abdurahman Baadiyow, page 46, made the time of the expedition, 1493 BC:31. The queen Hatshepsut (1507-1458 BC) was in power 1493—1479 BC (24 years though the last 4 years are in dispute of her reign).

The exact location of the Land of Punt is still disputed by some historians, scholars, archeologists, and others in the present day. It has been cited as part of the Arabia, present-day Somalia (most eastern of Africa) of Puntland State of Somalia at the Horn of Africa, the Sudan, Eritrea, Djibouti, or some other internal region of East Africa. The debates continue as to where Punt located with scholars, and others. The Egyptology (the study of the origins of the ancient Egyptians (pharaohs)) is mainly alive from the side of the Western historians and scholars.

Though many of those (western) historians and scholars are now in the final process of sorting out where in Eastern Africa the Pharaohs originated, seven decades ago, they could not accept that such a sophisticated and great civilization of Egypt was born and developed in Africa. Western archeologists, scholars, and historians were looking for a "Master race" which conquered Egypt and ruled. Genesis of the Pharaohs: Dramatic discoveries That Rewrite the Origins of Ancient Egypt, 2003, by Toby Wilkinson, p187:

Archeologizing and rewriting some pieces of the world history is an ending and tiresome human endeavor. Pharaonic civilization is an Egyptian civilization, indeed is an African Phenomenon, yet, there has still been a huge 'missing link' in the evolution of ancient Egypt. Scholars have had to take it on trust that of the most characteristic elements of Egyptian art, religion and symbolism must have originated within the northern-most corner of Africa; but there has been no proof until now. The Eastern desert rock art described and analyzed in this book "represents nothing than the discovery of that missing link.

Not only the Horn of the African countries have no enough resources to take part in Egyptology, but they also may not give a keen interest in its importance. It is almost certain now that the historians narrow down where in Eastern Africa the ancestors of the Pharaohs originated, Sudan, Eritrea, or from Djibouti up to the Promontory of the Incenses (Raas Casayr region). Many believe that the Pharaohs were not sailing to the southern coast (Somalia waters) of the Gulf of Berbera just for incenses (Frankincense and Myrrh).

Above: Queen Ati and King Perahu of Punt and their Attendants as depicted on Pharaoh Hatshepsut's Temple at Deir El-Bahri (Genesis of the Pharaohs).

The below (figure): The present-day inhabitants of the Eastern Desert. Three generations of a Bedouin family eke out an existence, a simple portable hut of mats and animal skins providing the only shelter from the intense sun and heat. This traditional way of life is increasingly
rare in modern Egypt (page 33). ****

Courtesy of Genesis of The Pharaohs by Toby Wilkinson

In the Somali inhabited areas, this way of life is very common. Camels are the most means of rural transport.

There was also a time that some of the outsiders had unknowingly called the inhabitants of the Horn of Africa as only Ethiopians (61, The Horizon History of Africa), but the eastern tribes were independent communities of their own. Also, Richard Burton characterized the Somalis as "A fierce and turbulent race of republicans when men were characterized as warriors (Waranle) and a man of religion (Wadaad)."

However, the two eastern groups of tribes knew each other as of Ethiopians (Greek term for black skinned people, ancient kingdom of Aksum) and Somalis. The oldest known kingdom in the Eastern Horn was Ifat. it flourished from 1285 to 1415 as an independent and uninterrupted kingdom when even the king, Saad-adin was killed. The Kingdom did not die for good until mid-16th century.

Chapter one referenced notes

Somaliland with Addis Ababa and Eastern Ethiopia by Philip Briggs, 4
The Holy Land of Punt, 4
A Voice for Somalia, Preface (12) by Mary Therese Robinson, the president of Ireland December 1990 to September 1997 who has observed the disaster in Somalia—in October 3-4, 1992.
Oxford Atlas of the World, 1490 BCE:284 and Modern Middle East Nations and Their Strategic Place in the World: Somalia by LeeAnne Gellettly, 2004, Mason Crest Publishers, 1493 BCE:31.
Rambles, 14
Futuh Al Habash Or the Conquest of Abyssinia
The Consul at Sunset, 1951 by Gerald
The Horizon History of Africa, 142
Portuguese East Africa by Reginald. C. F. Maugham, 259
Tanzania Notes of Records: The Journal of the Tanzania Society, p97
Somaliland with Addis Ababa and eastern Ethiopia by Philip Briggs, 2012, 7
The Horizon History of Africa of American Heritage Publishing, volume 1, 160161
The Economist, July 10[th,] 1993
Douglas Jardine: 315
Mad Mullah: The Sword of rebellion by Julian D. Warner, 217-218
The portion of Somali Territory Under Ethiopia Colonization: Somali Government Publications 1974, 25
Somalia: The Untold Story, page 5
Twentieth Century Atlas __Death tolls and Casualty Statistics for Wars, Dictatorships and Genocides
(www.users.erols.com, Conflict Trends (no. 23)) Real-Time Analysis of African Political Violence, February 2014
Somalia: The Untold Story, page 209
Wolfgang Weber of Die Zeit (World Press Review, March 1988)
Resolution # 733 on January 23, 1991 about the chaos in Somalia
In the Company of Heroes by Michael J. Durant, 2003, p.2 Current History: 201, May 1993

Chapter TWO

Ancient Egyptian and Puntites

"Dr. Neville H. Chittick of Britain (1924 –1984) led a British-Somali archaeological expedition in the northern half of Somalia. Members of the party included the Director of the Somali National Museum in Mogadishu, Said Ahmad Warsame, as well as 'Ali 'Abdirahman and Fabby Nielson. Particular emphasis was placed on the area near Cape Guardafui (Raas Casayr) in the far northeast—the eastern-most Horn of Africa. The reconnaissance mission found numerous examples of historical artefacts and structures, including ancient coins, Roman pottery, drystone buildings, cairns, mosques, walled enclosures, standing stones and platform monuments.

Many of the finds were of pre-Islamic origin and associated with ancient settlements described by the 1st century *Periplus of the Erythraean Sea*, among other documents. Based on his discoveries, Chittick suggested in particular that the Damo site in the Hafun peninsula likely corresponded with the *Periplus'* "Market and Cape of Spices". Some of the smaller artefacts that Chittick's company found were later deposited for preservation at the British National Museum.

A Site near Daamo, a town of 5 KM west of the Guardafui corner is found depictions of a hunter on a horse. However, it is not clear for this author whether the group of Chittick found that artefact (rock-art) at the location of Dhambalin in Togdheer or at the Daamo site, at one of the many others. According to www.wondemondo.com, there are known locations with rock art, and few of them are Karin Heegan of Sanaag, Jaleelo (paleolithic period) and Abaasa of Awdal, etc. Ancient rock paintings, which dated back between 9000 BC (Neolithic New Stone Age) and 3000 BC, have been found in the northern part of Somalia. These engravings depict an early life in the territory. The most famous of these is the Laas Geel complex. The domestication of cattle (3700 BC) is around the same time. Laas geel contains some of the earliest known rock art on the African continent and features many elaborate pastoralist sketches of animal and human figures. Laas Geel rock arts are sometimes termed as the most vivid in Africa. The quality of the rock art is also very high—specially the originality of the presentation of the cattle.

The general stability of the peninsula which is not appreciable limits further archeological works right now (2020). The artifacts excavated at Laas-Geel near Hargeysa are discussed in the *Mystery of Land of Punt Unravelled* by Ahmed Ibrahim Awale.

The most famous cities of the Bar Ajam (Land of heat) or Northern Somali Coast were Saylac, Berbera, Xiis (His), Maydh and Xaafuun (Hafun). The water was also the Gulf of Berbera and Gulf of Saylac along Saylac area. The chief town and harbour of British-Somaliland from late of 19th century, "Berbera" lying in 10° 26' North Latitude and 45° 4' East Long (Green witch), The Periplus of the Erythraean sea, as well as Ptolemy (Claudius, a Greco-Roman geographer and astronomer of Alexandra around 100 AD) and Cosmas (Cosmas Indecopleustes, 6th century AD was theologist and geographer, and traveled along the shores of Indian Ocean) gave the name "Gulf of Berbers" to the coast of the Land of Frankincense (Somalia) which is one of only four places (Somali section of Ethiopia, Yemen, Oman and Somalia) in the world that Frankincense trees are found; the town itself is probably identical with Μαλάω ἐμπόριον (Berbera).

There is one more clue that may pinpoint that the Land of Punt is the northern regions of Somalia. According to Mystery of Land Punt Unravelled by Ahmed Ibrahim Awale, 2013, page 24, *Boswellia Frereana found in Egyptian Tombs*, which is a member family of the general Frankincense species, "is only found in the northeastern mountain ranges facing the Gulf of Berbera."

When a Greek Empire in Egypt broke up at Alexander's death, Ptolemy became the ruler of an independent of kingdom. The ruling dynasty of the Ptolemies encouraged trading ventures, setting up new ports on the Red Sea coast and extending trade toward the east (east of Red Sea) which becomes the Gulf of Berbera, (V1.62 of The Horizon History of Africa.))

The claim that the pharaohs originated from the Horn of Africa, present-day Somalia, in particular, is unmatched. Before the travels of Periplus of The Erytharean sea (around first century AD) and the rise of Islam (6th century AD), the Pharaohs had been sending expeditions to the Gulf of Berbera. Part of *General Historical Collection of British Library, "The Holy Land of Punt": Racial Dwarfs in the Atlas and The Pyrenees, etc. by Robert Grant Haliburton p.3*:

The Expedition of Hanno to Punt (God's Land) had been hitherto supposed to have been the earliest. But that of Hurkhuf dates back between 5000 and 6000 years. A thousand years separate it from the second expedition of Hatshepsut–that of Hanno which in its turn was a thousand years earlier than the mission of Queen Hatshepsut, so boastfully avowed to be a wonder to gods and men. As her mission went in entirely different direction. From that taken by Hanno, it must have gone to a different country.

Other than those not yet known voyages tried by the pharaohs aimed for the Land of Punt, Hatshepsut took the right route. That route made possible her expedition to get to the Land of Sacred Gods (the land of the Blessed), The Land of Puntland (present-day northern Somalia.)" "Those expeditions searched for the Land of Punt went to west of Egypt—some through the Straits of Gibraltar and down the west coast of Morocco (the Holy Land of Punt, 3)."

From the land of Punt, Queen Hatshepsut returned with exotic trees, exotic animals, minerals and spices, beehive houses, shown in reliefs adorning the southern colonnade of the temple at Dar Al-Bahri (figure below).

Beehive-house shaped Dervish look-out towers (also used as granaries)

Courtesy of The Warrior Mullah: The Horn Aflame 1892—1920 by Ray Beachey (Raymond Wendell Beachey, a Canadian of 1915— 2010).

The Somalis in rural and small villages still use beehive houses. They carry on their camels when moving away for pasture. Which brings us once more to the voyage of Hatshepsut to the Land of Punt, the parents celebrated the birth of their baby-girl Hatshepsut, who later became a very famous queen. The perfumes of the sacred trees used at the celebration were from the land of Punt. We can say then, the dream of the Pharaohs to sail to the Land of Punt was the tale of the ancient dynasties, Queen Hatshepsut in particular. It is also mentioned in certain books that she came back with slaves including "Dwarfs (very short people)". Thirteen years after the death of the Pharaoh Queen Hatshepsut, a group led by a young adventurous Egyptian girl set an expedition to the Gulf of Berbera. Nora to The Land of Punt:

Nora, a young and wealthy Egyptian girl, is bored with the everyday routine of her life. Nora yearns for an exciting adventure like her parents had before she was born. Accompanied by her friend, Dakar, she secretly joins a dangerous expedition to the mysterious Land of Punt. Nora gets more than she bargains for though, like death and disaster plague the expedition. No longer just an exciting adventure, Nora must now fight just to survive.

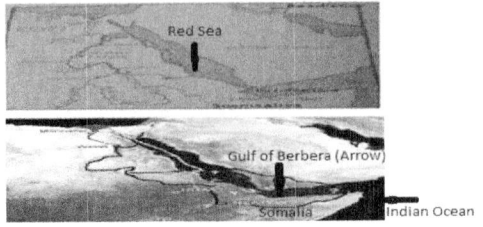

Top: Nora Expedition to The Land of Punt (see Gulf of Berbera).
Bottom: The Ancient Lost Kingdom of Punt is Finally Found: Tarek El-Diwany 2016 (Arrow: Gulf of Berbera).

Nora group started the journey from the top left of Egypt where at the bottom right you see "Land of Punt," the northern coast of Somalia. That was the end of the adventurous journey. The little book, *Nora to the Land of Punt*, talks about slim people who chew khat. They captured them, but they overslept when they ate too much Khat. That gave the Nora group a chance to escape.

Nora to the land of Punt is a fiction book. However, the story which the Ancient Egyptians made expeditions continually to God's Land (Gulf of Berbera), present-day Somalia is written widely. And the book also talks about some habits and the cultures of the Puntites which goes along with other scholarly researches. Not only that. As the book states, the girl used to hear stories about the Land of Punt from her parents, and in that regard, it just adds spices to the main story.

Also, this article which is a scholarly research is identical with to the Nora Expedition (www.ancient.origins.net/*Somalia: The Ancient Lost Kingdom of Punt is Finally Found?, 2016, Tarek El-Diwany*). Hathor Rising: The Power of the Goddess in Ancient Egypt by Alison Roberts, 8 "A great lady of Punt, she (Hathor) is the patroness of the fabulous land of Punt where the Egyptians went in quest of sweet smelling incense, myrrh, gold, spices, and exotic animals."

The theory that the Pharaohs originated from the Eastern Africa, around the Gulf of Berbera gets stronger and stronger and comes from various sources. Rambles in Lion Land by Francis Barrow Pearce, 1893: 232-3:

I discussed a somewhat fanciful theory that the Ancient Egyptians obtained their idea of their obelisks (a stone pillar) from ant-hills similar to those we saw in such numbers (Northern and Western Somaliland). A famous Egyptologist mentions a theory, that the Egyptians before the era of their settlement in the Nile valleys arrived in Africa from the East, crossing over by the straits near the present island of Perim (figure). They occupied, it is stated the land of Abyssinia, and the neighboring lands, and at last found their way to the Nile, where they have us such tangible proofs of their greatness.

The Perim island is between Djibouti and Yemen where the narrowest distance between the countries is 18 miles as mentioned earlier. A private company proposed to build a bridge for about 20 billion US dollars. More clarity of the Perim island, see also where the arrow crosses (figure).

Originally, the cover page map was a British-made and that was how the ethnic Somalis lived in the Peninsula. But there are pieces of history that the British did not state in the way they were. Before 1839 which is the time that Britain captured Aden, the waters currently most people know as the Gulf of Aden and the

Arabian Sea were the Gulf of Berbera and the Somalian Sea (the water of Berbers). Nothing from the human mind is 100% true. History is always open for critique and correction.

There is a reason we took the above (above the figure) statements. No historian can escape from the claim that the Pharaohs came to Egypt from Eastern Africa. The Egyptologist kept going and said (*Rambles in Lion Land, 233*):

They copied in granite these strange natural pillars (Ant-hills (Duddumo (Duddumo-Yulug is the thin tall one (figure coming))), which are such a feature in the landscape. It is accepted now that the ancient kingdom of Punt was situated in the country now known as Somaliland. During the Eleventh Dynasty, the Egyptians penetrated as far as land, and many curious details are known now to their reception, and of the visit of the princess and Queen of Punt to the Egyptian court, in the most approved of modern styles. So, it will be seen that Egypt and Somaliland have had communications even from the dawn of time.

Ant-hills or termite towers are common in northern and western Somalia. Left: Courtesy of Somalia in Pictures by Janice Hamilton and the two in the right are the courtesy of Curious and Googlist Somalis.

More than that, many historians believe that the series expeditions of Ancient Egyptians to the land of Punt were more than looking for Gods and sacred trees (Frankincense and Myrrh). One of the few Somali writers who stands to righteously change the face of Somali history is environmentalist Ahmed Ibrahim Awale. He always looks for historical artifacts and talks about the beauty and the structure of Somaliland (Somali inhabited area in general). In his book, The Mystery of the Land of the Punt Unraveled, second edition, 2015, p. 29-30:

A straight forward answer is that the land of the punt is where ancient Egyptians originated.

E. A. Wallis Budge confirming this claim said "Egyptian tradition of the Dynastic Period held that the aboriginal home of the Egyptians was Punt"; and historians point out that the Egyptians always seemed to be able to remember the way to Punt, even when there had been long periods without contact between the two peoples.

On the same subject, one of the defeats that the Exile Government of Sayid Mohamed Abdulle Hassan suffered at the Ilig, a location near Eyl of Nugaal region, the British talked about the forts of the Daraawiidh, some were as high as 60 feet. The Mad Mullah of Somaliland by Jardine, 282:

The deepest interest attaches to the fortresses which were the lairs of the Mad Mullah's raiding bands. Tale, his principal stronghold, consisted of a stone wall-ring of enormous strength and thickness, with a most elaborate system of guard-chambers and bastions.

The problem of the origin of these great stone-built strongholds in an almost desert land is one of extraordinary interest. The ramparts, with their projections and re-entrant angles, suggest a comparison with the ancient Egyptian forts on the Nile. It seems almost impossible that these buildings can be as ancient as the twelfth dynasty (about 2000 B.C.). Yet we must remember that Somaliland is now generally considered to be the land of Punt which the Egyptians regarded as their motherland, and for which they ever retain a religious veneration.

A landscape of Punt, showing several houses on stilts, two fruiting date palms, three myrrh's, a bird (Hedydiona metallica), a cow, an unidentified fish and a turtle, in water which in the original was green to show that it is salt ot tidal, [1] in a sketch from the walls of the mortuay temple of Hatshepsut at Deir El-Bahri, depicting a royal expedition to Punt.

Below: see details of the depictions

One of the questions being asked by the historians is the first contacts between the Ancient Egyptians and the people of the Land of Punt. Though some notes state that the expedition of Hanno ordered by Pharaoh Sahure got lost, it is almost unanimous that the earliest recorded ancient Egyptian expedition to the Land of Punt was the one organized by Pharaoh Sahure of the 5th Dynasty of 25th century BC. Some even put the dates back to 3700 BC (5,700 years ago from 2020 AD). 4th millennium BC is credited to major changes of human progress including the Bronze Age and the Invention of Writing. When the connection of ancient Egyptians and the people of the Land Punt are concerned, historians and archeologists try to finally agree on the exact location of the Land of Punt. Abdurahman Baadiyow, page 45, "Punt was not only a significant partner in trade, however; it was also a source of cultural and religious influence and a land which the Egyptians viewed as their place of origin and blessed by the gods." Historians are too close to each other to shut that door. If you check website "www.livescience.com," there is a question which is: Are Somalis from Egypt? The answer: Conclusion: Somalia is, now, the ancient Land of Punt: Homeland of the Ancient-Egyptians.

Top left: Ancient Somalis dancing
Bottom-left: modern Somalis dancing
Top-right: Ancient Egyptian dancing
middle-left: Ancient Somali
middle-right: Ancient Egyptian
Bottom-right: Ancient Egyptian adancing

Punt: The land of Punt, which is mentioned in the Bible and in
ancient Egyptian historical works and Hieroglyphics, was probably the area reaching from Eritrea eastward to perhaps the Bari-region of Somalia. Somalis often refer to the Horn of Africa as the Land of Punt. __Historical Dictionary of Somalia by Margaret Castagno, page 128. The word "Punt" in the Bible is not of a surprise since the Christianity religion came first AD century and Islam 6-7th AD century, while Hinduism is the oldest religion in the world, born between 2300 BC and 1500 BC.

Chapter two referenced notes

Periplus of the Erytharean Sea
Black Ancient Egyptians: Evidences of the Black African Origins of Ancient Egyptian Culture, Civilization, Religion and Philosophy , 2006, by Muata Ashby
Baadisooc, Ali Abdigir, 2018
Understanding the Somalia conflagration by Afyare Abdi Elmi:16   Somaliland with Addis Ababa and eastern Ethiopia by Philip Briggs, 2012, p. 7-9
Inside Al-Shabaab: The secret History of Al-Qaeda's most powerful Ally by
Harun Maruf and Dan Joseph, 2018, 279
Somalia in Pictures
The Horizon History of Africa of American Heritage Publishing, volume 1, 164165   Slavery in The Arab World by Murray Gordon, 224
Aksum and Nubia
The Periplus of the Erytharean Sea
The Mad Mullah of Somaliland by Jardine, 225
Archeological Expedition Dr. Neville H. Chittick of Britain (1924 – 1984) with Somali Experts __Making Sense of Somali History, Abdurahman Abdullahi Baadiyow, 2017

CHAPTER THREE
Modern Footprints

Ruins of the Adal Sultanate in Zeila, a kingdom led in the 16th century by Imam Ahmad Ibn Ibrihim (Ahmad Gurey). Remnants of Adal Sultanate, other Somali and Muslim groups in the area, with the help of Ahmad fought back.

The Somalis have a glorious history of struggle for the maintenance of their national independence but not fully documented. 1533, Ahmed Ibrahim Gurey with joined men of the defeated kingdom (Adal) was in complete control of the south and the center of Abyssinia including the highlands of 6000 feet to 8000— some being inaccessible, then further penetrated to the North and effectively occupied almost the whole of Abyssinia for nearly two decades. That campaign of penetration to the northern Abyssinia is known as The Conquest of Abyssinia. There was a time that some Arabian civilizations such Egyptian and Syrians used to call south-eastern Ethiopia as "Country of Zeila (Saylac), because of its commercial importance.

Those obsessed with power may not care about anything but how to rule. There is another side of about the historical background of Ahmed Gurey (1488—1544, or 1506—1543). According to *Futuh Al Habash Or the Conquest of Abyssinia* page V:

Before entering upon the history of the actual conquest of Abyssinia our author devotes a few pages to the early life of his hero. Ahmed began his military career as a knight in the service of Jarrad Abun king of Barr Sa'd (Sacad) Al Din, that is the country called Adel (present-day Saylac region and eastern Ethiopia) in the Ethiopia chronicles. After the death of Jarrad Abun, who was killed in battle with the Sultan Abu Bakr, Ahmed established himself as an independent sovereign. This involved him in a long series of hostilities with Abu Bakr; but eventually, after more than one abortive attempt had been made to bring about an alliance between them, Ahmed succeeded in killing the Sultan, whom he replaced by his brother Umar Din (*the brother of Sultan Abu Bakr whom Imam Ahmed killed (the Conquest of Abyssinia, 16th century, 2003, page 22*). The Iman now felt himself strong enough to assert his power against another and more reputable foe. The Batriq, a relation by marriage of the king of Abyssinia, had advanced into the territory of the Muslims, and, after ravaging the country, was making off with an enormous booty, when Ahmed heard of his movement and determined to pursue him. A great battle was fought, in which the Batriq was completely defeated. This exploit, the date of which is preserved in the Ethiopic annals, marks the definite entry of the Imam upon the conquest of Abyssinia, and the rest of first volume is simply the record of an unbroken series triumphs, which ended in the subjugation of almost the whole country to the invader.

In order to defeat the Islamic invaders, Abyssinian Emperors and other leaders buried their differences. Therefore, regrouped Ethiopians and rallying behind their fugitive king with a Portuguese expedition of 400 musketeers sent in response to desperate appeals for aid led by Christopher Vasco da Gama, the son of the famous explorer attacked Ahmed Gurey army near lake Tana. Ahmed Gurey lost his life in 1543 in a decisive battle which the Futuh Al—Habasa: The Conquest of Abyssinia, 16th century, 2003 Translation by Paul Lester Stenhouse page "Note on Title," makes on February 21, 1543, whereupon his army almost immediately disintegrated.

However, according to the *Conquest of Abyssinia (Futuh Al Habash)*, first printed in 1894, p IV-vii (4-7):
Wanag Sagad, the royal tile of the king Lebna Dengel (better known as Dawit I or II) who succeeded his father in 1508 whose reign lasted 1540 and Imam Ahmed confronted each other in 1529 in their first time. With the help of the Portuguese the Abyssinians were enabled first to stem and ultimately to roll back the tide of Muslim invasion; and the Imam Ahmed himself perished ignobly, <u>shot from behind an ambush by a Portuguese marksman who had been a valet de chambre.</u> Sir Charles Eliot, 13, the Foundation of Portugal's power in Africa and the East were laid by Prince Henry the Navigator 1394—1460.

Note: The place of the battle is known as Shimbiro (birds in Somali) kore (climb in Somali). It is not clear if the place is bird-climbing (shimbiro kore in Somali), or a coincidence with something else, since Amhara nation inhabits the region.

Although the struggle continued sporadically for some years, the strong Adal Sultanate could not recover. The Portuguese took and burned the city of Berbera (Rambles:47) in 1567 which shows that it was 25 years after the death of Ahmed Gurey. As soon as Ifat kingdom was born, branched out from Shoa, the fights between Abyssinian Emperors and Islamic/Somali Sultanates had no breaks. Burning the town of Berbera cannot be seen as an isolated incident. According to War Clouds on The Horn of Africa by Tom J. Farer (page 8):

During the third decade of the sixteenth century, Ethiopian culture came close to the breaking point when the legendary Imam Ahmed Ibn Ibrahim Al-Ghazi, or Ahmed Gran (the left-handed) as the Ethiopians called him, or Gurey by the Somalis came storming up from the Somali coast in a Jihad (crusade) which marked its passage by pillaged towns, burned churches, and forced converts to Islam. In ten years of unremitting conflict, his ethnically mixed force— including a large contingent of Somalis and stiffened in one crucial battle by 900 Arabs, Turkish, and Albanian musketeers— poured over the central highlands and streamed north into Christianity's redoubt.

Other than the burnings the Churches and the Mosques of one after the other, in general, the sailors of Portugal used to sail along the coasts of Africa looking for gold, ivory, slaves and other resources. Even there are some mentions that the *Greeks used to hunt elephants around Bab al-mandab and beyond, along the Somali east coast*. But much later, 1884—1886, British hunters and gamers used to shoot elephants in the hill country behind Berbera, and described the bush around Berbera in the range of 30 miles in, as very beautiful and wild (Harald Swayne: 7)."

Even today, many Somalis do not understand the preservation of the ecological balance. They do not like the large carnivorous animals which kill both themselves and their animals, domesticated or wild. Page 142 of Horizon History of Africa states that the Turks occupied Saylac in 1516 and gave way to the Portuguese. Why the Turks transferred Saylac and the real truth of it is subject to further investigation. However, the Portuguese burned it." At that time, the occupiers used to sell the occupied to anyone who could handle and pay for it. Sometimes, colonizers used to exchange with another land. We will see some examples of how France and British, or British and Italy, or British and Germany exchanged parts of the Somali lands in between.

Perhaps, there had been other reasons of why the Portuguese burned Berbera. In 1660, also the Portuguese soldiers burned Baraawe and looted.

In those sailings along the coasts of Djibouti, Berbera, Somalia sea and the Indian Ocean, Portuguese sailors used to have problems with the Somalis.

"Throughout the country (East Africa) at this point, and especially in the port of Beira (a city in Mozambique, see the map below, Cyclone (tropical storm) Idai hit the city badly, March 2019), probably every race and tribe of East, Central, and South African native may be daily encountered, from the tidy, alert, respectful Somali," (*Portuguese East Africa by Reginald. C. F. Maugham: 259*).

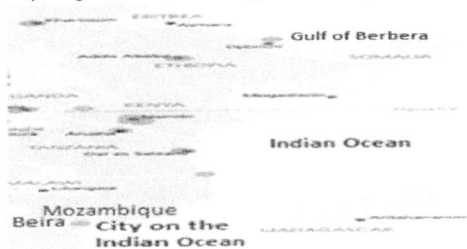

The word "Alert" that author Reginald used is also a metaphor for violent. The reason is that in 15th and the 16th century the Portuguese fought with the Somalis in Sofala (current: Nova Sofala, a region of Mozambique where the
Somalis controlled some time an area of gold business). [Tanzania Notes of Records: The Journal of the Tanzania Society, p97 and page 16 of The Golden Years of Somalia by Mohamed Ali Hamud] wrote, "In 1660, the Portuguese in Mombasa surrendered to a joint of Somali—Omani force." The communication was through the water. We can say also that the Portuguese used to deal or hear about Eastern Africa before the British, Italians and the French. Page 7 of Briggs:

BY the 10th century traders of Somali and Arab origin are known to have been active as far as Sofala, near the Zambezi mouth in present-day Mozambique. By the turn of millennium, an elaborate gold trade linked southeast Africa in the Persian Gulf via the Somali region. The gold derived from alluvial sources in the highlands of present-day Zimbabwe, from where it was transported via the Zambezi valley to Sofala, and then shipped northwards to Mogadishu through chain of medieval city-states that the Swahili coast of Mozambique, Tanzania and Kenya. These self-governing trade ports, inhabited by a cosmopolitan mix of indigenous and foreign merchants, the latter mostly hailing from the shiraz region of Persia, were united by their common adoption of Islam and the wide spread use of Kiswahili (an indigenous African tongue strongly infused with Arabic words) as a lingua France. Mogadishu remained the most important African trade emporium until the mid-13th century, after which improved navigational and shipbuilding techniques allowed the Arab merchants to sail further south in one season, and the focal point of trade relocated closer to the source of the gold, to Kilwa in present-day Tanzania.

The Somalis and the others in the business (Nova Sofala and other east Africa places) took a responsibility to defend the gold trade against many threats. About the relationship of the gold of Sofala and the Somalis, The Horizon History of Africa of American Heritage Publishing, volume 1, 160-161:

Around the first quarter of 12th century, when the Sultan/King of Kilwa learned of gold rich Sofala and promptly secured what amounted to a trade monopoly, the first people on this coast who came to the land of Sofala in search of gold were the inhabitants of the city of Mogadishu (present-day capital of Somalia). It was part of the agreement between these Gentiles and the moors of Mogadishu that every year they should send young moors so that there should be some of this race there.

Charles Eliot, 40, during the 17th century, "an Arabian group called Nabahan Princess captured Pate Island in Kenya and wanted to extend its influence into the neighboring communities. "The inhabitants invoked the aid of the Somalis to assist them against the aggression of the Nabahan Princess of Pate. The Somalis agreed, and the Nabahan princess were repulsed. A government was then established, consisting of a Famao (a descendent of Asiatic colonists) and a Somali Sheekh, which lasted until 1842."

In his book of Africa (Journey into Africa), Keith Johnston (Scottish explorer, cartographer and geographer) who visited Somaliland in 1875, said, "Though brave and clever, Somalis are fanatic Muslims and that "Murder and Theft (probably camel looting) for them are no bar to the gates of paradise (The Economist July 10, 1993)." If murder and theft are not a naked accusation, then, can the Somalis claim to be Muslims? On April 24, 2020, Farah Mohamud Mohamed (author of many books) forwarded from the Acclaimed Somali writer and Bard Professor Nuruddin Farah on Somalis and religion: Can anyone dispute about Nuruddin Farah's argument? Nuruddin Farah:

My true feeling is that Somalis are the least religious people on earth. How could anyone manage the destructiveness of Somalis towards each other? The killings that have been committed, the massacres within the country. If they believed in Allah, as truly as they should, they would not commit such atrocities among each other, especially among fellow Muslims. Therefore, I question their honest when they talk about religion, it is lip service that they pay to the faith.

Many Somali believe that what happens to them is a punishment for being bad Muslims. Another British, an officer who loved the Somalis, fought with them and ate with them in the World War Two, and authored *Warriors: Life and Death Among the Somalis (Originally: Warriors and Strangers)*, Gerald Hanley (1961, 992), 149, cover (back):

Somalia is one of the world's desolate, sun-scorched lands, inhabited by fierce and independent-minded tribesmen. Of all the races of Africa, there cannot be one better to live among than the most difficult, the proudest, the bravest, the vainest, the most merciless, the friendliest: The Somalis.

Relating to that, one of the worst human rights violations that people can commit is enslaving or killing another human being—a subject that Somalis do not fully commit to shun. Also, The Warrior Mullah: The Horn Aflame 1892—1920 by Ray Beachey Raymond W. Beachey) "The Somalis are proud (some would say 'vain') people." Others say "proud and individualistic." Others say "the struggle for survival against harsh condition make them as proud and individualistic."

Gerald Hanley, also the author of *The Consul at Sunset (published 1951)* said a lot about the Somali character which did not change much since 1941 when he was in the lands of the Somalis. On page 29, he said:

I never saw a Somali who showed any fear of death, which, impressive though it sounds, carries within it the chill of pitilessness and the ferocity as well. If you have no fear of death you have none for anybody else's death either, but that fearlessness has always been essential to the Somalis who have had to try and survive hunger, disease and thirst while prepared to fight and die against their enemies, their fellow Somalis for pleasure in the blood feud, or the Ethiopians who would like to rule them, or the white man who got in the way for a while.

The Somalis cannot challenge "*Murder and Theft for them are no bar to the gates of paradise*" when their religion is concerned. It may seem that being a Muslim is: "I am proud and fearless" to kill my brother and resulting someone else will do us part. "Theft" is the looting of camel which the Somalis believe it belongs to the stronger.

what should be the role of Islam in the Somali society? According to The World's Most Dangerous Place: Inside the Outlaw State of Somalia by James Fergusson, one Somali pirate was asked to relate his religion with his actions. He said, "In Somalia people are born muslim and they know how to recite the Koran. But everybody forgot what the actual principles are."

Here is another British (British, Irish or Scottish). John Buchholzer says that he has been told once that "The brave men were merely people who were so stupid that they could not see danger." Does the Somali see the danger of killing his/her fellow Somali, or any other human being? Fighting and killing among the Somalis is easy to start—but does not stop until a big number of the Somali youth is out of the window.

We touched earlier that the Somalis used to protect an area of Mozambique for their own businesses and received some respect from the Europeans and others alike. But what is the cost of "To fight and die against their enemies, their fellow Somalis for pleasure in the blood feud." That fearlessness of them destroyed a nation to killed over 700,000 of their own.

We cannot say the Somalis kill for pleasure but fighting and defeating their adversaries—which are mostly Somalis has strong roots in the Somali culture. The nation of poets, Somalis say a lot about the bravery and cowardice.

The death of the Dervish (the word is a Persian meaning a beggar and I do not understand in what way the British used) brought tranquility to the central and the northern regions of Somaliland but his struggle encouraged another generation which organized the mass to demand independence from the European colonizers. Though warned not to be a political organization like told to SNL (Somali National League and formerly Somali National Society) in the north in 1936, British Military Administration was well aware of the formation of the Somali Youth Club (SYC) in the South, and encouraged the youth to proceed the idea with caution. 15 May 1943, the formation date of SYC was also the same date that the Germans and the Italians were defeated in East Africa (A Pastoral Democracy by I. M. Lewis, 304). The news quickly reached the nomads in the farthest countryside looking after their herds and gave the young SYLs something to be fighting for and be proud of.

British Military Administration also doubled the size of the elementary school system and allowed the Somalis to staff the lowers levels of the civil service and gendarmerie. That was after the British defeated Italy in East Africa during the World War 2 (*chapter 5: World-War Two and The Rekindle of Somali Nationalism*).

Mohamed I. Egal (1928—2002) was the leader of the northern politicians who rejected to delay discussions of the unification even for a week for reasons we will touch in "The New Republic" chapter. It may be some kind of suspicion that Egal was indirectly behind an attempted coup in the north by junior officers of 1961 but not a universal view. But there is an undisputed understanding that Egal had a bigger ambition than being a number one politician of the north. He always dreamed of being either the president or the prime minister of Somalia. He was the last prime minister of publicly elected democratic administration.

And if the democratic system stayed uninterrupted, Egal was contemplating to run for president which he could win it. Before he passed away in 2002, the world was dealing with him behind the scenes to help him recreate the Somalia. He was the last of senior politicians who knew how to handle crisis.

During the Tiih (years from 1988 to present), especially after Egal, nobody stood as a trustable leader. One of his speeches include "Somalia will unite one day. When they clean their home, we will talk to the southerners."

1969 was famous for presidential assassination and a wind of military takeover which was also blowing throughout the African continent. The second president of Somalia, Abdirashid Ali Sharmaarke (1919–1969) was assassinated in Laas Caanood. That gave a chance the military which took over the administration with a bloodless coup on October 21, 1969.

The Supreme Revolutionary Council (SRC), a military junta led by Major General Barre, Lieutenant Colonel Salaad Gabayre Kediye, Mohamed Aynanshe and Chief of Police Jama Qorshel, assumed power and filled the top offices of the government, with Kediye officially holding the title of "Father of the Revolution," although Barre shortly afterwards became the head of the SRC.

SRC, subsequently renamed the country the Somali Democratic Republic, arrested top members of the former government, banned political parties, dissolved the parliament, the Supreme Court and suspended the constitution. Until the mid-1980s, the public saw many good deeds about the military administration. The SRC introduced the needed Somali script in 1972 and improved the education system in all levels.

Mainly, there are two Somali dialects, Maay (mainly Bay and Bakool (Rahanweyn regions)), and Maxay (Northern-Central Somali). There is a Banaadir dialect (also known as Coastal Somali dialect) which is spoken on the Banaadir coast from Adale (Somali: Cadale) to south of Marca (Somali: Marka), including Mogadishu, as well as in the immediate hinterland.

The common and the current Somali script was developed by the Somali linguist *Shire Jama Ahmed* specifically for the Somali language. It uses all letters of the Latin alphabet, except P, V, and Z. Besides the Latin script, other orthographies, there were scripts sections of the peninsula used for centuries for writing Somali include the long established Arabic script and Wadaad writing (mixture of Somali and Arabic).

Other writing systems developed in the twentieth century include the Osmania (1920), Boorama (1933) and Kaddare (1952) scripts. Osman Yusuf Keenadiid, Abdurahman Sheikh Nuur and Hussein Sheikh Ahmed Kaddare invented them respectively. None of those reached universal usage as a writing tool.

Except Wadaad-writing of much earlier than the three, the scripts had clan names like Osmania, Gudabursi (Boorama), Kaddare and so on. In the modern world, it is an honor to give the name of the invented thing to the inventor. Even today, clannism taints the Somali thinking.

The real Somali civil war started in 1988. Any administration of Somalia before that was better off of whatever came after 1991. The military administration killed less than 60, 000 (50,000+ in the north (Somalia: The Untold Story, page 5)), but in Mogadishu alone, in 1991, 200,000 were killed. [Twentieth Century Atlas __Death tolls and Casualty Statistics for Wars, Dictatorships and Genocides (www.users.erols.com, Conflict Trends (no. 23)) Real-Time Analysis of African Political Violence, February 2014), from 1991 to 2013, the people killed in Somalia are 510,000. Add that to 50,000 killed in the north in 1988-1990, more than 2000 persons in Gaalkacyo and the surroundings including clan-war fares].

The Civil War caused the deaths of more than 600,000 people, and unfortunately, it is not something only in the past and we will cover appropriately. Its root causes are weak Islamic foundations and highly polarized clan sentiments. Let us add another important point. Mogadishu's explosive growth after independence produced a rapid process of urbanization—a move that resulted in a great neglect of the rest of the country, central and northern regions in particular.

The northern population was around 1.8 million in 1988 (Somalia: The Untold Story, page 209). The residents of major cities of Sool, Sanaag, and Awdal regions were not the target. Around 50,000 of Hargeysa, Burco, and Berbera residents were killed while 600,000 escaped to refugee camps in Ethiopian, Djibouti and the rest to their relatives in the countryside. Then those cities became deserted.

"After ten years of the Somali-Ethiopian war, there were 40 refugee camps in Somalia, and more than 800, 000 people needed help. Most of the people in the camps were women and children. The men were either killed or went to the cities to work, and their dependence on international aid became debilitating," (Wolfgang Weber of Die Zeit (World Press Review, March 1988)).

After president Barre fled Vila Somalia (the Whitehouse of Somalia) on January 27, 1991, all the social services went with his system while fighting and fighting related diseases and hunger became inescapable. Before the president Barre fled the capital, the UN Security Council passed Resolution # 733 on January 23, 1991 about the chaos in Somalia, but nobody had ears for it. The United States and many other Coalition states were busy with Desert Storm, the attack of Iraq of Saddam Hussein.

The situation in Somalia was almost hopeless for intervention. According to the International NGOS, "When more than 30% of a given population are suffering from acute malnutrition, and when the mortality rate surpasses 2 out of 1,000 people per day, then there is a famine (Fergusson 161)." In August of 1992, in the Southern regions, the death rate was way above that level. In Baidoa, at least 100 people and probably more, used to die each day, a few of them in the town's only hospital. In Baardheere (Bardera), the number was 30-40, starving in their homes, or in the streets, since they had nowhere else to go.

The more than 600,000 that the Civil War claimed, the famine caused in excess of half. In the Company of Heroes by Michael J. Durant, 2003, p.2, Hanley 226: "Already a famine of Old Testament proportions had swept the country, starving more than 300,000 Somali to death."

According to *The World's Most Dangerous Place: Inside the Outlaw State of Somalia by James Fergusson, p154*, from May 1992 to July 1992, 29,000 children under the age of five died.

There is a quotation from the mouth of a well-known Somali leader who when asked to ease the suffering of his people said, "Those are not my people." That politician wanted to be the president of Somalia. Luckily, we do not put the owner of that quotation into this book right now but will one day. We even have the recorded voice.

It is for sure that the warlords who placed their families in save countries had not the same feeling as those whose loved ones were in exile or killed. Baydhabo (Baidoa) had the name of City of death at that time. Somalia Diary: 58, "fifty people a day were said to be dying in Bardera (Baardheere in Somali). Sometimes, nomads would reach the village—food within hands' reach—and drop dead. Fifty a day in a nation that has already lost hundreds of thousands to famine a tribal war."

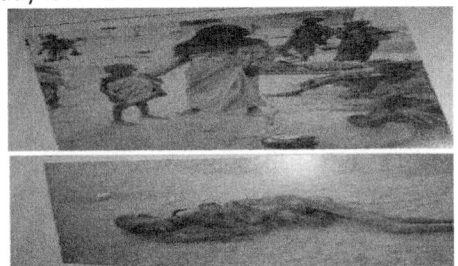

Courtesy: Somalia Diary by Philip Johnston

When that so-called Somali politician said "Those are not my people, "Mary Therese Robinson, the president of Ireland December 1990 to September 1997 was observing the disaster in Somalia—in October 3-4, 1992, she said in her book, A Voice for Somalia, Preface (12):

The suffering I encountered in Somalia offended all my inner sense of justice, a sense I had acquired partly through the practice of law but mainly through a simple human sense of what is right and fair as against what is profoundly unjust. I saw children die. I saw their mothers and fathers powerless to help them. I observed the life-and-death significance of items such as food and medicine—and often crude versions of each— whose abundance we take granted.

Current History: 201, May 1993, "Fundraising is typically centered around pictures, with only minimum story. The picture is usually of a hungry or suffering child (usually black), often with an aid worker (usually white) who is providing food, medicine, or comfort."

Major credit went to the former president of Ireland. That was one of the best examples of how the foundations of intervention were laid out. Many nations took part in that operation and saved thousands of lives, but some committed crimes against the natives including Canadian army members stationed in Beledweyne, the capital city of Hiiraan region.

Members of the group who committed crimes against the natives were court martialed. CHAPTER 19 (Canadian Role of Operation Restore Hope) completely covers how Canada punished the violators of the rule of law.

Let us close this chapter with a conversation between Philip Johnston of Care International president and General Mohamed Farah Aideed in Mogadishu during the Famine of 1992—1993 (Somalia Diary: 21:

General Aideed said, "You know, there is a problem, Mr. Johnston, a very serious problem now in Somalia. We are suffering. Our people have suffered so many years under a terrible dictatorship. So, we expelled him and now we suffer more. Drought has hurt us and the international community does not care."). The words of Johnston, "I knew better. I had seen the stealing and the corruption in the harbor. Aideed militia controlled the harbor."

Chapter three referenced notes

Periplus of the Erythraean Sea, www.wondemondo.com,
The Mystery of Land of Punt Unraveled by Ahmed Ibrahim Awale
The Periplus of the Erythraean sea, as well as Ptolemy, Claudius, Cosmas   Indecopleustes
The Horizon History of Africa, Vol. 1. 62
Travels of Ibn Battuta in Asia and Africa by H. A. R. Gibb., Dwarf Publishing Ltd., 1983, p. 110-111   Yakuts (iv, 602, the book of the cities)
The East Africa Protectorate of Charles Eliot, 1905,
[Fihrist of Al-Nadim, 1970 by Bayard Dodge, an Encyclopedia of 1149 pages
A historical encyclopedia and First Encyclopedia of Islam by 1913-1936 adds
Somaliland with Addis Ababa and Eastern Ethiopia, 106
The Muslim migration of 613 AD-615 AD
The Horizon History of Africa of American Heritage Publishing, volume 1
A Pastoral Democracy by I. M. Lewis
The Golden Years of Somalia, 2014, Mohamed Ali Hamud

CHAPTER FOUR

Modern Footprints 2

History feeds our curiosity with more questions, and there are no alternatives except to make further examinations of the questions. Just two things handicapped the documentation of the Somali history, lack of written script and no funded historians or archeologists.

When the ancient history of the East African Coast is analyzed, the best-known history is the Periplus of the Erytharean Sea. It is the reference that no historians can ignore.

The word "Erytharean" means red in the Greek language. And for the merchant, the Erytharean Sea consisted of the Red Sea, the Persian Gulf, the Gulf of Berbera, the Somali Sea and the western Indian Ocean coasts (Nine Faces of Kenya, Elspeth Huxley, 1991,9)). Periplus gave full accounts of the customs, cultures, and political institutions existing at the time in the Eastern-Horn (present-day Somalia).

One example of how Periplus talked about a town of Somalia (Baadisooc (back cover), Ali Abdigir, 270): "And then, after sailing four hundred stadia (6000 meters) along a promontory, toward which place the current also draws you, there is another market-town called Opone (present-day Hafun (Xaafuun)), into which the

40

same things are imported as those already mentioned, and in it the greatest quantity of cinnamon is produced, (the arebo and moto), and slaves of the better sort, which are brought to Egypt increasing numbers; and a great quantity of tortoiseshell, better than that found elsewhere."

We had not figured out yet what Peryplus meant of "Slaves of the better sort." The most important reason that Somali history is mostly unwritten is the lack of written script before 1972 as previously stated, and very few were also proficient with other languages such as Arabic and English. Those two factors played the greatest role to handicap the documentation of the Somali stories. When the military administration introduced the script in 1972, scholars started to develop the proper writing of the language. Unfortunately, within less than 20 years, 1991, and about 30 years as an independent unitary state, the Somali civil war broke out. Everything came into a hold. People ran away for safety to all over the world.

Today, 2020, an estimated 2 million Somali ethnic lives outside of East Africa, 1.5 million in North America, Western Europe and Oceania (Australia and New Zealand). In North America, the United States and Canada, they contribute to the nation's strives. Ilhan Omar became a US congresswoman, and Ahmed Hussein is Somali-Canadian senator and a minister.

In general, the Somalis are not well-liked in some of those communities. It is not because of a lack of contribution, but they are accused of not assimilating enough regardless of the communities' religion. A big chunk of the Somali diaspora lives in Minnesota state of the USA. The president of the United States of America (2016-202X) campaigned against the presence of the Somalis in 2016.

During his campaign in 2016, Donald Trump (*Inside Al-Shabaab: The secret History of Al-Qaeda's most powerful Ally by Harun Maruf (Macruuf) and Dan Joseph, 2018, 279*) said, "The influx of Somali refugees into and Muslims Minnesota was a disaster "Disaster" for the state. You have seen first-hand the problem caused with faulty refugee vetting, with large numbers of refugees coming into your state without your knowledge, without your support or approval, and with some of them joining ISIS and spreading their extremist views all over our country and all over the world." He used the extremist views of some misled youth for the Somalis as a whole. About the brain-washed young men, I even heard that the would-be suicide bombers are drugged to wrap up their genitals before their missions in order to preserve them for the promised 72 virgins in the heaven.

That influx itself was a brain drain and further complicated the livelihood, culture, religion, language, education and development projects both external and internal. It took a while for the people to reevaluate those things. But one Somali educator said about the Somalis all over the world, "We saved our selves, eliminated the possibility of being parts of killing, and we almost sustained the livelihood of the Somalis left behind."

When the original inhabitants of the eastern horn are concerned, still, some historians question the indigenousness of the Somalis. "Early European writers called Somalis a mixed race of Arab and African origins but more reasonable accounts suggest that Somalis are related to other ethnic groups in the Horn of Africa (Understanding the Somalia conflagration by Afyare Abdi Elmi:16).

Some observers even called them a half-caste offshoot of the great Oromo race, allied to the Caucasian type by a steady influx of pure Asiatic blood (*The Unknown of Horn of Africa: An Exploration from Berbera to the Leopard (Shabeelle) river in 1884 by Frank Linsley James, James Godfrey Thrupp, published in 1888*).

But, some pieces of Somali history are certain. Archaeological records shed light that people lived in the Eastern-Horn of Africa, present-day Somalia over 100,000 years. Or to state in another way, people inhabited Eastern Horn of Africa—present-day Somalia for as long as humans lived anywhere on earth. And there are no reasons, however, to disqualify that those were the Somali ancestors. Ifat/Adal Sultanate in the northwest and Ajuuraan Sultanate around Banaadir region flourished during the Middle Ages, and their successor states continued to thrive through the 19th century.

The Warsangeli Sultanate is another kingdom not many authors say enough about it. According to Somaliland with Addis Ababa and eastern Ethiopia by Philip Briggs, 2012, p. 7-9:

The Dominant late medieval entity in eastern Somaliland was the Warsangeli Sultanate, an Islamic state founded in the 13th century. Warsangeli sultanate incorporated much of present-day Puntland administration, as well as the Somaliland province of Sanaag. Despite the sultanate's great extent, it evidently less expansionist than Ifat and Adal, and its leaders tended to focus—in particular frankincense grown at the base of the Daalo (sometimes written as Daallo) escarpment—as opposed to the conquest of Ethiopia. Warsangeli sultanate remained fully autonomous sultanate until the end of the 19th century.

The Warsangeli Sultanate which came into existence in 1298 did not use to rule a large area. We can think of a couple of reasons it expanded not enough. It had no adversaries since Ifat-Adal Sultanate was in between itself and the Abyssinians. Also, both Berbera and Saylac had far netter commercial importance than Laas Qoray, the base of the Warsangeli Sultanate. Much is not known also if the Sultanate had expanded its influence to the northeastern regions, which later had a new kingdom, the Omaniyah.

There were two more Sultanates around the southern Somalia. Ajuuraan Sultanate came into existence on late-13th century or early 14th century. It flourished until Gelledi Sultanate overthrew it on the late of the 17th century. Gelledi Sultanate controlled the watering places, the agricultural centers and the

42

trade routes to the coastal cities of Marka and Mogadishu. Then, the Gelledi sultanate finally succumbed to the Italians in 1908. Adal/Ifat, Warsangeli, and Ajuuraan Sultanates, all came into life during the 13th century, and we can say that a wind of the Sultanate was blowing on the Somali peninsula.

Somalia in Pictures which cited the 1961 publication of *A Pastoral Democracy by I. M. Lewis*, "The word Somali appeared in writing for the first time in 1415, in an Ethiopian hymn written to celebrate a victory against the Somalis, the Ifat/Yifat Sultanate which progressed into Adal Sultanate."

The Sultanate of Ifat which used Amharic, Harari, Afar, and Somali, and even Tigrinya languages ruled part of Ethiopia, Eritrea, Djibouti, and northern parts of Somalia. It existed over from the late 13th century to the 16th century separate from Showa/Shaba Kingdom—sporadic existence in the early parts of the 16th century. Saylac was its main base. It was a rich city where its richness came from the slave trade in which the Arabs and the Persians have trafficked in many centuries.

Then, Ifat became a powerful kingdom. It dominated the old Showa from 1285, and had a close co-operation with the Showa Kingdom before they became independent entities. Ifat Sultanate which developed into Adal Sultanate has been more accomplished and more sophisticated than we put into this book. Horizon, 141, "The beginning of the Muslim state in eastern Showa date most probably from the late 9th century AD.

In 1285, however, the Showan imamate was overthrown and absorbed into that of Ifat, the predominant Muslim state of Abyssinia (Eastern Abyssinian (present-day Somalia))." The power struggle in the horn never stopped.

When Adal sultanate lost the fight and the king, Saad-adin lost his life, the remnants regrouped and threatened the existence of the Ethiopian Kingdom. When Emperor Amda Seyon came to the throne in 1313, his kingdom was in a threat from the east. The Horizon History of Africa of American Heritage Publishing, volume 1, 164-165:

When this king came to the throne in 1313, his country was being seriously threated by Muslim attacks. The first leader to campaign against him was Sadra-din, the Muslim ruler of the Muslim principality of Ifat, to the east of Showa (present-day Somalia). When Islam was introduced to the Somali coasts during the 7th century, slave trade which existed before A. D. further flourished. The
Arab dealers and their Somali associates started going deeper and deeper into Africa to find slaves.

The Ifat Sultanate dominated the slave trade business which flourished in the area and made the Christian rulers in the Horn too angry. That was not for hatred of slavery but not dominating or taking a lion's share of the slavery business itself. "A Jihad, mounted from the Islamic sultanate of Adal from the 1520s, temporarily overran Ethiopia and resulted in the deportation of thousands of slaves across the Red Sea into Arabia," (Slavery in The Arab World by Murray Gordon, 1989, p131.

With exception of the Romans and Greeks, the east coast of Africa was unknown to Europeans, such as the British, Italians, French, Germans, Spain and the Dutch until the Portuguese Vasco Da Gama opened up the road to the Indian Ocean round the south of Africa in 1498. The hinterland lands of the Somalis were

Vasco Da Gama (first European reached Somalia by other route other than through Arabian) visited the island of Zanzibar in 1499, Mogadishu and bombarded from the sea. He came back again to Zanzibar early in the 16th century. That is when the Portuguese which had not been pushed out of East Africa 1728 (Somali history: origins, migrations and Settlement by Sampson Jerry, 9) became the masters of both Zanzibar and east African coast (p152 of Journey into Africa by James McCarthy, 20014).

Let us jot a bit why the Horn of Africa was unknown to the Europeans till the 15th century. Both Asia and Europe connect through the land, but Africa, Australia, explored in 1606, New Zealand in 1642, and North America explored in the 15th century have big oceans in between.

In 1884 when Harald Swayne of *Early Days in Somaliland and Other Tales* was fascinated by adventure in wild and hunting big game was surveying some parts of northern Somalia, the interior of Somaliland was unknown to the west. Elephants, Lions, Rhinoceros, Hippopotamus, and Oryx were abundant in northern Somaliland. None of those animals are available in the northern Somalia today.

One of the very historical benefits that many Somalis may not much consideration about the struggle of Daraawiish was stopping the cannibalism of the wildlife. Geoffrey Archer (55), "In the happy days before the rise of the Mad Mullah here (Somaliland) was the Mecca, the magnet of attraction, for the sportsman naturalist from Britain and the continent. British Somaliland, the Haud and the Webi Shabeelle area all provided grand-hunting long before East Africa had come into the picture."

In addition, even before that, thousands of Africans were being exported through the Somali coast, most of them Ethiopians. The Arabs, Jews, Persians and the African themselves practiced slavery many centuries. As many as 600 people were used to put into double-deck dhows when the Europeans became whole-buyers.

In the middle of 19th century, Livingstone estimated that, every slave sold in the Zanzibar market, five died on the way (James McCarthy: 157). In that Island of Zanzibar, the Somali used to live in their dominions as stated "Wild-looking Somali from the far north of the Sultan's dominion" were with the Omani Sultans in the slavery business in east Africa. Though the Netherlands, UK, USA, France,

Italy, Portuguese and Spain made a fortune of the slave trade, at the same time, they were the first who started fighting against the practice.

In the Somali peninsula, the biggest and the deserved credit of campaigning against that horrible culture goes to UK with the help of other Europeans. Emperor Haile Salasse silently acknowledged the wide spread and deep-rooted nature of the problem (slavery) in his country. A delegation of the Anti-slavery and Aboriginal Protection Society visited Ethiopian in 1932. The King (Haile Selassie) who was crown in 1930 asked for another 20 more years to get rid the country of slavery (Slavery in The Arab World by Murray Gordon, 224).

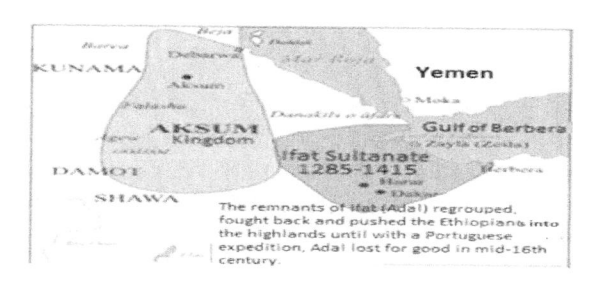

King Amda Seyon defeated king Sabra-adin of Ifat and tried to rule the peninsula of the defeated kingdom. He was not capable of occupying the land with force, and as a desperate choice, he nominated Jamaluddin as a ruler (governor) in the position of his brother, Sabra-adin. That move of trying to put brother against brother increased the hostilities. Nor the Somalis forgot about the power struggle in the Horn. Adal remnants and other Somalis in the area regrouped and joined the army of Jamal-adin.

The worst fights between the Ethiopian Empire and regrouped Somali and other Islamic forces (Turkish and Egyptian) had taken place in the early 16th century. With the leadership of Ahmed Gurey, Somalis fought back. But, with Portuguese expedition which sided with the Ethiopians, they defeated the Somalis again in mid-16th century.

However, Somali historians reject any suggestion that the word "Somali" came up in the early 15th century. But it is safe to say that was when the Ethiopians achieved their much celebrated and unbelievable victory against the
Somalis.

It is the nature that neighboring communities to fight each other for resources. Ethiopians and Somalis are a pure example. They had known each other for many centuries as Ethiopians and Somalis. The author of The Periplus of the Erytharean sea mentioned two Berber people in Africa. Northern Berbers are the indigenous people of North Africa such as Libya, Morocco, Algeria, Tunisia, Niger (landlocked), Mauritania (Atlantic coast), and the rest on the Mediterranean coast.

The eastern Berbers (Somalis) are along the Gulf of Berbera coast up to the Arabian Sea or the Somalia Sea and along the western Indian Ocean coast. How the northern Berbers got to North Africa or where they originated is not too concrete. But that may be same to everyone else in the world.

In the 3rd century, Ezani, an Aksum Kingdom of AD320 – AD360, conquered some portion of Beja territory (Beja: an ethnic group inhabiting Sudan, as well as parts of Eritrea and Egypt). Then, in the 4th century, the Aksum also tried to conquer the Eastern desert tribes (Somalis), but they posed a serious threat to the Aksumite state (Aksum and Nubia).

We can understand now why the Ethiopian Empires exploded with jubilation when they defeated the powerful Somali Kingdom in the early 15th century, and the fight was not over until in the mid of the 16th. The Periplus of the Erytharean Sea (a merchant based in Alexandria) explained clearly the locations of the two Berber people. He wrote, "The Cape of Spices is later named "Cape of Guardafui" (look and escape) by the Italians in the late 19th century and is known Raas Casayr by the locals. Italy built the coming Lighthouse on the cape in 1922 – 1924 (See the figure)."

Geeska Raas Casayr
Cape Guardafui

Italy built the Lighthouse on the tip of the Cape of Guardafui in 1924 and had not been maintained since then. The tip that faces the water (Indian Ocean), the locals (Somalis) call Libaax Yuurura (sitting lions), and that is why the Italians said: Look and escape (Guardafui). The town has some residents all the times. The term "Cape of Spices" is not suggesting that spices were the product of the promontory but the region was a market of exchange. The Mad Mullah of Somaliland, 16:

French Somaliland formed part of the land of Cush mentioned in Genesis, and was known as the Land of Punt to the early Egyptians about 1700 BC. To the Greeks and Romans, it was the Regio (Latin word for 'region') Ctnnatnomifera, Although there is little doubt that Cinnamon was never a product of Somaliland but was imported from Southern India and Ceylon (Sri Lanka now) to Berbera (Malao: Present day Berbera) and the other ports on the Somali coast, and there retailed to the Greeks who never traded further east or south than Cape Guarda Fui. To the Arabs of six century A.D., it was known as Bar Ajam, the "Land of Heat."

About the origin of the word "Asayr," there are some unanswered questions. In the Somali language of the word "Asayr" is Casayr. "Cas" means red and "Sayr" throw away. I am not sure if we can derive something from that. Omar Abdi Iidan is a tireless researcher and academic. One time I discussed with him about the originality of the word, he believes that Arabs came up with the name Ras Asayr meaning the difficult corner.

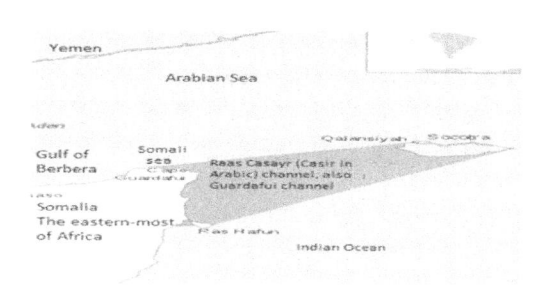

Raas Casayr means Deegaanka Casayr in Somali (Raas Casiir in Arabic which means difficult corner and Cape Guardafui means look and escape in Italian. Viewing the figure, this oceanic strait (Guardafui Channel) connects the Gulf of Berbera to the north with the Somali sea to the south and to the Indian Ocean. It experiences cyclones that emerge from its southeast in the Somali Sea, and that is one of the reasons that Arabs used to call it "The difficult corner." Different than how the figure looks, Xaafuun is not cut off from the mainland of Somalia yet.

To say Somali seas means: The waters of Gulf of Berbera, Somali Sea (on top of Cape of Guardafui) and the Somali Economical Zone of the Indian Ocean.

Sailing further to the end of Gulf of Berbera, along the southern coast of the Arabian (Somali sea which is below Arabian sea), and the Cape of Spices, present-day of Cape of Gaardafuu (Guardafui), up to Xaafuun (Dante by the Italians), the easternmost projection of the African continent had rich historical connections to Madagascar (biggest African island and four largest in the world), Maldives Islands on the Indian Ocean and the Bay of Bengal which India, Sri Lanka, Bangladesh, Myanmar (Burma) and other islands share.

In 1346, Ibn Battuta, a Moroccan traveler met Abdul-Aziz AlMaqdashawi (From Mogadishu) as a ruler of one of the Maldives Islands (Travels of Ibn Battuta in Asia and Africa by H. A. R. Gibb., Dwarf Publishing Ltd., 1983, p. 110-111). The name of the "Gulf of Berbera" had been known to Phoenicians and Arab sailors before the Europeans came to know anything about Somaliland.

The older Arab geographers knew only a land of the name of Berbera, after which the Gulf of Aden is called Bahr Berberā or alKhalīdj al-Berberā. The land owes its name to the natives who are called Barbars or Berbers. They are Somalis, and they are the people whom Yakuts (iv, 602) describes them as barbarous negroes, amongst whom Islam had penetrated.

The full name of the explorer is Yakut/Jakut Al Hamawi while his book is "Mu'jam (Mucjam Al Buldan (the Book of Cities)). He started writing his traveling experiences in 1224 AD and completed 1228—while he passed away in 1229. He was an Arab geographer of Greek ethnic born in Aleppo (Xaleb), Syria [Fihrist of AL Nadim, 1970 by Bayard Dodge, an Encyclopedia of 1149 pages].

The Somalis were known to the Phoenicians (Mediterranean civilization), Mycenaeans (Bronze age), Babylonians and some other groups of sailors. However, the name "Gulf of Aden" is less than two centuries old, and this is another explanation of how Arab and Greek travelers explained it as "The sea of Berbera goes up to Aden, and this sea stretches further until it reaches the ocean (Indian Ocean)). Maqdisho (Mogadishu) is situated on the mainland of the Barbar/Berber who are a tribe of nomads, not those whose country is the Maghrib (Algeria, Morocco, Tunisia, Libya, and Mauritania)."

A historical encyclopedia and First Encyclopedia of Islam by 1913 to 1936 adds "Historically, the Gulf of Aden was known as "The Gulf of Berbera," named after the ancient Somali port city of Berbera on the south side of the gulf. However, as the city of Aden grew during the colonial era, the name of "Gulf of Aden" was popularized from 1839. The name of the Gulf was inspired by the former British Crown Colony city of Aden, now part of Yemen."

The capture of Aden in 1839 and its establishment as an important British port and garrison town is one of the most important factors that increased British interests into the southern coast of the Gulf of Berbera. The surveys of the western Indian Ocean and the familiarity with the Red Sea Route also played vital roles in knowing more of Somaliland. Somaliland with Addis Ababa and Eastern Ethiopia, 106: "The name Berbera is truly antiquated, the Ancient Greeks and Phoenicians referred to the inhabitants of the Somali Coast as Berbers, a name referenced in the Medieval Arabic name for the Horn of Africa, Bilad al Barbar (literally, "Land of Berbers").

Back then, the name was applied to the entire southern coast of the Gulf of Aden, and it is unclear when it became associated with one specific port."

We presented many examples about that the Gulf of Aden was known as the Gulf of Berbera before 1839. This author had been using Gulf of Berbera in his last 15 books published.

The history that states that Islam came to the Somali coasts as early as the 9th century is also very premature. As mentioned earlier, the middle eastern travelers, or merchants used to sail regularly to the Gulf of Berbera before the birth of Islam. That could have paved the way for the Muslim migration of 613 AD and 615 AD. More than a decade before he passed away, the Prophet advised a group of his first flowers to go to King Negus of Ethiopia for asylum.

Most likely, they came first to the familiar ports of Gulf Berbera, and up to the Cape of Spices. Since the oldest transport vessels are boats and the Somalis have the longest coast of Africa, from Gulf of Tojorrah to Raskamboni of the Somali-Kenyan border, it is arguably logic that all or most expeditions to the Horn of Africa used to come first to the Somali coast.

Exotic animals such as the giraffe caught and sold by Somali merchants were very popular in medieval China [Color, Confusion and

Concessions: History of the Chinese in South Africa 2005, Melanie Yab, Dianne Long Man, page 3]. Medieval China, Yuan Dynasty 1271-1368. It is believed that the Chinese had made three visits to the Somali coast in the early 1400s. The Horizon History of Africa of American Heritage Publishing, volume 1, 163: "Before the Ming Dynasty of 1368-1644, the Chinese did not know anything about the Somaliland. During the 1400s, Chinese travelers reached Malindi, Brava (Baraawe) and Mogadishu.
That expedition got a gift of giraffe for the Chinese king from an African ruler in 1444. The story had been revealed by a Chinese professor at Leyden University in London in 1947."

And it is well-known that the Somalis used to sell all kinds of animals to the visitors. In 1996, I went back to Somalia after being away for more than 16 years. I encountered with a relative in Gaalkacyo who had a young Tigers for sale. I threatened her not to sell the treasure of the nation. I have been harassed to say that, and I have no idea where that young Tiger ended up.

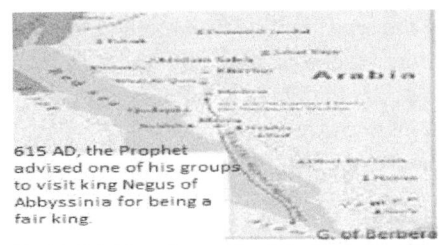

The Muslim Migration to Abyssinia or the first Hijra

615 AD, the Prophet advised one of his groups to visit king Negus of Abbyssinia for being a fair king.

Even Islam get introduced into the Gulf of Berbera earlier than thought. Frictions among the Islamists during the campaigns of spreading the religion which existed during the leadership of the Prophet exploded after the death of 632 A.D. For safety with new campaigns of introducing the new religion, many Muslims traveled to various places of the world. Because of its proximity, Somalia was one of the earliest to visit and settle. Africa was the first continent into which Islam spread from Arabia, during the early 7th century.

Today, more than third of the Muslims in the world live in the continent of Africa. *Before Blackhawk Down by Abdurahman Sharif Mahamud, page 16:*

After the assassination of Caliph Uthman Ibn Affan in Arabia in 656 A.D., Arab leaders failed to agree on the choice of a successor. As a result, the Muslims were divided into contending groups during the Caliphate of Ali Bin Abi Talib, with many wars arising. Because of these events in Arabia, many "Sunni Muslims" came over and settled in Somaliland at the beginning of the 9th century. These Arab migrations and the building of settlements along its coastal region obviously led to the spread of Islam among Somali.

That was when it almost spread to the coastal cities, northern and northeastern regions in particular. But, as a matter of fact, Islam was introduced to the northern Somali Coast early on from the Arabian Peninsula, shortly after the Hijra (from 622 AD). Saylac had remains of two-mihrab Masjid al-Qiblatayn (two directions to pray) dates back to the 7th century. It is the oldest mosque in the city (Somaliland with Addis Ababa and Eastern Ethiopia, 149).

The early contacts with the Somalis were initially at the coast. As mentioned earlier, some of the early visitors were the Pharaohs, Greeks, and the Persians. The connections between pharaohs and the people of the Land of Punt had existed as far as we can trace the ancient Egyptian history itself. They used to call it: Paradisal land, Land of Gods, the Sacred Land, the Land of Exotic Trees and other names as mentioned earlier.

There is another point of history that we will talk briefly. Café drawings (The Mystery of the Land of the Punt Unraveled by Ahmed Awale, Making Sense of Somali history by Abdurahman Baadiyow, 42, Baadisooc by Cali Cabdigiir), and archaeological findings hint that the Ancient Somalis are the first people who domesticated the camel during the 3rd and 2nd Millennium BC and developed a profitable trade system. The Dromedary or one hump camel is 95% of the world's camel population.

The Horn of Africa hosts 80% of the Dromedary. The Camel is the most important animal of the Somalis, almost to a point of worship. After so many centuries of camel domestication, in the Somali culture camel belongs to whoever can keep it. It seems that religion does not prohibit Somalis from looting or taking camel by many means.

The Islamic religion was introduced to Somalis before the death of the Prophet Mohamed. However, the Somali mythology did not fade away even today, 2020. The public modified much of the religion in terms of their situations, cultures and customs. It is not also controversial to say that Somalis adopted the religion to be safe from enslaving. "As part of the Islamic world Somalis were at least nominally protected by the religious tenet that free Muslims cannot be enslaved—but Arab dhows loaded with human cargo continually visited Somali ports," (Besteman, 51 which also cited Cassanelli).

About the Dromedary camels, more than 7 million of the 80% belongs to the Somalis. In 1941, British estimated the camel, cattle and sheep of the Somalis around one million each (The First to be Freed, p64`). After some time, the domestication culture spread to ancient Egyptians, then to southern Arabia. Both feral and the domesticated, one hump or two humps, the total population of the camel in the world is about 18 million. There is one more domestication credited to East African civilization. Historians and archeologists believe that the domestication of cattle started in the Nile Valley of lower Nubia (present-day of northern Sudan) as early as 7500 BC.

Another area of interest that some historians think that people first learned how to domesticate camel is southern Arabia, such as Yemen, Oman, and Saudi Arabia. If that claim had a big weight, even, Horn of Africa is the second place that further developed the practice and made a very sound trade. There is even a joke of comparing of East African camel to an Arabian camel by a world traveler (Rambles in Lion Land: 26): "The East African camel (he-camel) is a gentleman in manners and bearing, compared with its cousin of Asia."

One of the first elements of the Somali culture which the British learned was their love towards the camel, and we will see later why the Colonizer created the Somali Camel Corps. Camels used in the expeditions of fighting against the

Daraawiish came in some distances from places far removed from Somaliland; Abyssinia, Arabia, Egypt and India.

The Warrior Mullah: The Horn Aflame 1892—1920 by Raymond Beachey, page 8:

...., the camel stood out predominantly. It is the most cherished of all livestock –so much so, that the highest benediction bestowed by camel herders was 'my God grant you camels and sons.' Camels are the most highly esteemed and valued animals in pastoral in Somalo society, and they figure prominently in Somali oral literature and are the subject of many proverbs: 'Give away camels never! No camel means no milk and no milk means no life." Nowhere in the world, except, perhaps, in Bikaris, India, or Arabia, does the camel (camels dromedarius) reign so supreme as in Somali land, which today has Bakari's the largest camel population of any country in the world.

If the tribes had been willing to assist the expeditions against Daraawiish, there would have been no difficulty in obtaining sufficient animals (Hamilton: 157). The author writes, "The Gudabursi, whose chiefs had promised to produce a contingent of horsemen, failed to do so, although Mr. Keyser, His Majesty's Consul at saylac, used every endeavor to include them to come forward. The tribes in this part of the Protectorate had not suffered from the Mullah's raids, and being of separate origin to the Isaaq tribes, were affected by the latter's misfortunate."

Last 20 years, a new generation of Somali writers show interests of gathering Somali stories from various languages and websites. They sometimes translate from other languages and put into Somali websites. The Horizon History of Africa by American Heritage Publishing Co., Inc., New York, Volume 1, a package of 2 volumes of more than 560 pages with editors of about 16 scholars, page 141:

Shortly after the rise of Islam, Muslim Arabs and Persians created a series of coastal settlements in the region that came to be called Somalia. In these towns, Arab and Persian merchants settled as local aristocracies, into a process of Islamization, and by intermarrying with local women formed a mixed Somali-Arab culture. The prolonged period of contact between the Somali and the civilization of the Arabian coasts—a contact that had brought Islam and many other elements of Muslim-Arab culture to Somaliland flourished. Such cultural borrowings betray themselves (Somalis) in the Somali language, which contains numerous Arabic loanwords. However, the Somali language retains its unique character as a separate and vigorous tongue possessing an unusually rich oral literature. Poetry among the Somali is not merely the private medium of the author, but frequently the collective tongue of the Somalis.

Islamization of the interior was a slow process. In some inhabitants it reached in the 15th century. [*Oxford Atlas of World History: From the Origins of the Humanity to the Year 2000, General Editor Patrick K. O'Brian, Institute of Historical Research, University of London, p.62*], Islamization reached Western Somalis around 1250-1450. Also, page 82:

To the east and southeast of the Christian Empire (Ethiopia), Islamic trading settlements were established along the coast and along the trade routes leading into the interior from the major ports, of which Saylac was perhaps the most important. As the Muslim population increased, the creation of a number of Islamic sultanates lead to conflict with the Christian Ethiopian Empire. During this period the Somali slowly expanded from around the Gulf of Berbera, along the coast north to Saylac and south to Mogadishu, and into the interior – to occupy much of the Horn of Africa. By the 12th century Siamization of this area had become well advanced. *"In East Africa, Muslim Arab traders settled along the coast from 900 AD and created City-states such as Mogadishu"* Encyclopedia of Islam, 2009, by Raana Bokhari and Mohammed Seddon, page 95.

We have seen how the Sultanates of Ifat-Adal, Warsangeli and Ajuuraan came into power. That was way before the Europeans began to know more about the Eastern Horn of Africa. Ibnu Batuta (1325-1354), a Moroccan Berber, and one of the most famous travelers of the world wrote about the Land of Punt [Wikipedia, the Free Encyclopedic in reference to 1. Versteegh, Kees, 2008, Encyclopedia of Arabic Languages and Linguistics, volume 4, Brill, In Search of a State]:

From Aden, mid-January 1331, Ibn Battuta embarked on a ship heading for Zeila (Saylac) on the coast of Somalia. He then moved on to Cape of Spices, present-day Guardafui, present further down the Somalia seaboard, spending about a week in each location. Later he would visit Mogadishu, the then preeminent city of the "Land of the Berbers" (Balad Al Barbar), the medieval Arabic term for the Horn of Africa).

Other than Saylac and Mogadishu, traveler Battuta stayed on another location of Somalia, around Raas Casayr or the Guardafui area which we could not name. Though they get into a same branch of DNA, according to the history books, the Somalis had not been part or confused with the Ethiopians. Arab scholars such as Al Masudi (935), Al Bakri (1067), Al- Idris (1154), Al-istakhri (960), Ibn Hawqal (977), Al-Burruni (1030), Al-Bakhri (1067), AL Idrisi (1154), Ibna-Said, Ibn-Harrarani (1344), all assert to the actuality of a rigorous, alert and independent Somali culture. Ibn Khaldun of late 14th century mentioned that the Somalis were completely independent of foreign rule. All those Arab travelers described the Somali peninsula as extending throughout the length of the Horn of Africa. They called the peninsula as Bar-Ajam, or the "Unknown land," the inhabitants "Berri-al-Somali, or the "Land of the Somali."

Piracy off the coast of Somalia shocked the world in a sudden wave at the closing of the 20th century and the first two decades of the 21St century. Foreign fishing boats and mega-ships overfished in the Gulf of Berbera (Gulf of Aden as the British popularized after 1839), Somali channel and Somali sea, in Somali territorial waters. They came within a few kilometers to Somali towns like Eyl of Nugaal region. Local fisheries reached a point of marginalization and fought back with highjacks and kidnapping. It resulted in a crisis of ransom business.

The route of the Gulf of Berbera, into the Somali sea and the Indian Ocean is one of the most important sea lanes in the world. The vessels which go through that channel are over 30,000 each year.

One afternoon of 2000 in Garowe, I was sitting with Mohamed Abdi Hashi, vice president from the formation to October 13, 2004, and president from October 4, 2004 to January 8, 2005 of Puntland administration. I reminded him of a ship hijacked on the Somalia waters by Somali pirates. The vice-president was well aware that grievance has developed into greediness. With a frowned face, he said, "Politically, we cannot say certain things, but the foreign vessels are making illegal and unscrupulous fishing in our waters, and there will be ecological damage." Pirates: A New History, From Vikings to Somali Raiders by Peter Lehr, p.140:

On 15 August 2005, a pirate gang calling itself the National Volunteer Coastguard of Somalia captured three Taiwanese-owned trawlers that were fishing in Somali waters. The pirates brazenly declared that they had not hijacked but 'impounded' these vessels, and that the $5,000 they demanded from each of the forty-eight captured crew members was not a ransom demand but a 'fine' for their participation in the crime of illegal fishing.

Somalia waters are rich in large pelagic fish, diverse tuna samples such as *yellow fish, longtail, and bigeye tuna, anchovies, Sardines, herring, and mackerel in the nearby waters. Bottom—dwelling fish, include flounder, groupers, porgies, and snappers. Sharks and Rays are abundant.* These untapped waters with no or weak local defenders attract mega-fishing foreign vessels. They had no fear of fishing illegally in Somalia's exclusive economic zone. Sometimes, illegally fishing ships on the Somalia waters were estimated at any time around 300 plus. During the outbreak of the Somali piracy, the academic world on the other hand tried to know about the sailing history of the Somalis. We learned that the Somalis used to make their own boats and were good sailors.

Some Greek sailors called the Eastern Horn of Africa inhabitants as "Nomad savages and ferocious wild beasts haunt the shores on either side of the sea." This tells that the Somalis were sea traders and used to protect themselves. Let us recall the quotation of *Reginald. C. F. Maugham in his book, Portuguese East Africa: 259,* "Throughout the country (East Africa) at this point, and especially in the port of Beira (a city in Mozambique), probably every race and tribe of East, Central, and

South African native may be daily encountered, from the tidy, alert, respectful Somali."

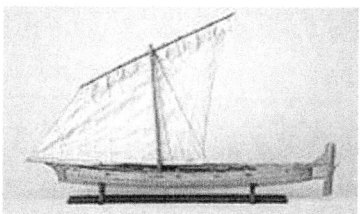

Somali Beden ship from Fra Mauro's Map

The Fra Mauro Map is "Considered the greatest memorial of medieval cartographer," is the map of the world made around 1450 by the Italian cartographer Fra Mauro.

Baadisooc by Ali Abdigir: 310 {www.wikipedia.org which refers (*Chittick, Neville (1975, an Archaeological Reconnaissance in the Horn: The British-Somali Expedition, 1975. p. 127, Johnstone, Paul (1989, The Sea-Craft of Prehistory. Routledge. pp. 180–183. ISBN 0415026350. Chittick, Neville (1980). Sewn boats in the western Indian Ocean, and a survival in Somalia*}:

The Beden', *badan*, or alternate type names Bedenseyed and Beden-safar, is a fast, ancient Somali single or double-masted maritime vessel and ship, typified by its towering stern-post and powerful rudder. It is also the longest surviving sewn boat in the Horn of Africa and the Arabian Peninsula. Its shipyards predominantly lie in the northeastern Hafun region of Somalia (notably Bayla), as well as Muscat. There are 2 types of Beden ships, with one type geared towards fishing (the Beden-seyed) and the other, trading (Beden-safar). The average trading Beden safar ship measure more than 15 m (49 ft.) in length, and are significantly larger than the fishing Beden-seyed ships, which measure 6-15m (20-49 ft.) on average, but both are dwarfed by a much larger trading variant called the 'uwassiye, the most common trading and voyaging ship, with some measuring up to 77+ ft. The ship is noticeable and unique in its strengthened substantial gunwale, which attached by treenail . Originally, all Beden ships were sewn with coiled coconut fibre, holding the hull planking, stem and stern-post. But Omani variants, beginning in the 20th century, began nailing instead of sewing the planks.

Chapter three referenced notes

What Led to The Discovery of the Source of The Nile, Journal of Adventures in? Somali Land, page 86, Edited and Published by Erik Publication

Africa, Keith Johnston, 274 *www.kaisercroos.com,* Article: The Soldier's Burden: A Punitive Expedition on the East African coast, 1890 (WITU article 1890]. Maqaddinkii Xeebaha Birri-Soomaal, Axmed I. Cawaale, 2014,52

Saylac and its people, April 1887, Baadisooc by Ali Abdigir, Amazon 2018, ISBN: 9781983449703 (the black and white one, and the color one, 136-37

Early Days in Somaliland and other Tales by Harald Swayne, 53

www.kaisercroos.com, Article: The Soldier's Burden: Somaliland: 18841898; The early British years

CHAPTER FIVE

Treaties Betrayed

In the history of the two neighboring African nations, Ethiopia and Somalia, 1897 was a glorious year for one and black one for other (Somalia).

Until the rise of Islam in the 7th century, Europeans knew very little about Somaliland. They read about Arab and Phoenician travelers' notes about the Somalis and their land. The Horizon, 159 states, "The first Western notice of the East African coast occurs in the writings of Al-Idrisi, a twelfth century Moroccan muslim scholar who spent most of his life in Palermo at the court of Roger II, a Norman ruler of Sicily."

From there on, European explorers took risks to know more about Somaliland. British involvement in Somaliland began in 1825. That was when British Ship Mary Ann was robbed and sunk near Berbera (Mad Mullah). After the incident, the navy of the Government of Bombay of Great Britain blocked the southern coast of the Gulf of Berbera.

Through the intervention of Hagi Sharmaarke Ali Salah (1776-1861), the governor of Saylac (1839-1861 (History of Hagi Sharmaarke by Ahmed Awale, 58)), the survivors of the Mary Ann were recovered, and the Somali bound over to abstain from future attacks on the English vessels. Those discussions resulted in the first treaty that the British had180 with any Somali group. The year was 1827.

The 30 years after that treaty, Britain was sending explorers to the eastern horn of Horn of Africa. *John Hanning Speke* who later discovered the source of the river Nile joined the Burton group in Berbera from Nugaal. The group hab been attacked in Berbera, Abriil 18-19 of 1855. *What Led to The Discovery of the?*
Source of The Nile, Journal of Adventures in Somali Land, page 86, Edited and Published by Erik Publications:

January 29, 1855, Lieutenant William Stroyan and lieutenant Herne were now both employed at Berbera or in its vicinity. The former (Stroyan) had been making slight excursions inland, shooting, and had killed three elephants; whilst the later (Herne) was purchasing baggage-cattle for the expedition transport. John Hanning Speke was instructed to lead an expedition himself to the Wadi Nugaal (Waadiga Nugaal) before joining the others at Berbera. He failed with this adventure and that is one of the main reasons that Majeerteenya ended up being part of Italian-Somaliland.

Ten years before "when John Hanning Speke was instructed to lead an expedition himself to the Wadi Nugaal (Waadiga Nugaal)," Africa, Keith Johnston:274, in 1875 wrote, "Beyond the abrupt of the Abyssinian highland lies the eastern promontory of Africa, which still appears on our maps on a dreary empty waste land." Then, Somaliland became grab-a-land arena. The Europeans were in a competition that each wanted to colonize as many nations as possible.

The Turks were there as well. The Germans were also searching this area to put a foot on somewhere of it. When they could not grab any spot around northern Somaliland, they (Germans) moved to Kismayo side through the Omani Sultans in Zanzibar which is the second largest island in the east African coast. The region fell under the Sultan of Zanzibar in 1892 after a year after Banaadir became under the rule of the Zanzibari rule.

The British again kicked the Germans out from Kismayo area in 1890. They signed a treaty called Heligoland in which Germany gave up Kismayo area for a British concession of two small islands in the North Sea off the mouth of the river Elbe and the Caprivi strip of between today's Botswana and Zambia to Germany [www.kaisercroos.com, Article: The Soldier's Burden: A Punitive Expedition on the East African coast, 1890 (WITU article 1890, Anglo—German treaty of July 1890]. There is a statement the reader has to keep in mind. Regardless of the magnitude of the resistance, no foreign power ever entered Somali peninsula with no fight.

1866 Khedive of Egypt obtained firearms from the Ottomans and established a control over on the Red Sea on the African side and then moved up to Hafun. But the Grab-a-land game of Khedive of Egypt ran out of gas. Egyptians did not get only firearms from the Turks but also purchased Gulf of Berbera ports (Somali ports) for an annual payment of 15,000 British pounds. That move could not help the Egyptians in occupying Somali ports from 1870-1884 because of more problems with the Mahdi of Sudan.

There were other problems as well. Egyptians were unable to come up with the running capital of the territory while on the other hand, the British pressured them out with power and money to give up the occupation. The British control of the Northern ports of the Gulf of Berbera from the Egyptian government became final in 1884.

Till 1889, the British governed Somaliland from Calcutta of India—a British colony (James Fergusson, The World's most dangerous place: Inside the Outlaw State of Somalia, 2014, page 244). According to Somaliland by Angus Hamilton, the administration of the Somaliland Protectorate was transferred from the Government of India to the Foreign Office in 1898.

Even while the Egyptian still had their feet on from Saylac to Raas casayr (Guardafui), Britain had been already dealing with the Somali clans and signed some treaties with them as mentioned. In the south, in 1892, an Italian Explorer first called Horn of Africa Banadir. From there on, Banadir region was administered by "Compagnia Leonardi (1892—1905), then "Societa Anonima Commerciale Italiana Del Banadir" 1899—1905 until Italy got the whole Banadir from Omani Sultanates which Britain helped Italy to close a deal with the Oman Sultanate in London, January 1905 for 144,000 Sterling Beachey, 17). Before that deal was closed, Italy leased from Omani slave traders, so-called Zanzibari sultanates the towns Baraawe, Marka, Muqdishu and Warsheekh.

1888, Sultanate of Hobyo (1845—1911) of Yusuf Ali Keenadiid entered into a treaty with the Italians, making his realm an Italian protectorate. During the expeditions against the crusade of the Daraawiish—especially the third expedition (Daratoole), the British asked Sultan Yusuf to sell camels and horsed to them. Though he said yes in the beginning, Yusuf ordered that no horses were to be sold to the British or to the Italians except by his express consent.

Though there was no love between them, Sultan Yusuf was not happy with any attack by the Europeans against Sayid Mohamed and the Daraawiish. However, though cutting Jubbaland into two was after World War One, Europeans had completed the process of separating the Somalis into five mini—Somali lands: British Somaliland (north central), French Somaliland (east and southeast); Italian Somaliland (south); Ethiopian Somaliland (Ogadeen, Haud and Reserve), and the Northern Frontier District (NFD) of Kenya during the first two decades of the 20th century. Not much earlier than 1872, the British India Steam Navigation Company (Charles Eliot, 26) established regular communication between India, Zanzibar and Europe; and from that time on, the Europeans were dethroning the Omani Sultanates in East Africa.

According to Somaliland by Angus Hamilton (first publication 1911):198, Hobyo is the first spot or port that Italy set foot in Somaliland, 8 February 1889. With an agreement with Yusuf Ali, the Italian flag was raised. However, on January 31, 1903, Sultan Yusuf and his sons were embarked on board "Nowshera," Italian boat, at 6 a.m., in charge of Italian guard. They will be handed over to the Italian Resident at Aden and from there they were exiled to Eritrea. That was when the Sultan became uncooperative with the Europeans. Hamilton, p214: "31 January,

Yusuf Ali and his sons embarked on board Nowshera at 6 Am, in charge of an Italian guard. They will be handed over to the Resident at Aden until their destination is decided by the Italian government. Nowshera sailed at 9 am Newark Castle was shifted in for discharging at 2pm, and a few stores were landed from her. The wind and sea were bad on this day."

Before the exile of Sultan Yusuf Ali (Angus Hamilton: 214), the Italian government never exercised any great authority in this portion of its protectorate. After the exile of the sultan Yusuf and they empowered his son, Ali Yusuf Ali, the Somalis immediately began to bring in a variety of supplies (ponies, horses, camels) which were offered to the British authorities at reasonable prices. Since the sultan had men including cavalry, forts and ammunition ready for use against the Europeans, his arrest was a well calculated option. Hamilton, p224:

The manner in which the arrest was affected impressive and, at the same time, nicely calculated to overawe any native resistance that might have been offered. Invited at daybreak one morning to go aboard the Italian gunboat, the Sheikh (sultan Yusuf) and his son were detained while a cordon of troops was placed around the village. In the search after arms and compromising correspondence, which then took place, unsuspected reserves of rifles and ammunition were discovered. All together 100 rifles, of the 1874 Gras pattern, and 20,000 rounds of ammunition were recovered, among the weapons being a magnificent bejeweled sabre engraved with the name of Ali Yusuf, and gold-mounted Mauser pistol engraved with the name of Ali Yusuf, the son, the trophies being gifts from the Italian government.

The Italians brought back Sultan Yusuf a year later after no Sultan, king, or any other leader had power. "The Italian deported Sultan Yusuf to Aden and then to Massawa, Eritrea and replacing him by his son, Ali Yusuf. Yusuf Ali was brought back to Hobyo in 1904, much broken in mind and body and nearly blind (Beachey, 51)."

At the northeastern region (Bari), Italian relations with Osman Mohamoud, Sultan of the Majeerteen, and Sultan Yuusuf Ali of Hobyo were limited to the payments of annual subsidies of 1800 dollars to each. The main interest of Italy in her Somali Protectorate lied in the Banaadir. This territory belonged to the Sultan of Zanzibar. It is not very clear if the Zanzibari Sultan was Said Bin Barqash, but the British and Italians dealt with him in gaining control of the Banadir coast.

The Italian Protectorate had been proclaimed in November of 1889. However, that position of Italy was fully recognized August 12, 1892. The rival of the Sultan Yusuf, Boqor Osman (established mid-18th century) also signed a similar agreement with the Italians at Bender Alula (Caluula), 7th April 1889 (1306, Shaban, Hijrah). It states:

We, Sultan Osman Mohamoud Yusuf, Sultan of all the Majeerteen, have our own free will put to this Act our hand and seal. We have placed our country and all our possessions, from Ras Auad-ral-el-Kyle (Uadi Nugaal (Waadi Nugaal) being the furthest limit),) under the protection and government of His Majesty's Ship Taffeta. We declare that we will not make treaties or contracts with any other government or persons.

However, when his rival, Sultan Ali Yusuf Ali Keenadiid was also made powerless, Boqor Osman tried to resist the Italian but it was too late. His son, Hersi Boqor tried to fight against the Italians. He was overpowered that Italy established complete control over king Osman territory at the end of the first quarter of the 20th century.

But in 1862 (Beachey, 16), a treaty had been signed with Great Britain in which the Majeerteen undertook to protect the lives of passengers wrecked on this somewhat dangerous coast. In 1879, and again on May 1885, the agreement was renewed, with further stipulation that 360 dollars should be paid annually to the Majeerteen and to Yusuf Ali of Caluula (Alula).

That was a chance that Great Britain missed with an error to sign a treaty of protection with the Caluula (Alula) kingdom—a possibility that present-day northeast (Bari), parts of Mudug and Nugaal regions could be a part of British Somaliland—as one British author said, "The whole land of the Somal should have been opened up by Englishmen to English commerce many years ago."

Note: Sultan Ali Yusuf Ali inherited the Sultanate from his father, Yusuf Ali Keenadiid who created the rulership around sometime of 19th century 1870s).

Ruins of King Osman's castle in Baargaal, said it was built in 1878, a seasonal capital of the Osman's Sultanate/kingdom

Sometimes, a love for power or rule does not know blood relations. Both Majeerteen rulers entered the protectorate treaties with the Italians for their own expansionist objectives with no cooperation between them. If the opportunity knocks the door none would forgive to overthrow the other. Keenadiid wanted to use the support of Italy to overthrow the Sultan of Zanzibar who controlled Warsheekh (part of the ex-Mudug region) and a surrounding area. Italy completed the occupation of Italian-Somaliland under terms of 1889 protectorate in 1925.

France had the same interests as the other powerful European states to take a share of the Red Sea and the Gulf of Berbera ports. French Explorers such as Robert D'hericourt and Heneri Lambert were coming one after the other to the area. Charles Guillain, a navy captain traveled along the southern coast of the Gulf of Berbera in 1847. He "awakened French interest in acquiring a base in the Gulf of Tojorrah (Raymond Beachey, 12-13)." That was an intimidation treaty that the locals had to sign when a French official was murdered in the area in June of 1859. The incident resulted in the France purchase of Obock in 1862 (Maqaddinkii Xeebaha Birri Soomaal, Axmed I. Cawaale, 2014: 52).

Let us see one treaty between Issa Chiefs or Sultans (Danakil and Somalis) and France government at Obock (Obokh), 26 March 1885, "There shall henceforth be eternal friendship between France and the Chiefs of Issa. The Chiefs hand over their country to France that she may protect it against all foreigners." The word "May" made that treaty unbinding. France was also trying hard to put a foot on the coast of Saylac. Finally, on 9 February 1888, France and Britain concluded an agreement defining the boundary between their respective protectorates. Of that treaty, Zeila (Saylac) and its eastern neighbor Berbera came to be part of British-Somaliland.

Also, Britain ceded Ras Jibouti to France as a part of boundary settlement (Saylac and its people, April 1887, Baadisooc by Ali Abdigir, Amazon 2018, ISBN: 9781983449703 (the black and white one, and the color one, ISBN: 9781983592713: 136-37)). Berbera remained the capital of British protectorate until 1941.

Christian religion became the faith of the Ethiopians in the second half of the 4th century. Then Islamic religion was first introduced to the Somalis by the Prophet's followers in the 7th century and spread faster. Ethiopian Empires started to claim that Ethiopia is a Christian island in an Islamic sea—though Geoffrey Archer (84) put as *"In a sea of Pagans by*

Menelik in 1891." But, before the British came to the Horn of Africa, Ethiopian kings were not in a position to grab any portion of Somaliland. That appeal of a "Christian island in an Islamic Ocean" got European ears. Therefore, British made it possible that the Somali regions are today a part of the Federal Democratic Republic of Ethiopia.

Early Days in Somaliland and other Tales by Harald Swayne, 53, "Prior to 1887, we had not heard of the Abyssinians, for Harar, the Mohammedan state, was between us and Abyssinia and was governed by Mohammedan Amir Abdullahi. All the Abyssinian troubles were to come four years later."

The year of 1897, Menelik captured Harar. In addition, the British encouraged him not to stop there but move into Ogadeen land (www.kaisercroos.com, Article: The Soldier's Burden: Somaliland: 1884-1898; The early British years). They signed an agreement which Menelik had to keep the captured portion and more. A real betrayal took place.

The British Government had signed similar protection treaties with the following Somali tribes: Gudabursi (1884), Issa (1885), Habar-Toljecla (1884), Habar-Garhajis (1885), Habar-Awal (1884), Warsangeli (1886) and Ogadeen (1896). United Kingdom did not respect those protection treaties.

These four sultans whose pictures are displayed and Boqor (king) Osman, signed treaties with European colonizers. Sultan Abdullahi Deria, Sultan Abdullahi Sultan and Sultan Mohamud Ali dealt with the British, Sultan Yusuf Ali, and Boqor Osman Mohamoud with the Italians. The rest of the country which became Somalia in 1960, various local Somali authorities, Sultan Osman Ahmed of the Gelledi Sultanate and Zanzibari Sultanate, which controlled an area including Warsheekh (now part of the middle Shabeelle region), signed with the Italians.

The traditional leaders of the Issas and the Afars of the Jabuuti peninsula had signed off their land to France as well.

With or without the signatures of the traditional leaders, the Europeans had the will and the other resources to occupy. But those leaders had the same choices as Sayid Mohamed Abdulle Hassan. Therefore, that is why Tom J. Farer, the author of War Clouds on The Horn of Africa: A Crisis for Détente wrote, "No account of Somali modern history would be complete without some reference to the unsuccessful war of independence organized and led by Sayid Mohamed Abdulle Hassan."

Of all the ex-colonizers, Englishmen know the Somali even better than themselves. They call them merciless, proud, curious, volatile, friendly, generous, independent and sensitive. We will see such characterizations when the British generals talked about them.

Born and raised as a Somali, it is true that the Somalis are sometimes deceitful, violent, curious, and not easily trust anyone. I believe that these pragmatist elements should be researched openly and honestly. However, most of what the British authors say about the Somalis are unchallengeable, but cannibalism is not common in their stories.

There are many documented stories of cannibalism in all over the world, from Fiji to the Amazon basin to the Congo to the Maori people of New Zealand. Until 12 years of age my family lived in the countryside. Sine the main Somali culture is based on nomadism, I used to hear few cannibalism stories being told to the children in the rural life— especially when nomadic families move for water and pasture, which used to absorb the life of the Somali nomad.

Though it is important to conduct more researches, I believe that cannibalism does not have strong roots in Somali culture.

The English man, Douglas Jardine, the author of The Mad Mullah of Somaliland (cited Warriors) states, "The Somalis, of course, are not, and never have been cannibals. In Fact, considering their antecedents and their amazingly strong prejudices in regard to food, they would be less likely than most European nations to give way to cannibalistic practices in circumstances of dire necessity."

Though what others had said about them do not necessarily materialize, Richard Burton was an early British explorer who had been in some parts of Somalia in 1854-55. He wrote "The First Footsteps in East Africa" about his journey. Somali: The Enchantment of the World by Marry Virginia Fox quoted Richard Burton as, "The Somalis are full of curiosity and travel the world accepting any job without feeling a sense of inferiority, perhaps because they believe that they are superior to anyone else." They were aware of the Europeans expeditions to their land.

The Horn of Africa by John Buchholzer, 109, towards the end of the 19th century, a certain expedition had penetrated a good distance into the Horn of Africa where it came across some Somalis. Somalis asked what all the white men were doing here. "We just want to have a look at your country, replied the leader of the expedition. "That is all very fine, "said the Somalis. "You people always come and say that you just want to have a look at our country, but you look at it so long that in the end we shall have none of it left for ourselves."

When it comes to travelling, according to *The World's Most Dangerous Place: Inside the Outlaw State of Somalia by James Fergusson, 245*, the Somali and Yemen people built the first Mosque in Cardiff (Cathays district which also I. Lewis said in his book "A Pastoral Democracy" that first Somalis settled also in London and Marseilles of France) in 1860. Hanley on page 205:

A free Somali race will be good for Africa. Their bright intelligence, their courage and their confidence will be of value to the new Africa shaping now, if only because they never for a moment felt inferior to any white man, and were never tiresome about being black, or about you being white. They would like Emperor Haile Selassie to give them the camel wilderness of the Ogadeen, which by its bitterness belongs to the Somali people and to their famished camels.

In 1875, about 20 years after the wounded Richard Burton sailed from the Gulf of Berbera back to Aden, British had no control of any place in Somaliland. Africa: Keith Johnston, 275 (PDF) said, "1875, the only secure harbor all along the northern Somali coast of Saylac to cape Guardafui is that port of Berbera 500 large crafts and is safe in all winds (Africa, Keith Johnston, 274 of the PDF version)." More concretely, Rambles:15 "The British took over the Gulf of Berbera ports from the Egyptian Government in 1884, a statement we had seen earlier."

The Somalis at the coastal cities hated the systems of administration of the Egyptians and the Turks for reasons not yet fully known. Those hatreds, financial resources, and advanced weapons helped the British to take over. 1866 (Margaret F. Castagno, 153), Turkey transferred African Red Sea ports to Khedive Ismael of Egypt and gave him ammunition. Khedive then extended his power to the Gulf of Berbera. Geoffrey Archer: 53, "The first clearly established historical facts are the invasion by the Turks from the Yemen in

1500 and the capture and burning of Berbera by the Portuguese fleet in 1516."

The Somali character is sometimes unpredictable. Another British who had been in Somalia in WORLD WAR TWO and wrote a lot about the Somali character (*Warriors and the consul, Gerald Hanley*) states:

Any lingering ideas I had had about some races, religions, colors, or what have you, being better than others, vanished after a year in those wastes. Excellence and the lack of it are everywhere, and I knew nomads (Somalis) with qualities of natural intelligence and vitality far greater than hordes of white men I had known.

Unfortunately, many times, ignoring what they inflict on themselves, the Somalis take their failures to the West without telling some good things that Europeans introduced to them. Because of the past, of course, colonialism is distasteful to many now. At the same time, the Europeans introduced good cultures to the Eastern Horn of Africa.

Having written extensively about them—though I think it is in all cultures, Somalis have an ideological sense of racism. They always find ways to despise other races. If you are not warlike in their terms, they accuse you of cowardice. If you have kink hair and a flat nose, and you are darker in color than them, they accuse you of not good looking. If they are comfortable with your look and character, then, they accuse you of being an infidel.

In general, the Somali culture and customs are based on the nomadic life which is a struggle by itself. Though women are the backbone of the society, sexism is very strong. Bravery is another term they still misuse. To be brave you ought to be a fighter or a killer, or say strong and harsh words when in front of others on behalf of yourself or of your clan.

"*Justice delayed is justice denied*" is a quotation by Martin Luther King Junior. When the colonial powers came to Eastern Africa in the early of the 19th century, they intervened a major catastrophe which was going in the area for centuries. Slave Trade was flourishing. There was a big slave trade market in Mogadishu— the capital of Somalia. The word "Shangaani," a village in Mogadishu is "Shan gee
(take five to the market of slaves)."

Both Saylac and Berbera were also important ports of slave export. So-called Muslims were the biggest slave traders. Rambles in a Lion Land: 47), "In 1848, Berbera was an emporium amongst other chattels for slaves, where the slaves were marched from Harar and the interior. These slaves were shipped to Arabia and the Persia." Slavery in the Muslim world, Arabia, in particular, is very well known, but most Somalis do not like to talk about it, and its effects either.

The Doctrine of Slavery: An Islamic Institution, by Bill Warner, PHD, p1, "There is a big connection between Islam and slavery. Almost every slave sold to the Europeans, mainly UK, Italy, Portugal, Spain, Netherlands, France and USA, or white slave trader was purchased from a Muslim wholesaler." Slavery was a common practice of life in pre-Islamic Arabia and surrounding lands.

It is discouraged but there is no absolute nullification of slavery in the Islamic religion. *"Ye who believe the law of equality is prescribed to you in cases of murder; the free for the free, the slave for the slave, the woman for the woman. But if any remission is made by the brother of the slain, then grant any reasonable demand, and compensate him with handsome gratitude. This is a concession and the mercy from your Lord (2.178)."* From the Arabian point of view, there were two norms— black were negatively associated with slave—and being black and non-Muslim was the worst.

The British fought hard with the Somali clans to stop selling their own people. The main reason that Aw-Ali group (Aw-Ali: The man who killed William Stroyan, a British lieutenant killed in Berbera) attacked the Richard Burton group in Berbera in April 18-19, 1855, was that the Somali chiefs believed (that Burton and his men were spies working for the British Government against the slave trade (Africa Explored, 206)). "Arab dealers and their Somali associates had to go deeper and deeper into Africa to find slaves. Area after area was, in consequence, depopulated, villages burned, as long trains of people, bound or chained together by the neck, slowly made their way to the coast (The Horn of Africa by John Buchholzer, 19)."

Britanica.com: Slavery Abolition Act, August 28, 1883, effected on August 1, 1834 (Royal Assent), "In British history, act of Parliament that abolished slavery in most British colonies, freeing more than 800,000 enslaved Africans in the Caribbean and South Africa as well as a small number in Canada." Slavery became illegal in Qadar in 1952, Yemen which still practices under the rag in 1962, United Arab Emirates in 1963, Oman in 1970, Saudi Arabia in 1962.The Holy Quraan talks about slavery in many verses, such as 2:177-178, 4:25, 4:92, 5:89, 14:31, 24:33, 58:3, 9:1-12 and many more.

In 1981, 147 years after (1981-1834) when slavery was outlawed by the British, Mauritania on the Atlantic Ocean Coastline made slavery illegal, the last country in the world to do so, and Saudi Arabia in the 1960s.

Some slavery events which used to take place in the 1800s, this one in 1872, *The last Slave Market, Alastair Hazell, 2011: 233,* "Slaves had been exported from the East African coast for thousands of years. When the British ships blocked the Indian ocean, slaves were transported by land to Somalia from where they could be sent elsewhere. In Somalia, prices were high, annual fair at Berbera off Somali coast went on for months, creating a huge demand. From there, many slaves were shipped on up the Red Sea, across to Arabia and into a wider world.

Young Somali mother and Babe: Aden, National Geographic magazine, Photographed June 1917 by Mrs. Charles K. Moser. Even the primitive heart of a Somali woman is instinct with a sense of protection for the innocence and helpless of a child.

Islamic religion openly speaks about slavery. The same people who claim that religion came through them to refrain from inhumane cultures and customs and the men who were capturing and selling their own people kept practicing the horrible business. In reference (thanks to Ahmed Awale for this piece) to *Faculty of Oriental Studies of University of Oxford, the dissertation of D. Phil, April 2010, with the original source: The Red Sea Region During the "Long late Antiquity (AD 500—1000)*:

An 11th century Arab treatise on slave girls, written by Ibn Butlan of Bagdad (d. 1050) pays special attention to the slaves produced by this region (East Africa): "Most of (the Ethiopian women) have a smooth, soft body, but are weak and often suffer from consumption …. They are good natured and gentle, self-restrained and reliable…. (Beja women) have a golden complexion, beautiful faces, delicate bodies and smooth skins; they make pleasant bed-fellows if they are taken out of their country while still young and whole…. of all blacks, the Nubian women are the most agreeable and tender. The African slaves exported from Saylac 'included both broadly 'Ethiopian' peoples brought down to the coast from the interior, and Berbers (Somalis) from the regions of modern Somalia. Muslim merchants were apparently active in the procurement of slaves from the interior, as already noted.

Schooling was another culture not rooted in the Eastern Hornites. There were constant raids of camels among tribes which the British government worked hard to reverse. Next is one of the warnings that the British Government had given to one of the Somali clans to abstain from all offensive practices, mainly slavery.

According to (www.allsanaag.com and www.somalilandpress.com), January 26-27, 1886 in Bunder Qoori (Laas Qoray), "The traffic in slaves throughout the territories of the Warsangeli shall cease forever, and the Commander of any of Her Majesty's vessels, or any other British Officer duly authorized, shall have the power of requiring the surrender of any slave, and supporting the demand by force of arms by land and sea." Main raids of the Daraawiish started in 1900.

When the Somalis understood that the Europeans pretended superior to other races, Puntites rejected that characterization. But, instead of denouncing the whole notion, they made the situation worse and called themselves superiors as well. They claimed that they were superior to other Somalis, and some other nations. One letter written (in English) by Somali Darood elders in 1922 to the Chief Native Commissioner says *((Unravelling Somalia, Catherine Besteman, 1999, 119:*

The Government officials who have visited our country know we are decedents from Arabia, and this we have already proved and we can prove we assure you we cannot accept to be equaled and compared with those pagan tribes either with our consent or by force even if the government orders this we cannot comply with, but we prefer death than to be treated equally with these tribes for as the government knows well these tribes are inferior to us and according to our religion they were slaves who we used to trade during past years.

In 1897, a powerful Biyomaal elder (a Somali clan), Xaaji Cali Ciise wrote to an Italian Administrator, in his book, *Xusuusqor, p.23, Farah Mohamud Mohamed* writes, "Our slaves escaped to Marka, and we cannot do anything without slaves. If you try to run the country without slaves, there is a destruction to the country, and to your administration as well." "Equality complex" was absent from the Daarood elders and elder Xaaji cali Ciise. It is a known factor that animals mostly fear the unknown where the humans, the most sophisticated animals known so far are searching for the truth.

Dr. Alfred Alder (1870-1937) was an Austrian medical doctor and psychotherapist. He said, "The person who feels superior to others has an inferiority complex which he wants to overcome." The answer you would have possibly liked to know is how the feelings of superiority and inferiority complex are acquired. We could only find: "Superiority complex is either developed from a defensive need to overcome inferiority or constant overwhelming feelings in which an individual feels truly superior to others.

It is usually said, "European dismemberment of Africa," but in the case of Somaliland, Egypt, and Ethiopia, two African countries were there. Britain kicked Egypt out of northern Somaliland before the real partition.

Conflict in the Horn of Africa: The Kenya-Somalia Border Problem 1941-2019: 235, Vincent Bakpetu Thompson, "Hence, France which was previously kicked out of Egypt by the British, Britain, Italy and Ethiopia which instead of being dismembered participated in the partition, have disjointed the Puntland from 1880 to 1897. That was when the Europeans have had signed all the main treaties with the Somali clans." We close this chapter of with an admittance of the British government.

In February 1955, the British Minister of State for the Colonies stated in front of the House of Commons (The Betrayal of the Somalis: 32):

Three rival European powers in the Horn, and two African powers, Egypt and Ethiopia, the region was still strategically important for the powers seeking to retain and expand their respective spheres of influence. I think that in many ways the 1897 Treaty with Ethiopia was unfortunate, but it suffered from our limited knowledge of Somaliland at the time and we must see it against a background of that knowledge and the expansionist tendencies of Ethiopia.

The treaty which the minister was referring to is from The Betrayal of the Somalis by Louis Fitzgibbon, p.28, "On May 14, 1897 Britain also concluded an agreement with Abyssinia, despite the treaties of protection signed with the Somalis in 1884-1885 and 1886, thus effectively "giving way" parts which never hitherto been under Abyssinian control."

In the history of the two nations, Ethiopia and Somalia, 1897 was a glorious year for one and disaster one for other (Somalia).

Now we can recall that When Menelik captured Harar in 1897, it was the British who encouraged the Ethiopians to move into Ogadeen land (www.kaisercroos.com, Article: *The Soldier's Burden: Somaliland: 18841898; The early British years*). Aside from the Sudan consideration, the main preoccupation of the British with Somaliland was to secure fresh supplies for the garrison at Aden and to secure the safety of their ships on the way to India and the Far East. It was for this reason that British concern was always for the coast and not for the hinterland. While on the hand Some British politicians claimed that the campaign of the Sayid disrupted the development of Somaliland.

Angus Hamilton said in his book of *Somaliland*, "The Somali is a born trader; and, if we could content ourselves with establishing our authority our own spheres and define our economic policy by the development of the ports of Bullaxaar, Saylac, and Berbera, and the provision of a light railway between the coastal contents and the interior, the trade and produce of the country must continue to develop." The railway between Djibouti and Addis Ababa started in 1897 and completed in 1917.

If the British built just one railway from Berbera to either Burco or Hargeysa, a distance of fewer than 200 KMs, that would have played a vital role in the development of the protectorate.

But in reality, for the British, the coastal area of Somaliland was always of interest for strategic and commercial reasons because of its location near the Bab Al-Mendab straight at the entrance to the Red Sea (Suez Canal), and proximity to Aden which is only 160 KM from Berbera. "Interior Somaliland was of a little political or commercial interest," Aden Second Assistant Resident, Langton Prendergast Walsh (www.kaisercroos.com, Article: The Soldier's Burden: Somaliland: 1884-1898; The early British years).

Though the British signed most of the treaties with the Somali clans earlier of late 20th century, the boundary lines were not clearly done until mid of the 20th century.

In Mogadishu, on January 15, 1948, Brigadier General R. H. Smith, the Chief Administrator of the British Military Administration of Italian-Somaliland said in front of Four Power Commission or The Big Four Commission, "The boundary with Kenya was demarcated during the years of 1925-27 (between Somali-Kenya and Italian-Somaliland).

That with British-Somaliland (between British-Somaliland and Italian-Somaliland) was demarcated during the years 1929 to 1931 with the exception of the last few lines near the coast where agreement could not be reached on the subject of the position of the frontier relative to Bender Zeida (present-day Qaw), west of Boosaaso and part of Boosaaso district. 60 years before that, Colonel H. G. C. Swayne, Early days in Somaliland and other tales–A Pioneer's Notebook, Volume 1, 18841892, 1996 edition, p. 53:

I had now surveyed the greater part of the Habar-Awal country, the hinterland of Berbera and Bullaxaar so far as Guban, the lower country west and had produced a "Map of the Habar-Awal country" three miles to one inch. I had also surveyed Eilo Range and the Bullaxaar to Saylac Route and produced a "Map of Eilo Range, Gudabuursi Hills and Bullaxaar to saylac Caravan Route." These maps were sent to Poona and one of the Habar-Awal countries was printed there during 1886. So far, my only (and the only, except James' Route) exploration beyond Guban (the low country) had been my two dashes to Jerato and Murgo. I have not yet shot a lion, Leopard or Elephant and of course, had not heard of rhinoceros.

The original purpose of Captain Harald G. C. Swayne and his brother Captain Eric of Royal Engineers was hunting. Harald Swayne came to the Somali lands at least 17 times. Both brothers also contributed significantly to the surveying and mapping of the interior. Eric Swayne returned to Somaliland as the British commander in the 1901 and 1902 campaigns against Daraawiish crusade, Ilig (a location near Eyl of Nugaal region) Expedition Third, in particular which the Daraawiish lost heavily. One time, Daraawiish were trapped between Abyssinia and the British. "Showed his genius for war for a daring move, following a heavy rainfall, when pools of water aided moved, he moved to Nugaal Valley (Roy Irons, 69)."

Hamilton, p55, "Fortunately, the newly appointed commanding officer, together with his brother, Major Swayne, of the Royal Engineers, was familiar with the region and was known to the tribesmen, while the two officers had rendered valuable services to the Imperial Government during the course of various hunting expeditions which they had made there." The majority of the Somalis were not very aware of the ramifications that future ecological imbalances would bring. Even there was a time they asked Richard Burton to help them kill the lions and the elephants.

Chapter five referenced notes

The Holy Land of Punt
Nora to the land of Punt (cover)
Hathor Rising by Alison Roberts, 8
Rambles in Lion Land by Francis Barrow Pearce, 1893, 232-3
The Mystery of the Land of the Punt Unraveled, second edition, 2015, p. 29- 30
The Mad Mullah of Somaliland by Jardine, 282
The Mystery of the Land of the Punt Unraveled
The First to be Freed, p64
Rambles in Lion Land: 26
The Horizon History of Africa by American Heritage Publishing Co., Inc.,
New York, Volume 1, a package of 2 volumes of more than 560 pages with editors of about 16 scholars
Versteegh, Kees, 2008, Encyclopedia of Arabic Languages and Linguistics, volume 4, Brill, In Search of a State
The Doctrine of Slavery: An Islamic Institution,2010, by Bill Warner, PHD,
Before Blackhawk Down by Abdurahman Sharif Mahamud
Douglas Jardine, the author of The Mad Mullah of Somaliland states
Dawn from the Civilization to the Modern Times by Mohamed Farah Aideed and Satya Pal Rubella on page 83 quoted Burton

James Fergusson, The World's most dangerous place: Inside the Outlaw State of Somalia, 2014, page 244

Pirates: A New History, From Vikings to Somali Raiders

Africa: Keith Johnston, 274-275 (PDF)

Warriors and the consul, Gerald Hanley

Rambles in a Lion Land (p.47

The last Slave Market, Alastair Hazell, 2011, 233 National Geographic Society, June, 1917   www.allsanaag.com and www.somalilandpress.com   Unravelling Somalia, Catherine Besteman, 1999, 119

Timelines of Somali History, p.23, Farah Mohamud

Conflict in the Horn of Africa: The Kenya-Somalia Border Problem 19412019: 235, Vincent Bakpetu Thompson

The Betrayal of the Somalis, 32,28

www.kaisercroos.com, Article: The Soldier's Burden: Somaliland: 1884- 1898;

The early British years

Colonel H. G. C. Swayne, Early days in Somaliland and other tales—A Pioneer's Notebook,

Volume 1, 1884-1892, 1996 edition, p. 53

The East Africa Protectorate by Charles Eliot, 1905

Chapter SIX

The Exile Government of Sayid Hassan

No account of Somali modern history would be complete without some reference to the unsuccessful war of independence organized and led by Sayid Mohamed Abdulle Hassan. __Tom J. Farer, the author of War Clouds on The Horn of Africa: A Crisis for Détente.

For two decades prior World War 1, Mohammed Bin Abdulle Hassan, the self-proclaimed Mullah of Somaliland, was a persistent thorn in the side of British colonial authorities in the arid, sweltering East African protectorate. To the British he was the "Mad Mullah," a quasi-religious bandit leader intent on plunder and disruption who imposed his will through savage execution and mutilations. To his adherents he was a messianic Sunny holy man, jihadist and freedom fighter. Regardless, the Mullah and his ferocious Islamic fundamentalist dervishes survived four major military expeditions sent against them by the British, in fighting so intense that no less nine Victoria Crosses (Medal of bravery) were awarded. Although the Mullah was defeated in battle several times, he was never captured. __The Hunt for The Mad Mullah of Somaliland by Derek O'Connor.

Somalis had many great heroes. Unfortunately, their histories are not fully documented. The one most written and talked about is Sayid Mohamed Abdulle Hassan. Heroes are not limited to Ahmed Ibrahim (Ahmed Gurey) and Sayid Mohamed Abdulle Hassan. The Somalis must write about Omar Samatar, Sheekh Bashir, Sheekh Hassan Barsame, Farah Oomaar, and the generation of SYL and SNL.

There are at least three major chapters that we say a lot about the freedom fighter which the British called his struggle "The Exile Government of Sayid Mohamed Abdulle Hassan." We touch from his arrival and anger in 1895 to his death in 1920. Soon after the Europeans almost signed treaties with the Somali clans, and divided the land with their own borders, the Sayid started a crusade campaign, mainly Britain and Ethiopia. The struggle took longer than thought until Britain used modern technology.

Though there are more unanswered questions, it is believed that Sayid Mohamed came back with hatred of colonization and more education than most of the local religious leaders in 1895. But when he decided to build an army with a clear intention of freeing his country from occupation is another broad subject of research. Author Farah Mohamud Mohamed believes that Sayid Mohamed was against the old establishment in the land, whether Sultanate, kingdom or any other system of rule.

Whether he wanted to acquire power or a unified for the colonizers is not clear. *"You are with us, or against us"* is a quotation very known for George W. Bush during the September 11, 20101. That term was used centuries before 21th century. Nobody fully analyzed whether the Daraawiish used to raid only the neutral and European-friendly clans or any clan to feed his army?

In 1899, a letter to Sultan Abdullahi Deria, Sayid Mohamed said, "The British *have destroyed our religion and made our children their children.*"

Another episode that added to the anger of the Mad Mullah and raised the public awareness in general took place in 1902. There was a famine taking place in northern Somalia. People were coming to Berbera for food being given by a missionary. Father Etienne, the head of the French Catholic missionary was mixing the help of the needy with teaching of Christianity principles.

The news of the Christianization reached Sayid Mohamed Abdulle Hassan. That did not help the British to quell the cry of the public in general and Sayid Mohammed. Hamilton, p115:

By January, 1902, Berbera was crowded with refugees clamoring for food, and imploring the missionaries to take care of their starving children. Unfortunately, the good fathers of French Mission, having barely what would feed the children already under their care , were compelled to refuse many of these supplicants .The head of the French Catholic Mission (established in 1891) in Berbera at this time was Father Etienne, whose gospel of humanity, preached to all alike, was imbued with the finest principles of *Christianity....As it was, by March so intense was the famine, that a woman and girl were discovered devouring human flesh, having actually roasted a small child. This occurrence, though reported by Father Etienne, was an isolated incident of the ravages of the famine; for while many people died of starvation and distress was general, the missionaries contrived to rescue a good number of the victims.*

Happily, the famine was but a phase of the conditions which the activities of the Mullah set up in the protectorate and the British forces had to surmount.

The Europeans constantly fought among themselves to grab the lands of other weak nations. Both Menelik and Haile Salasse dealt with the Europeans with their own political doses, and the British were always lenient for the Ethiopian kings. Also, French policy with regard to Abyssinia was one of obtaining favorable treatment in furthering her interests in the Nile waters through strong ties of friendship. The railway which connects Ethiopia to Djibouti was one piece of favor.

In his early 30s, the Sayid as a religious scholar came back home from Arabia. He was the right man at the right time. Some Somali clans had too much anger towards the Ethiopian Kingdom.

From there onwards also observing the British occupation and Ethiopian's expansionist conquest, he started his campaign in the north with raids first against Somali clans friendly with British. Having known the history of Ahmed Gurey (lefthanded Ahmed, a Somali nationalist and Islamic scholar who fought against Ethiopia from 1506-43), the news of the Sayid's nationalist activities greatly annoyed Menelik, the King of Ethiopia.

British on the other hand had not yet viewed the Daraawiish as more than a "Mad Mullah" (a name given to him by a Somali interpreter, not a British during his return from Arabia through the Port of Berbera) until his forces had overrun an Ethiopian expedition. Menelik decided to silence the new movement and sent an expedition to kill or capture the Dervish leader. The campaign did not succeed to achieve that goal but took many animals most of them camels from the Somalis. That had further revived the previous tensions of the 13th century between the two African nations.

Before going further with the Sayid's struggle, according to the folktales, we have to explain how the name Mad Mullah might had come up.

When Mr. Hassan landed at the Berbera port in 1895 (the day is unknown), he was asked to pay a head-tax. There was a Somali interpreter. Mr. Hassan said, "Ask him (a British man) if he paid head-tax when he came to this land." The British man did not like that challenge and ordered his arrest. But the interpreter was a smart man. He said to his boss, "Let him go, he is just a Mad Mullah." Nonetheless, being asked head-tax when he came back to his soil annoyed him.

The early years of his teachings, local religious leaders pushed him out of Berbera and Beer near Burco because of conflicts with the teaching of the religion. It is not clear if the first place he moved to was Daymoole where he met some Somali children at the care of a Catholic Mission.

After some time, the British authorities also kicked him out at Sheekh in the Golis range (4,000—6,000 above sea level) 40 miles south of Berbera before he could be arrested. Musa Farah Egarreh was the officer (native political officer) who later became Risaldar—an army rank equivalent to a captain was assigned to arrest the Mullah (Beachey, 77, Geoffrey, 58). That is one of the colonial double standards of how they denied the merits of even those who were loyal to them.

Though the sequence of the dates is not too clear, he then moved to Qoobfardood, about 170 miles from Berbera, Dhulbahante grazing land. He was hungry for reputation and acceptance both from his people and from the colonizers as well. That was also a decade after when the Mahdi of Sudan died (1885).

To rid of the crusade of the Sayid Mohamed Abdulle Hassan which became a reality in 1920, the Great Britain had been in constant touch with Italy: "Berbera, 1April 11, 1901, and signed by J. Hayes-Sadler, His majesty's Consul-General, Somali Coast Protectorate"; then again, Great Britain Foreign, August 9, 1902; Italian Embassy in Aden replied August 25, 1902; then Great Britain Foreign Office, October 10, 1902; Italy replied on October 30, 1902 and so on. At the battle of Gumburo which we will see the details, there were no survivors on the British side, or six survivors according to the Governor of the Protectorate.

During the process of Jidbaale campaign—Expedition Third, in early November of 1900, the British Consul-General talked to Emperor Menelik to cooperate with a large force. After that Expedition, the Campaign of Jidbaale in connection with Ilig base of the Daraawiish near Eyl, General Egerton sent a letter to the Founder and the Head of the Daraawiish to surrender in full, in which his life and the lives of his family would be spared. Daraawiish lost more than 57 men, dead and wounded. British asked Sayid Mohamed to be exiled to Mecca, but never replied that offer.

During that campaign of Ilig, Italian navy bombed from the sea, Ethiopians to Garloogubay, some ships of East Indies station from Berbera to Ilig and the British forces on ground collaborated. The nationalities of colonial armed men against the Daraawiish were Britons, Central Africans, Sudanese, Indians, south Africans (Boers (descendants of Dutch and French protestants)), and Somalis who were always the majority.

The first publication of "Lion Hunting in Somaliland by Captain C. J. Melliss" was 1894. The wild animals of the nation that the British people used to hunt in Somaliland were Lions, Warthog, hyenas, rhinos, ostrich, Elephants, land Turtles, Oryx (Biciid), Goodir (Kudu forest) Garanuug (one kind of Gazelle), Dabotaag (Gazelle), Deer (Deero in Somali, all kinds). We quote this book because Europeans were not afraid of organized forces until Sayid Mohamed Abdulle Hassan challenged them. The cover, "Somaliland By Hamilton, today the Somali Democratic Republic, was once a favorite hunting ground for British officers stationed there or in Aden."

According to Medieval China (Confusion and Concessions: History of the Chinese in South Africa 2005, Melanie Yab, Diane Long Man: page 3), the Chinese used to come to the Gulf of Berbera, the Somali Sea, up to the Northeastern area, all the way to Hafun and used to buy exotic animals such as Giraffe which were caught and sold by the Somalis.

Note: Somali sea is the main water that borders the eastern coast of Somalia, and the entire coastlines of the Somali peninsula (Gulf of Berbera, Somalia sea and the Somali water of the Indian Ocean. The water of the Gulf of Berbera water turning to the Indian ocean is uniquely also called the Somali sea, that is before going further into the Arabian sea. The route of the Gulf of Berbera, into the Somali sea (corner of Raas-casayr (Guardafui)) and the Indian Ocean is one of the most important sea lanes in the world. The vessels which go through that channel are over 30,000 each year. Indian Ocean Monsoons push boats to sail north from April to September, and December to February southwards.

The British carried at least five well-prepared expeditions against the struggle of the Daraawiish. After almost 200,000 (Douglas Jardine: 315), "deaths for 21 years, even in his last days of bad defeat, he refused to dismantle his forces but was ready to regroup and build Daraawiish again."

To Walwaal of the Daraawiish stronghold, the British forces moved through Gaalkacyo, camped at Beyra (15 miles north west of Gaalkacyo) in 27 March of 1903, then to Dhudub, and Gallaaddi to assist the Ethiopians in their operations against the Daraawiish—while the Sayid had established a strong outpost at Jidbaale (*Somaliland, first published in 1911: 305 by Angus Hamilton.*) In general, in 1903, it was not safe for the Europeans to go a few miles into any part of Somali inhabited areas without the help of an armed escort.

On page 315 of The Mad Mullah of Somaliland, Douglas Jardine whose country, Britain used World War 1 fighter planes against the Somali freedom fighters on January to February (some British authored books made the days January 21 to 18 February 1920) the air po of 1920: "His extraordinary tenacity of purpose, faced by a European power, which at once strong and anxious for peace, he (Sayid Mohamed Abdulle Hassan) was never apparently tempted to abandon his ideals and to come to terms."

Ethiopia and the Europeans witnessed his vision of "This is my country you occupy by force which I have the right to defend and rule," at the same time the derogatory names they used to call him include barbarian, butcher, fanatic, tyrant, zealot, madman, bandit and many more. I discussed this with a young Somali author. He put it into this way: "You concurred my land. I asked you to leave. You refused, and I fought back. Many perished in the process. Then, you called me a bandit."

As a refreshment, Dr. Yusuf Abdi of Rutgers University reminded me two achievements that humans invented in an unequal capacity. First, they invented fire which helped them to cook food. Second, they learned how to make bullets and guns. They occupied nations like Somalia. But, Sayid Mohammed was one of those visionaries who refused to take that as a quid pro quo. Killing Somalis in both sides in big numbers started.

Once committed to colonize, the British did not care much about the Somali casualties that more than 98% of the 200,000 were Somalis. It is also a well-known claim of occupiers that they civilized savage people, and we have not analyzed the colonization only from the disadvantage point of view. Europeans occupied Somali lands without the will of the natives. When the Somalis asked them to leave, colonizers refused.

As a last resort, people tried to resist the occupations in many different ways, Daraawiish being the strongest. The result of the born confrontations, 200,000 perished. Hence, to blame Daraawiish and the others who took part of the resistance for the deaths is very much misleading and distorting the history.

In November of 1900, the British decided to recruit, train and arm thousands of Somalis and put against the Dervishes. Mad Mullah: The Sword of rebellion by Julian D. Warner, 217-218:

The best men to wage war in Somaliland were the Somali's themselves. The new recruits would have to be trained quickly to take over from the King's African Rifles. The response to the call for volunteers was truly staggering. On the first day of recruiting alone 1,200 men came forward. The rate of pay for the levy was to be unusually low. Only 12 Indian rupees a month (less than a dollar). That was four rupees less than the coastal police earned.

Colonel Eric Swayne who came up with the idea defended his choice of recruiting Somalis. Since both the men and the horses of the country were accustomed to travelling long distances without food or water, Colonel Eric "too much dependence was placed at first upon the levies—Somalis in this case." Geoffrey, page 55, quoted Douglas Jardine: "They are truly a hardy and frugal people, these Somalis. Inured to danger and fatalistic to a degree, they are more completely at home in the bush, which is at the breath of life to them, than almost any other African race." On page 81, Geoffrey also quoted Jardine, "It is freely admitted by experts that of all Africans he (Somali) is the most difficult and consequently the most interesting to govern or control." But on another angle, according to what the British (Eric Swayne) wrote about the Somali as a military man, "the Somali lacks a sense of discipline; he is prone to idleness, and addicted to boastfulness; and though possessing courage, dash, and even resource, he is so excited as to be beyond control when employed in any considerable strength."

On another issue, any time you see the European phrase "African race," remember that it is a racist term in itself—since they do not say "Any other race, or the human race." The third and Fourth expeditions did cost much the British, in treasure, no less than five million sterling; in blood, the lives of many valuable British officers whom our <u>small professional army could</u> <u>ill afford</u> <u>to lose</u> (The portion of Somali Territory Under Ethiopia Colonization: Somali Government Publications 1974, 25).

Great Britain decided to recruit Somalis to use against the Sayid campaign. But that was not that a Somali man was any Somali man. In selecting them, only those vouched for by responsible chiefs and those belonging to trustworthy tribes were enlisted. No Dhulbahante men were allowed to enter the ranks (Hamilton: 56). Also, those tribes who did not suffer from the Sayid's raids did not come forward to participate the campaign.

British calls the Daraawiish (Dervish) struggle as an exile government, and it was structured into four groups (*Oral Poetry and Somali Nationalism by Said S. Samatar: 119-120*).

1. Khusuusi: Men of impeccable character and selection into the council depended on religion, prowess in warfare and generosity.
2. Gaarhaye (bodyguard): Matters of security in the Sayid's households and generally for order in the capital.
3. Maarraweyn (regular army): Comprised the third branch of the Dervishes, tightly organized.
4. Reer-Beede (general population): The fourth body of the Exile government, the most unstable segment.

Most of the Somalis know Sayid Abdulle Hassan as the father of Somali nationalism. He was the first one who put all the all available resources together and tried to free his country from foreign occupation by force. But there is another chapter of his character to mention.

His poems, killings, alienation of certain clans and robing camels and other kinds of livestock are enough to portray him sometimes as a rude, badmouthed and merciless crusader. Those actions of prejudice against a group or clan were one of the most important bases of rejecting or not welcoming his ideology. But it is not fair how some people because of an anger towards him portray his dislikes towards them. As a matter of fact, Sayid Mohamed badmouthed, raided, and fought against any clan which did not welcome his ideology, regardless of how the

Somalis group themselves into clans or tribes—the records should be set as such.

To sidetrack a bit, in 1995, a cousin of mine had a wedding in Toronto, Canada. He asked me to have a role in facilitation. My first advice to the newly-wed couple was not to allow any kind of poem to say at the wedding. The best praises Somalis usually say are bravery—and such bravery is almost how one Somali killed another Somali. Hence, if any poem would have read at the wedding, for sure, some people at the wedding would have been offended.

But it is a fact as well that the death of the Sayid gave colonial powers more access into the remote areas. Therefore, there is no question that the elimination of his struggle was a sudden stagnation of Somali nationalism as well. When the crusade of the Daraawiish became a force to deal with in 1900, the interests of Italy, France and Great Britain in Somaliland already made the "Horn of Africa" a fully partitioned peninsula, and wanted to keep it that way.

The period (199 – 1921 since the struggle did not die immediately after the death of Sayid Mohamed), is best remembered as the struggle of the Dervish (Daraawiish), Sayid Mohamed Abdulle Hassan against the Somali colonizers, Italy, British, and Ethiopia, the last two in particular. Sayid's tireless struggles to free his country from foreign domination are known as the Daraawiish Fight for Freedom. As a matter of history, his dislike of the colonization arrived with him in 1895.

During the leadership of the young visionary, the Daraawiish had used all the resources available for them at that moment to educate the people about imperialism. The warrior's motivational speeches and poems firmly stay with the people. But many of his own did not get the message, and because of that, instead of siding with him, they have chosen otherwise.

Though one of the main reasons that resulted in the defeat of his resistance is partially attached to his policy towards certain clans starting from his own clan as mentioned earlier, for over two decades, the British and Ethiopia could not stop his struggle. He tried hard to drive the colonial powers, British in particular out of Somalia. His ability of a remarkable poetic talent, his unyielding refusal to submit foreign domination for a right cause, and his vision of Somalism, put him in a position to be recognized as the father and founder of modern Somali nationalism.

As any struggle in the world, there were inner tensions in the Exile Government of the Sayid. The most famous of the inside fights was Canjeel Talo-waa (The Tree of-bad-Counsel). The coup failed, and from there on, the security policy of the Daraawiish had changed. The resistance adopted strict and screening measures afterwards.

In 1908 when the Daraawiish was very strong, a letter came from abroad accusing the Mullah of being 'a sinner against Allah and the Prophet, a veritable kaffir, an unbeliever and a madman.' The letter was from Sheikh Salah in Saudi Arabia, the head of Salihiyah branch of the Islamic religion. The British looked for that letter very hard to use against the head of the Daraawiish, but was unsuccessful. It is believed that the circulation of the news from Sheikh Salah had played a role of failed coup of Canjeel Talo-waa (The Tree-of-bad-Counsel).

To recall how he became the father of the modern Somali nationalism, let us go back to late 19th century.

Ethiopia which was a kingdom for centuries had secured admission to the Brussels General Act with an Italian sponsorship in 1890. There was no special love between the Italians and the Ethiopians, but the Ethiopians were very clever to know what each European power was looking for to achieve through Ethiopian kingdoms. That gave her a right as a Christian state to an unrestricted purchase of European weaponry and ensured its superiority over Somali herdsmen with bows and spears.

At the expense of the Somalis, to please Emperor Menelik of Ethiopia, a British politician, Sir Alfred Peace who visited Somaliland in 1897:

We (British) have prevented them (Somalis) from acquiring arms and ammunition and having deprived them of all means of self-defense…. have left them at the mercy of raiding Abyssinians who have no other employment than that of making raids on Gallas (negative name for Oromo) and Somalis *(The Betrayal of Somalia: 24)*.

Even, in 1941 when the British defeated Italy in the World War Two in East Africa and freed Ethiopia from Mussolini, Britain freed Ethiopia for Ethiopians but not for themselves to colonize (The First to Be Freed, P6):

Ethiopia was never an Occupied Enemy Territory in the true sense of the term. As soon as conditions permitted, in accordance with Mr. Eden's statement of February 1941, the Emperor Haile Selassie retuned not only to his throne but to his power. Britain had redeemed the first of her pledges to free the conquered and to cast down the proud. Still, when the Somalis obtained firearms in other means, they fought back and defeated the Ethiopians in the East of Harar which was worrisome to the British in 1887-1888.

Ethiopia was always in a position to balance the power among the European powers. Since the opening of the Suez Canal in 1869, the interests of the British government were getting bigger, and beyond Somaliland. Britain always wanted to use Somaliland as a stepping-stone to Ethiopia, Sudan and to Egypt where it already pushed France out, or to make sure to prevent pirate attacks on the routes of Zanzibar, India and Egypt. Menelik, on the other hand, was too clever to engage in political tactics with the colonial powers.

The Emperors of Ethiopian never abandoned the ambition of getting a port on the Gulf of Berbera or on the Gulf of Tojorrah, and they could never do it by themselves. When the Europeans overpowered the natives and occupied the Gulf of Tojorrah and the Gulf of Berbera, the Abyssinian kings asked the Europeans for help to get access to Saylac or Berbera or both. This is one of the Menelik quotations: "If the government of Italy occupied Saylac and Berbera and gives the Harar, then we shall certainly have a good channel of commerce."

During the early years of the Somali dismemberment which was a process of 1830s—1900s, Italians generously used to give Ethiopian Emperors loans, arms and ammunition. Having acquired those resources which, the Somalis could not get from the Europeans, Ras Makonnen of Abyssinia (1852-1906) threatened to capture Saylac and add to Ethiopia in 1893 (Beachey, 20).

Even there was a time that the British allowed to give Saylac to Ethiopia, but King Haile Selassie was too greedy to accept the British conditions. *The Root Causes of Political Problems in the Ogaadeen, 1942-1960 by T ibebe Eshete, Northeast African Studies, Volume 13, Number 1, 1991, Asmara University (page 7)*:

There were discussions between Ethiopia and the United Kingdom regarding how to put pressure on the communities around Zeila (Saylac) so as to give the town and the port to Ethiopia: "It seems clear that ... would make it more difficult than ever for us to put pressure on the Essa (beesha Ciise) to hand over Saylac under any condition." Letter from military Governor's Office, July 10, 1947, FO 371/53526, UK National Archives.

[Africa's First Democrats by Professor Abdi Ismail Samatar, 2016, Indiana University Press, 243, *"More difficult than ever for us to put pressure...."* came later when the British realized that it betrayed the Somalis, and at the same time, could not change its mind on 1897 agreements.

Even one time, Ethiopia presented an argument of keeping Somalia and Eritrea. A quotation of Haile Salasse said, "Ethiopia is best fitted to administer Eritrea and Somaliland, the inhabitants of which are the same stock of ours."

Updating his superior in Aden on November 27, 1882 (the Betrayal: 14), a British politician in Somaliland said, "As soon as the port of Assab was opened the Italians began to pour arms through it in a steady flow into Shoa; the French the same through their protectorate, first at Obock and next at Tojorrah."

John Drysdale, 131:

These lands had, de Fact, been transferred by Britain to Abyssinia in 1897, without consultations with Somalis, in order to obtain from king Menelik assurances that would secure Britain's imperial interested in the Sudan and continue supplies of Somali mutton, largely produced in Haud, for Britain's coaling bunker in Aden. Two fruitless attempts were made by the British government to acquire area. First, Ethiopia was offered a corridor to Saylac but the French objected, and Ethiopia was occupied in any event, was interests in
Assap and Mussawa in Eritrea. There was an agreement of 1906 between France and Britain that would have been another obstacle for the British to close the deal. The second was at

straight swap by Ethiopia of the lands in exchange for cash payment or British battleship. The Ethiopians were not interested. Eventually, the De Jure recognition of Ethiopia's sovereignty over these lands, again without consultation with Somalis, Anglo Ethiopian Agreement of 1954, which was forerunner to Somali demands for independence and precipitate merger with Somalia 6 years later.

Some scholars say, however, that the British was not in full control of Berbera in 1895, and could not have the authority of imposing head tax, especially on the Somalis. The British Government concluded all protection treaties with the Somali tribes before 1895; Gudabursi (1884), Issa (1885), Habar-Toljecla (1884), Habar Gerhajis (1885), Habar-Awal (1884) and Warsangeli (1886). Then, we can say that the colonial power had inserted some kind of administrative control at the port.

In March of 1900, in retaliation, the Dervish fought back and recovered most of the animals, around two thousand camels from Menelik. And as a result, he earned a reputation of a warrior and a hero. So, the first campaign of the Sayid was mainly directed against Ethiopia and the Somali clans friendly with the British, or even neutral. The kingdoms then recognized that the resistance of a young freedom fighter was a power to deal with. Also, the European colonizers realized that the cause of the Sayid was real. His aim was just a great Somaliland without foreign influence, but the time was not ripe for that.

Though they underestimated the force he was putting together, they looked into the matter. The two kingdoms made a joint military force to crash the new nationalist movement. That campaign had opened the gate widely for what is known as the Daraawiish crusade (Exile government as the British calls it). British Lt. Col. Eric John Eagles Swayne assembled a force of 1,500 Somali soldiers led by 21 European officers and started from Burco on 22 May 1901, while an Ethiopian army of 15,000 soldiers started from Harar to join the British forces intent on crushing the 20,000 Dervish fighters.

Still, both the British and the Ethiopian Kingdom were not too serious about the Sayid's crusade. They woke up when he already built a formidable army known as Daraawiish. The period (1903 - 1904), he put together an army of 20,000 which 8,000 of those were cavalry (Said Samatar 122). That may be a bit exaggerated in accordance to their needs—which on the other hands hints why any livestock was to see and take.

Then, from 1895 to 1920, the Daraawiish conducted a war of resistance against the colonizers using guerilla campaign tactics and many times with conventional wars. British officers had superior schooling and firepower, including the first self-loading machine gun. But on the other hand, the cunning Mullah exploited his home field advantage brilliantly. During the struggle, the arms and ammunition were coming through Ethiopia, Jibouti and Laas Qoray as well.

Here are some factors which helped the Daraawiish to exist as a fighting army against a world power. They were familiar with the land and the people. They also believed that they were fighting for the right cause. The most effective weapon which, the Darwish had in poetic speeches used to attract the men, was picturing the resistance as a crusade against Christian invaders. The Somalis had an advantage over the British army because of the adaptability of the harsh factors of the land. The Daraawiish was easily adaptable to the conditions of the territory.

During the crusade, Europeans many times tried to trick him into peace treats but failed every time. There was ongoing communication between the Darwish, the Ethiopian and the British leaders of British Somaliland. Mr. Hassan never blinked that he wanted nothing, but his country free of colonizers. At one time, the British members of the protectorate stayed only at the port of Berbera. One of his famous letters to the colonial powers had said it all (Somalia: nation in Search of a State by Samatar and Laitin, 58): "*I have no forts, no houses, I have no cultivated fields, no silver or gold for you to take. You gained no benefit by killing my men and my count)" is of no good to you... The Country is jungle... If you want wood and stone. you can get them in plenty. There are also many antheaps. The Sun is very hot. All you can get from me is war. If you wish for peace, go away from my country to your own.*"

Though he wrote that letter around 1907 or 1908, the colonial powers could not easily contain the defiance of the Sayid more than another decade. Daraawiish had reached its best time in 1912. That was when they built stone forts at Labo bari, Buuhoodle, Dameer, and Taleex which was the biggest of all. Sayid Mohamed was not thinking very much that the British will use warplanes against him, and therefore, feeling proud and strong, he halted communicating with the Protectorate.

The country which the Sayid constantly used to advise the Europeans to leave is defined by the British as, P124, Roy Irons of Churchill and the Mad Mullah, "The country itself is barren. Certainly, all authorities agree that it has no commercial, no mineral, and no agricultural properties. The poverty of the land is extreme. It is a country valueless to all except the wild inhabitants who live in it, and to them it is dearer than life."

Since the British committed itself to stay in Somaliland and realized that the fight with the Dervish was costly and took longer than thought, it decided to be serious about one of the longest and bloodiest conflicts in the annals of sub-Saharan resistance to alien encroachment. The more than two decades that Dervishes were trying to kick out the colonizers from Somaliland, Britain had four prime ministers, and for sure, the Mad Mullah annoyed all of them.

Finally, Prime Minister David Lloyd George (1863—1945) of 1916-1922, signed the go-ahead attack. For the planes used for the First World War, Britain bombarded Taleex, the headquarters of the Sayid, and other important Daraawiish strongholds in northern Somalia.

According to various notes, the number of the royal air force planes used against the Daraawiish strong holds of Taleh and other forts was 10-12. Some were also used as air ambulances which was also one of the first times of the world's air ambulance. "Whatever the many explanations for his fortress-building, Taleh was an impressive structure by any standard (Beachey, page 93)." The height of the forts was 40-60 feet and 12-14 feet thick.

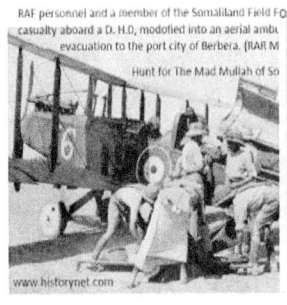

RAF personnel and a member of the Somaliland Field Force casualty aboard a D. H.0, modofied into an aerial ambu evacuation to the port city of Berbera. (RAR M Hunt for The Mad Mullah of So

The man whom the British had known him as The Mad Mullah (the religious fanatic), but in reality, in the Somali society was the Father and the Founder of modern Somali nationalism, the master of Somali poetry and a freedom fighter, the head and the founder of the Daraawiish, Sayid Mohamed Abdulle Hassan died of influenza in Iimeey in December of 1920 at the age of sixty-four. Though the idea lives, that was the end of the leader and his strong Exile Government as the British calls.

Daraawiish fought for 21 years for their fundamental right to self-determination against European powers which believed and said many times, "We are the people who brought civilization to Africa," Harold Macmillan (1920–1986) UK prime minister of 1957–1963, contradicting "We are a society which respects the rights of the individuals." The idea that the Europeans civilized savage Africans still lives in the minds of many. Not even many Somalis believe that the most heinous sin that Muslim people commit is enslavement.

Roy Irons, 22, "There was no greater poet among the Somalis, no greater orator, than the Sayid Mohamed Abdulle Hassan, the 'Mad Mullah.' He was highly intelligent, single mined, deeply religious, ambitious, persuasive…although it inspired fear, although it created an admirable military discipline, acted as a balance and a counter to all the rest, he was abominably, mind numbingly, brutally cruel."

But the date of the death itself is not crystal clear. Most of the writers took the date from each other and put November 23 of 1920. The Somali authors make it in the third week of December 1920. Both groups rely on the stories collected from the survived Dervishes—mainly those with him during his last days. Although the Italians had a non-materialized agreement with the Darwish, according to "The Mad Mullah of Somaliland: 15," since his rise in 1899 (though the rise is earlier than that), no Englishman ever set eyes on him."

Even the period of the Daraawiish resistance is more than 22 years.

The struggle did not immediately fall with the leader in 1920 but dragged till mid-1921. Many of his followers had also succumbed to the epidemic. Others returned to their tribal areas in Somaliland. Some remnants continued to roam the country. The hardcore and last diehards moved south into the region between the upper Jubba and upper Webi Shabeelle to dream of reviving the resistance to one day become again a force to respect.

Also, Sayid Mohamed started building Daraawiish a couple of years before 1899. That is another chapter of the Daraawiish that needs further investigations. In that year of 1899, stated by *Air Power in British Somaliland: The arrival of Gordon's Bird-men, Independent Operations and unearthly retributions by Brigadier Andrew Roe*, Daraawiish had 5000 men, of which 1500 were mounted men.

Churchill (1874—1965) who was the Secretary of State for War stayed two days in Berbera in October 1907 and suggested to occupy Somaliland or withdraw. Somaliland 1905-1913: Military Activities in the Somaliland Protectorate from 1905 to 1907 by Derek O'Connor:

In October 1907 the British Under-Secretary of State for the Colonies, 33-year-old Winston S. Churchill, made a brief stop in Berbera and travelled inland to see the country. He was not enthusiastic about what he saw, and recommended either a withdrawal to the coast or an occupation of the interior that, in an alliance with the Italians, would crush the Mullah. He deplored the lack of a submarine cable between Berbera and Aden, which would be a small investment that could be used to quickly request reinforcements. Back in London nobody was particularly interested in Churchill's report, and it gathered dust whilst its author moved on to become President of the Bord of Trade.

The recommendations of Churchill were "occupy effectively or withdraw to the coast." "For the British there was no retreat and no surrender for The Mad Mullah." According to the article of Military Activities in the Somaliland Protectorate from 1905 to 1907, in 1905 there was an agreement between the Italians and the Daraawiish that Daraawiish could live peacefully in the Ilig area.

Though it was a covert treaty between the Italians and the British, Daraawiish itself was very aware of the intentions of the Europeans and never stopped building Daraawiish. "British had covertly supported Italian ambitions elsewhere in Somaliland by influencing the Zanzibar Sultan to concede the Banaadir ports, and by recognizing an Italian land claim near Kismaayo."

We had seen earlier that the British mediated between the Italians and the Zanzibaris to reach a final agreement in London for 144,000 British bounds. When the British decided to stay in Somaliland and to face the Daraawiish, there took many events which the colonial power documented even when the Sayid had the upper hand.

One night, at the outskirts of Berbera in mid-1900, a British levy of more than 150 trained men had been firing for a while at a goat mistook an attack of the Mad Mullah men. Mad Mullah: The Sword of rebellion, 125: "Archie (British officer) to be confronted by hundred or more ghostly shapes of Dervish spearmen about to charge the perimeter. At first, nothing could be seen. Then to everyone's relief the intruder in the wire was spotted. Mr. McCorder (British officer) chuckled and then roared out. 'It is a bloody goat. A bloody stupid goat. It's got it self-caught up in the wire."

"It reached a point that the British completed its withdrawal from the interior of Somaliland on March 25, 1909 (Churchill and the Mad Mullah, p93)."

The rumor of the British withdrawing from Somaliland alarmed both the Ethiopians and the Italians. At that time, the businesses came into a halt. The caravans became good candidates for Daraawiish interceptions. No clan or group of clans could defend themselves since the British did not arm them with good fire powers, and the exile government of the Sayid was its best of force.

The British renewed the war in 1910 which did not become easy to crush the Dervish resistance. They fought at the war of Dulmadoobe (40 KM, southeast of Burco) where Britain lost officer Corfield.

The Struggle got stronger both in moral and force. Still, it was necessary for the British to stay in Somaliland to keep open Bab Al-Mendab straight at the entrance to the Red Sea, to Suez Canal, to Aden and up to Bombay.

To quell the anger of the public and the Daraawiish towards a possible Christianization, the colonial authorities closed the French Missionary (catholic orphanage) in 1910. In 1930, the missionary asked for reinstatement but the colonial authorities rejected. The losing of Richard Corfield in a battle with Daraawiish had also created a political stir in the UK. Some of the British papers stated that the colonial authorities let an inexperienced officer lead a battle.

Churchill (First Lord of Admiralty), recommended using air power. By May 1914, the Daraawiish was the real candidate of aerial bombardment, but World War One broke out. The British government got busy with the war, and the Sayid increased his fights against certain clans and some coastal towns of both British Somaliland and the Italian-Somaliland until early January 1920. During WW1, politically, the Germans and the Turks sided with the daraawiish. Turks took a position that Sayid Mohammed Abdulle Hassan was the leader (Amir) of Somalia.

Though some documents mention assistance in building military fortifications, financially or militarily, there was no tangible and known support given to the Daraawiish by the Germans and the Turks. During that time, many Dervishes were armed with rifles. Daraawiish used to acquire weapons from Turkey, Sudan and some other Islamic countries.

Even Emperor Lij Iyasu of Abyssinia who was a non-crowned ruler of 1913-1916, symbolically one time supported the campaign of the Sayid against the Europeans. Yasu was the grandson of Menelik II. Margaret, 96: "It is said that Lij Yasu converted to Islam in 1915 and that he was friendly toward Sayid Mohamed. He was deposed in 1916, at which time Ras Tafari (later Emperor Haile Selassie) became regent. In the conflict the coup in which Lij Yasu was deposed, his Somali followers were annihilated."

The British wrote many articles about the Exile Government of the Sayid and published many books. Almost all of them did look back at the man and his struggle almost the same way—better than how some Somalis do. Roy Irons, the author of *Churchill and the Mad Mullah of Somaliland: Betray and Redemption* makes parallelism of Sayid Hassan and Winston Churchill. On page 213:

Both men (Churchill and Sayid) had their own distinct view of the world as young men, which did not change as they aged. Both felt a sense of great destiny, an urge to advance their cause, and themselves, beyond the wildest dreams of most men. Both felt, or knew that they had been born for a great purpose. The paths which the Somali Mullah and the imperial aristocrat took to play out their destiny were necessarily different. Their tools—a commanding personality, a wonderful facility with language and an oratorical power unequalled among their peers— were the same.

However, after the British had silenced the Exile Government of Sayid Mohamed Abdulle Hassan, again, the Protectorate used Royal Airforce fighter planes for Somaliland. Churchill and the Mad Mullah of Somaliland: Betray and Redemption 1899—1921 (page 222) by Roy Irons, "In 1922, when Churchill was Secretary of State for the Colonies, a disturbance which resulted in the murder of Captain Allan Gibb was quelled by just two aero-planes which he allowed to be sent from Aden, the tribes agreeing to heavy fines rather than enduring air attack."

See the Retrieved article of 1922

HANSARD 1803–2005 → 1920s → 1922 → March 1922 → 14 March 1922 →
Commons Sitting → ORAL ANSWERS TO QUESTIONS.
SOMALILAND.   HC Deb 14 March 1922 vol 151 cc1953-4 1953   § 36. Major-General SEELY   asked the Secretary of State for the Colonies whether he can give any information as to the recent events in Somaliland; and can he state what is the present position?
§ Mr. CHURCHILL (Secretary of State for the Colonies)
On 25th February the Governor of Somaliland (Geoffrey Archer) telegraphed that an affray between tribesmen had taken place at Burao on the previous day, in the

course of which Captain Allan Gibb, D.S.O., D.C.M., the District Commissioner at Burao, had been shot dead. Captain Gibb had advanced with his interpreter to quell the disturbance, when <u>1954</u> (Column 1954) fire was opened upon him by some riflemen, and he was instantly killed.

The murderers escaped under cover of falling darkness.
Captain Gibb was an officer of long and valued service in Somaliland, whose loss I deeply regret. From the information available, his murder does not appear to have been premeditated, but it inevitably had a disturbing effect upon the surrounding tribes, and immediate dispositions of troops became necessary in order to ensure the apprehension and punishment of those responsible for the murder. On 27th February the Governor telegraphed that, in order to meet the situation which had arisen, he required two aero planes for purposes of demonstration, and suggested that two fighter planes from the Royal Air Force Detachment at Aden should fly over to Berbera from Aden. He also telegraphed that in certain circumstances it might become necessary to ask for reinforcements of troops to be sent to the Protectorate.

The Air Ministry entertained some doubt whether this flight from Aden to Berbera could be accomplished, as, having regard to the range of the aero planes at Aden, the risk involved was considerable, but on 2nd March a further telegram was received from Somaliland, stating that the flight had been successfully made and that the aero-planes had arrived at Berbera on that day. Telegrams since received from Somaliland report that the arrival of the fighter planes and a demonstration which they made on the following day have had a profoundly satisfactory effect upon the local situation. The Governor now considers that the dispatch of troops to the Protectorate will be unnecessary. The leaders of all the tribes concerned have come in and undertaken to carry out the terms imposed upon them, and the situation is well in hand.

Note: Captain "Alan Gibb had advanced with his interpreter to quell the disturbance, when <u>1954</u> (Column 1954) fire was opened upon him by some riflemen, and he was instantly killed." Allan Gibb took part of the battle of Dulmadoobe in 1912. And we do not know if the killing of captain Gibb was related to culminated anger of his participant of Dulmadoobe battle, the harsh bombardment and the defeat of Daraawiish, in January 1920 to mid-921, it was an isolated incident. Allan Gibb had worked in British Somaliland for over years. For the murder of the District Commissioner, Allan Gibb, 1,000 camels were imposed on the natives (details, Geoffrey, page 135—137). The most important question is: Who killed Alan Gibb and what do we know about him?

However, we are not done with this chapter yet. It is an important mind-feed to be persistent on certain curiosities. Some of the most appreciated money I ever spent on books is the one I paid on "Mad Mullah: The Sword of Rebellion" by Julian D. Warner. At the end of February of 2019, this book: The *Genesis of Somalia's Anarchy* was in its final draft.

I already wrote as you read about how the name "Mad Mullah" came into existence. To me, it was a childhood folktale which I never let it go but never saw it written before 2019. My mind was always speculating if there could ever be any trace of the Somali interpreter and the British officer at the dock of Berbera the day Sayid Mohamed Abdulle Hassan arrived in 1895.

One of those days of late February 2019, as I have been finalizing the first draft, I was checking the names of the old google books about Somalis or Somalia. Some of the books available only at Amazon.co.uk are restricted to be mailed to outside UK, which I (in Canada) was denied couple of times. I saw Warner's book and ordered from the Amazon.co.uk. Mad Mullah: The Sword of Rebellion by Julian D. Warner, 35:

In 1895 he (the Sayid) returned to Berbera. It was on his return that he obtained his name of The Mad Mullah from the British. On his arrival at the docks at Berbera a British custom official demanded that he paid a tax. The Mullah was outraged at such a request. Why should he have to pay an Infidel a tax for returning to his own country? Through an interpreter the Mullah argued with the official. The British were about to arrest him. But fortunately, the interpreter told the British official: 'Don't mind this man sir! He is just a Mad Mullah!' Convinced of the interpreter's explanation the official sent the Mullah on his way as arresting him would appear to create more problems than it would solve.

Sometimes being good to be persistent of good intentions, now we have some confirmation of how the name "Mad Mullah" came up—that it did not originate with the British or the Italians as is often thought. But, still, the most important piece of the puzzle is missing. And, we conclude a question with this chapter. Who were the Somali interpreter and the British officer at the dock of Berbera the day Sayid Mohamed Abdulle Hassan arrived in 1895? The history of the Somali interpreter at the dock of Berbera the day of the Sayid's arrival, to us, should be very important. So, as the British Customs officer.

Chapter six referenced notes

Oral Poetry and Somali Nationalism by Said S. Samatar: 119-120 Canjeel Talo waa (The Tree-of-bad-Counsel), well-known Daraawiish history
The Betrayal of Somalia: 14, 24
The Oral Poetry, the Case of Sayid Mohamed Abdulle Hassan by Said Samatar
Churchill and the Mad Mullah, 124

The Mad Mullah of Somaliland of Jardine, 15
Mad Mullah: The Sword of rebellion, 125
Churchill and the Mad Mullah by Roy Irons, 213, 222   HANSARD 1803–2005 →
1920s → 1922 → March 1922 → 14 March 1922 → Commons Sitting → ORAL ANSWERS TO
QUESTIONS. SOMALILAND, *HC Deb 14 March 1922 vol 151 cc1953-4* 1953
Mad Mullah: The Sword of Rebellion" by J. D. Warne, 35-36r
War Clouds on The Horn of Africa: A Crisis for Détente by Tom J. Farer, 1976.

CHAPTER SEVEN

The fall of Exile Government

Sayid Mohamed Abdulle Hassan (image)

His intimate knowledge of regional tribes' history, culture, and aspirations enabled him to build alliances and to ultimately prevail. Hassan and his ragtag forces hid in caves, survived long deserts crossings by drinking water from the bellies of dead camels and employed varied assortment of survival techniques that would make even American SEAL team units envious. He was a general, imam, politician and gifted propagandist all rolled into one who used poetry and oratory to both inspire his fighters and intimidate his European nemesis. __Oliver Leighton-Barret, a multi-Lingual researcher and decorated retired military officer.

Mohammed Abdulle Hassan, who fought a tenacious 20-year irregular campaign against multiple foreign powers, gained a special place in the British military aviation history due to a self-contained RAF (Royal Air Force, formed on April 1918) expedition employed against him in British Somaliland in the winter of 1919 to 1920. __Brigadier Andrew Roe

"Unbelieving men of religion have assaulted our country from their remote homelands. They wish to corrupt our religion…. Our aim is to cleanse the land of the unbelievers." __Sayid Mohamed Abdulle Hassan.

The first major expedition against the Exile Government of Sayid Mohamed Abdulle Hassan was in May 1901, the Second Expedition in 1903, the Third Expedition in 1903 and the fourth Expedition in 1904. There were other successive expeditions in 1912, 1913, and 1914. At the battle of Gumburo, there were few survivors on the British side. 48 men of 2 Indian Sikhs, a company of 2nd battalion of King's African Rifles (KAR) and their overall British officer, Lieutenant colonel Archer Plunkett were killed in a 2-hr fight against Daraawiish. But the governor of British Somaliland from June 1913 to January 1923, Geoffrey Archer states another side of the Gumburo battle.

But according to *Personal and Historical Memoirs of an East African Administrator* (1963) authored by the Governor himself, page 60, wrote, "Finally, the whole British was annihilated, the casualties amounting to 9 British Officers and 187 other ranks killed. There were only 6 unwounded Yao survivors (*Yao soldiers* in *British* service in Nyasaland (Malawi), 1895-1939. During the *colonial* period, the *Yao* formed the main of King's African Rifles). The whole bitter story was unfolded at the subsequent Court of Enquiry held at Gallaaddi. Daraawiish had a well calculation of that battle. Pages 51—52 of The Warrior Mullah: The Horn Aflame of 1892-1920 by Raymond Beachey, a Canadian wrote:

Unaware of the Dervish spy system and their use of bonfire signals to warn of British troop movements, Plunkett's force rashly pursued, and was lured into the dense bush of the Gumburo hills. The Mullah, choosing a well-sheltered spot, laid his trap, and was ready for them. The British was vastly outnumbered by the Mullah's horsemen and spearmen, and in the two-and-a-half hours of fierce fighting that ensued, it was virtually cut to pieces. News of the Gumburo disaster reached Ethiopians after they had withdrawn to Harar, although they tried to use it as justification for their withdrawal there, and also for their failure to link up with the British Forces.

Daraawiish reconnaissance men 1919, location not very known
www.alamy.com

The battle of Dulmadoobe (40 KM, southeast of Burco) in which Richard Corfield was killed, the commander of the army, 36 British troops get killed and 21 wounded, and the Daraawiish side in the hundreds. After that battle, Daraawiish advanced to control half of British Somaliland. The detailed portion of how Richard Corfield get killed in the battle of Dulmadoobe and the final fall of the Exile Government of Sayid Mohamed Abdulle Hassan is summarized and selected from various books and articles.

The battle of Dulmadoobe and the death of Richard Corfield is detailed in the following excerpts. However, that is from the perspective of the British. It is unfortunate that former Somali administrations did not give much interest in collecting the history. About 40 years before today there were people who had good memory of many events. Even there were elders who took part of the World War 2.

The excerpts of the Dervish State we put in this book are carefully selected and summarized mostly from the "The Mad Mullah of Somaliland by Douglas Jardine, Somaliland by Angus Hamilton, Somalia: A Nation in Search of a State by Said S. Samatar, Churchill and The Mad Mullah of Somaliland by Roy Irons, Mad Mullah: The Sword of Rebellion by J. D. Farer, Personal and Historical Memoirs of an East African Administrator by Geoffrey Archer (1882—1964 (Somalis used to call him Caarshe Dheere since it was not easy for them to pronounce Archer)) —though came to the land as an acting governor in June 1913, he was the British Somaliland Governor 1914-22, according to the book he authored, published in 1963 *"Personal and Historical Memoirs of An East African Administrator,"* Oral Poetry and Somali Nationalism: The Case of Sayid Mohamed Abdulle Hassan by Said S. Samatar, The Warrior Mullah: The Horn Aflame by Raymond Beachey and many more. In the following paragraphs, we will see how the battle of Dulmadoobe was fought in detail. Also, we will learn more about the Somaliland Camel Corps.

"The battle of Dulmadoobe: Command of the Somaliland Camel Constabulary was given to a 30-year old Political Officer, Richard Conyngham Corfield (1882-1913), who had previous service in Somaliland, South Africa and Nigeria. The two other officers appointed were Allan Gibb and Cecil de Sivrac Dunn. Riding camels and saddlery were obtained from India and musketry training was conducted near Berbera. By early December 1912 the Corps was based at Mandera, 68 kilometers south-west of Berbera and it went into the field to retrieve stolen stock from Suulagudub raiders. The operation was successful and 1,282 camels, 11,300 sheep, 170 cows, 17 donkeys, 6 horses and 16 rifles were delivered to cadaadley where a post of the Indian 119th Infantry was located. Thirty-eight of the raiders had been killed for no loss to Corfield's command. This type of low-level operation continued, to the satisfaction of the friendly tribes."

We may say a couple of words why the Somali camel was the ideal transport of the desert to use against the Daraawiish. Beachey, 55, "The Indian camel could carry a 400 bounds load, but could not go for long periods without water, as could the Somali camel. Egerton had bought up or hired over 4,000 of the latter. The Somali camel, although carrying only 160 bounds, was priceless for its power of endurance."

According to Douglas Jardine who authored "The Mad Mullah of Somaliland," for the 21 years of fighting with the Daraawiish, more than 200, 000 people perished inside the Somali inhabitants, most of them Somalis. The Europeans, British, Italian, France and Ethiopia have used to collaborate for the killings of the Somalis. For sure Daraawiish had taken a lion's share of the killings. But the Europeans used to recruit and train Somalis and put them against the Exile forces of the Sayid.

There is also a forgotten war in East Africa, World War 1 where Africans died in big numbers. France and Britain were allies in World Wars 1 and 2 while Italy was on the other side. All the Europeans recruited men for the wars where Ethiopians and Somalis suffered heavily in the Horn of Africa. Their history is not fully documented.

we have previously stated that when gunpowder, handguns and rifles were invented, war-fares entered into new stages and affected the battle fields. The rate of death had changed as well. Europeans first mastered how to use the gunpowder (invented by the Chinese) and the gun, then conquered the weak nations, dismembered among themselves and colonized.

The Somalis immediately learned it was the guns that made the Europeans occupy their land. The forgotten Front 1914-1918: The East African Campaign by Ross Anderson, p21:

In 1914, the KAR (King's African Rifles) numbered under 2, 400 men of whom 62 were British officers, 2 were British non-commissioned officers (NCOs) and 2,319 were Africans. Like other colonial forces of the period, British officers occupied all senior positions and were supported by African non-commissioned officers (ANCOs) who rose from the ranks. The theory of 'martial race' was still widely maintained and this meant that the troops were generally recruited only from traditional, favored tribes."

One time, during World War II, an army of about 600 men had 14 British Officers, one British non-Commissioned officer where other ranks were Africans, 554 mostly Somalis. During battles, you can figure out that the death had a direct correlation to the demographics of the army. Imagine then, the proportion of the death when two African armies of such magnitudes with few European officers face each other. Roy Irons wrote "Their knowledge of the country and ways of the enemy's fighting (daraawiish), wonderful sight, especially at night, and alertness were very strong points known for the Somalis."

The next picture shows the distribution of arms to the Somalis to face Daraawiish. Hence, they died on both sides.

Richard Corfield distributing arms in Burao fort.

Straight from British authors:

"In January 1913 the Corps occupied Sheikh and then Burao, but was not permitted to advance further south although it did move west to settle disputes at Hargeisa. But Corfield chafed at the bit and did move south to Idoweyne to search for Dervish raiders. This action resulted in a critical memorandum to Corfield written by the Acting Commissioner Geoffrey Francis Archer, who reminded Corfield that the Corps was to stay near Burao and was not to take offensive action.

Eight months later Archer visited Burao accompanied by Captain G.H. Summers, 26th (King
George's Own) Light Cavalry, Indian Army, who commanded the Indian Contingent in Somaliland. Archer's arrival was quickly followed by reports of Dervishes attacking friendly tribes between Idoweyne (Idoweyne), Burao and Ber. The friendly tribes requested British protection, and in order to discover the facts Archer authorized Corfield to make a strong reconnaissance towards Ber; Summers was ordered to accompany Corfield as the military advisor.

On 8th August a 15-man pony section from the Constabulary was order to reconnoiter, and shortly afterwards Archer permitted Corfield with 119 camel-mounted men to follow up the reconnaissance and observe the situation. The riflemen carried .303 Martini Henry rifles with 140 rounds in bandoliers plus a reserve of 60 rounds in their saddle bags. Also, one Maxim gun with 4,000 rounds of ammunition packed in cork-lined tin boxes was transported on camels.

Richard. C. Corfield of leading a Somaliland Camel Constabulary 1912. Corfield was killed by the Daraawiish in the battle of Dulmadoobe 1913

At 1900 hours that evening one of the pony reconnaissance party was met coming back to report. He stated that a large force of Dervishes was driving many herds of looted stock towards Idoweina (Idoweyne: Somali); the reconnaissance party had engaged the enemy, firing over 80 rounds each, and had hit several Dervishes who in retaliation had killed two ponies. Corfield advanced for a couple of hours and then formed a sareba with the camels sat down in the center. The fires in the Dervish camp could be seen about eight kilometers distant. The pony section returned with a Dervish strength estimate of 2,000 footmen and 150 mounted men, all armed with rifles. The Dervish leader was Ow Yusuf Abdulle Hassan, a brother of the Mullah. Local friendly Dhulbahante tribesmen assured Corfield that they would provide at least 300 men tomorrow, armed with rifles or spears, to assist in recovering their stolen stock.

Corfield expressed his intention of either attacking the Dervish camp that night or of intercepting the enemy during the next day, and he sought Summers' opinion. Summers was adamant that Corfield could not win a battle against such a strong Dervish force, and he urged him to stick to his orders and just reconnoiter. But Corfield wanted a battle and he decided to intercept the Dervishes the next day.

Corfield moved his men out at dawn, tracking the Dervish line of march by the dust clouds that the herds threw up. At 0645 hours near a location named Dulmadoobe (black hill, 40 KM, southeast of Burco) Corfield's men were ordered into a skirmish line to face the left flank of the Dervish advance, with the Dhulbahante tribesmen positioned on the left flank. Corfield attempted to advance his line through thick bush in order to reach more open ground ahead but the Dervish advance was too swift, catching Corfield in a totally unsound position where his men could not always see each other. Summers urged Corfield to form a square, the safest formation to adopt as it could not be dangerously out-flanked as a line could, but Corfield wanted all his riflemen to fire at the same time, and so he left them floundering in a skirmish line without a reserve of troops or flank or rear protection.

The Dervishes scented victory and charged forward, firing as they ran; nearly all the Dhulbahante tribesmen immediately fled the scene. The Constabulary line was quickly outflanked causing some of Corfield's men to disperse to the rear. The Maxim gun fired three belts but was then permanently put out of action by bullet strikes on the mechanism. Richard Corfield, who had positioned himself near the gun, was shot and died instantly at about 0715-hours." * ****

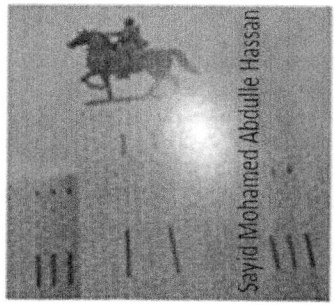

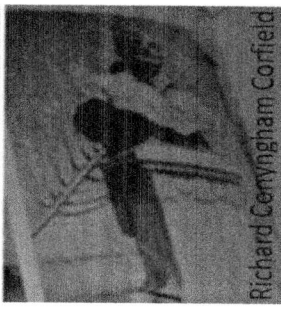

Sayid Mohamed Abdulle Hassan | *Richard Cervyngham Corfield*

There is a reason we display the attached statues (the oppressed and the oppressor). Though even the struggle of Sayid Hassan is not free of controversy, the worst irony of the monuments is that the oppressor (Corfield) who killed the freedom fighters of the colonized nation get rewarded with medals. Who did it? His country, the Great Britain. It is why that there is no total fairness on earth. The British officers with Richard Corfield were Assistant Commandant Mr. C. de. S. Dunn, temporarily attached Captain G. H. Summers, Rank and file 109 men and Followers 7. When he became the full governor of British Somaliland, 1914, Sir Archer established his headquarters at Sheekh (page 86), and that year was the first time that a wireless colonial station had been erected in British Somaliland, at Sheekh.

About the Dulmadoobe battle, 57 men out of 110 were killed or wounded. When the British first encountered with the Somalis, it immediately recognized the affinity between the Somalis and camel charges and that was one of the reasons of why Somali Camel Corps was created.

When the First World War was over, the last resort to defeat the Dervishes became an air power. 12 DH9 cockpit-open planes called Z-unit which two were later adjusted as air ambulances were shipped from Victoria Station of London via Boulogne and Marseilles of France to Egypt.

The major components of the planes were assembled in Egypt, then shipped to Berbera (Airpower in British Somaliland: The arrival of Gordon's Birdmen, Independent Operations and unearthly retributions by Brigadier Andrew Roe). They arrived in late December of 1919.

The technicians, pilots, and necessary know-how people came to Berbera through Aden disguised as geologists and oil drilling experts. It was told to the locals that the British are going to undertake an oil-drilling operation in the Protectorate. Geoffrey Archer, 101:

To give effect to this plan, I summoned the officials in Berbera and pledging them to secrecy, I informed them the operations were about to begin, and indicated the expedient by which it was hoped temporarily to keep the matter secret from the Somalis. We knew that the best way to spread a report was for the Europeans to talk about confidentially among themselves in the club in the presence of the servants. True to form, the "leakage" worked. Group Captain Gordon, with an advanced party of Royal African Rifles, were due in Berbera in November 1919, and to play their part in the game they arrived Aden by Dhow in mufti- disguised as oil experts.

Somalis had already seen airplanes at Aden, they neither knew for their intentions nor of the demoralizing effect of an air attack. According to *The Horn Aflame: 1892—1920 by Raymond Beachey, 131*, exploration was done in 1921 and 1924 and concluded that there was not worth exploiting.

The Hunt for The Mad Mullah of Somaliland has been retrieved from www.historynet.com*: Frequent contributor Derek O'Connor writes from the U.K. For additional reading he recommends:* RAF Operations 1918-39, *by Chaz Bowyer; and Personal and Historical Memoirs of an East African Administrator, by Sir Geoffrey Archer. The Hunt for The Mad Mullah of Somaliland was Originally published in the July 2012 issue of* Aviation History. *All or part of the article had been written in November 1, 1920.*

De Haviland D. H. Of the RAF's Z-Unit until the line up for a mission against Mohammed Bin Abdulle Hassan, who had defied British Colonial authorities in
Somaliland for two decades. Royal Air Force (RAF) Museum, Hendon Derek O'Connor

The photos in the article of the aerial bombardment of the Daraawiish bases are taken from the Royal Air Force (RAF) Museum, Hendon of UK. Suburban Hendon is known for the Royal Air Force Museum, with vintage aircraft, flight simulators, and a 4D Cinema. The article has been retrieved from www.historynet.com.

At least 300 men and 200 women were employed to clear 200 yards airstrip at Ceelduur Ceelaan, about 100 miles from Berbera. In parallel to that, reattaching the aero planes was completed during the third week of January 1920. The ground force was British Somaliland policemen, Somaliland Camel Corps which its headquarters was in Lafaruug (near Mandheera between Berbera and Hargeysa, 1939-1944), King's African Rifles and battalions of Indian army.

When the planes were assembled and tested, the protectorate prepared at least two more airstrips closer to the Daraawiish bases—Laas-Qoray being one of them. British informed the Italians about the operation. The Z-Unit squadron consisted of 36 officers and 183 other ranks.

Derek O'Connor of <u>The Hunt of Mad Mullah of Somaliland</u> states that air bombardment of the Exile Government of Daraawiish proved for the British to be an important step to subdue resistances against colonization. O'Connor says, "Although the Royal air Force (RAF) had been used in India to support the army in controlling local unrest, it was the campaign against the Mad Mullah that proved independent air power could play a vital role in suppressing colonial rebellions. Thus, it suppressing not only guaranteed the survival of the RAF as an independent service, it also set the pattern of air policing for the next two decades, notably in Iraq."

Chapter seven Chapter referenced notes

RAF (Royal Air Force) expedition employed against him in British Somaliland in the winter of 19191920. __Brigadier Andrew Roe

The Hunt for The Mad Mullah of Somaliland has been retrieved from

www.historynet.com: *Frequent contributor Derek O'Connor writes from the U.K. For additional reading he recommends:* RAF Operations 1918-39, *by Chaz Bowyer; and Personal and Historical Memoirs of an East African Administrator, by Sir Geoffrey Archer.*
__Air Power in British Somaliland, 1920: The Arrival of Gordon's Bird-Men, Independent Operations and Unearthly Retributions by Brigadier Andrew Roe who made around 90 citations. October 18, 2018. Brigadier Andrew Roe is the Director of the Higher Command and Staff Course
 and Assistant Commandant (Land) at the Defense Academy, Shrivenham.

__Moyse-Bartlett. H., The King's African Rifles. 1956, Gale and Bolden Ltd, Aldershot.
Reprinted by the Naval and Military Press Ltd.
__Jardine, Douglas, The Mad Mullah of Somaliland. 1923, Hebert Jenkins Ltd., London.
__Digest of History of Somaliland Camel Corps, KAR.
__3rd Battalion King's African Rifles Historical Record 1895-1928.
__ British Battles and Medals by Hayward, J., Birch. D., and Bishop, R.,

CHAPTER EIGHT

The proposal of Geoffrey Archer V The Counter proposal of Sayid Mohamed: March -April 1920.

New researches highlight that influenza or the disease that killed Sayid Mohamed Abdulle
Hassan on December 20, 1920, might be the Second Wave of the **Spanish Flu** of 1918— 1920 which 2.5% of the world population succumbed to it, and will see couple of citations at the end. The Governor of British Somaliland, Geoffrey Archer who defeated the Daraawiish with airpower in 1920 believes that Sayid Mohamed Abdulle Hassan died of influenza (Geoffrey: 113). It is said that Haji Waraabe whom Archer promised him of big reward if kills the Sayid was the last man who got close to kill the head and the founder od Daraawiish. One of the situations that helped the British was the landscape of Somaliland. Archer states that "The flat, open nature of the country, and the general absence of caves in a mountainous region were the greatest help in Somaliland, and for the R. A. F. (Royal African Rifles) the conditions and the terrain generally were truly ideal."

When the Daraawiish was defeated remnants of the Sayid, mostly Dhulbahante of Habar Jeclo dispersed inti their clans. Ray Beachey, a Canadian professor and an author of *The Warrior Mullah: The Horn Aflame: 1892—1920*, wrote, "Sayid Mohamed Abdulle Hassan was a man of immense charisma, a master of desert and querela warfare, an able politician and negotiator, a man of cruel and merciless temperament indifferent to human suffering." Douglas Jardine who was the secretary to the British Somaliland administration from 1916 to 1921 also wrote, "His extraordinary tenacity of purpose, faced by a European power, which at once strong and anxious for peace, he (Sayid Mohamed Abdulle Hassan) was never apparently tempted to abandon his ideals and to come to terms."

Douglas authored one of the best books ever written about the Sayid Mohamed Abdulle Hassan and the Daraawiish, The Mad Mullah of Somaliland. In reference to the book, 291-292, Geoffrey Archer, the Governor of British Somaliland sent this letter to Sayid Mohamed Abdulle Hassan on March, 1920. According to Geoffrey Archer (109), the Ergo had set out from Burco on the 9th of April, 1920. The where abouts of the Sayid his diehard followers were helped by the capture of the Mullah's second son Abdelrahman Jahid and his uncle Haji Osman (Geoffrey: 106).

The proposal and the counter proposals continued from March 1920 to May 1920. The last reply received from the defeated warrior, Sayid Mohamed Abdulle Hassan went to Geoffrey Archer, the Governor of British Somaliland on the second week of May, 1920 (*110 of Personal and Historical Memoirs of an East African Administrator*).

To Sayid Mohammed bin Abdullah Hassan. May God preserve him in good health. "After compliments, I inform you this letter is sent with important people, recognized leaders of the diin (religion), the government, and the tribes. Their names are:

Sheikh Ismail bin Sheikh Ishak, head of the Salihiyah tariqa."
"Sheik Abdullahi Bin Sheikh madder (Madar), head of the Kadarieh (Qaadariyah) Tarika.
"Sheik Mohamed Hussein, head of the Andawarieh Tarika."
"Akil (Caaqil" Ali Aden, Habi Yunin (habar- Yoonis), reer Sugulleh, Bah Diiriye."
"Akil Jama madar, Habar-Yoonis, reer Sugulleh of reer Rooble Sugelleh."
"Akil Hagi Ibrahim Warsame, Habar Yonis, Reer Sugulleh, bah Sugelleh."
"Akil Hersi Hussein, habar Yoonis of reer Hussein. "Akhil Hagi Abdillahi Jama, Habar Toljeclo, Sulamdoo.
"Akil Ali Guled, habar-Awal of reer Ahmed."

"These men are sent to you as an ergo to discuss Aman (peace) and to offer terms. And you are aware that under Somali custom and the Mohammedan Sharee as well as under Government practice, an Ergo has safe conduct from all, and is entitled to the hospitality extended to strangers, so do not abuse this rule. They are my delegates and the words they bring are sincere and true. If you do not accept the terms I offer, then return the Ergo in the way in which they have come, i.e. in safety. God is the judge of what is right. But if you accept my terms, then come with my delegates in Aman so that all men may know you come in this manner. I have treated your Ergo with kindness, and I now send them back to you. That is one thing.

"Now, with regard to your letter I need say thing, for it does not make your intentions clear; and in sending a reply many people advise I am wasting time. This may be true. But your Ergo swear Qur'aan that you desire Aman: and I feel it is better to effect peace by settlement than war, if it is possible. So, I have sent you this letter under my signature, offering you terms of peace in case you wish to end a quarrel of 21 years and live in immunity for the rest of your days. You have tested the bitterness of war. You will do well to try the consolations of comfort." "The conditions I offer are:

"First, I will assign to you a locality on the Galbeed (western) side, suitable for grazing stock and making gardens where, with your people, you can establish a Dervish Tariqa. And I will restore you you your children and your relatives now in my hand. Their names are recorded by your envoys Sheikh Ah (may be Ahmed) Gurhan and Osman Bin Sheikh Hassan.

"Secondly, the stock you bring with you will be yours, and if it is not enough then I will restore to you sufficient to meet the requirement of your people, stock, pay, and so forth, so that your tariqa will be on the same footing as other Tariqa under the protection of the Government. I will not interfere with your religion: and if you desire to go to Mecca you will be able to go as others, in raha (in luxury), Government affording facilities."

"Thirdly, you on your part will have nothing to do with the ordering of the tribes by Government; for this is a matter dealt with the Akils, no Sheikhs, who are concerned only with the administration of the Sariah Mohammedean.

"Fourly, if any disputes arrive between you and the tribes-people, the matter will be reffered for the orders of Government. And the court will be open to you as to others for hearing of cases and for the giving of fair and impartial judgements."

"It is now for you to accept these terms or to reject them. There is nothing between yes or no. And if you accept, come with me Ergo within a space of forty days.

(Signed) as G. F. Archer (Geoffrey Francis Archer).
     Governor, British Somaliland. Either commissioner or Governor, Archer was the head of the Protectorate from 1914 to 1922?

To my understanding, the simplest explanation of the Governor's letter is: "You lost the war and the British Government will dictate your future." The Governor had his intuition and prediction that Sayid Mohammed will not surrender. Expecting a rejection of his peace terms, he was putting a strong Somali arm to attack the remnants of the Daraawiish in parallel with his proposal.

Let us see the position of the Darwiish. Here is the Sayid's reply of the Governor's one.

"This letter is sent by me to His Excellency the Governor Archer. I inform you that your messengers reached me safely in good health and all here pleased them. I have accepted the peace terms they brought me willingly, but not under compulsion namely:

1. You are to return to me my stock, consisting of camels, cattle, sheep and goats, ponies, mules and donkeys, my <u>slaves</u>, firearms, coins, amber (scent), diamonds, pearls, feathers, reading books. The golden coins amounting to 100,00 Uk bounds, the feathers are the feathers of 900 ostriches.
"Piastres 30,000
"dollars, 20,000
"Other small coins not counted
"20 boxes of Amber (Scent
"Five boxes of Diamonds
"1,000 pearls
"two pieces of ivory
  "Very many firearms, among which there were four machine guns (two large and two small), four other guns (one of four shells, one of two, one of one, and the other small), thirty maxim guns, many revolvers, and all kinds of rifles. *

   "This is one condition."

2. The other is that you return to me all those of my men who may fallen into your hands either on desertion from me or captured by you in war.
3. The third condition is that you give me back all my land as well as the buildings demolished by you, and that you, and you also afford Aman with no enmity on the part of the Warsnagali, Majeerteen, or others. Further, there should be no trickery, or ill-conduct, and no one is to interfere with your religion or business, there should be no interference with this.
"Oh, Governor Archer, I am Sayid Mohammed. I know you. When lately I was illtreated by the Italian Government, who caused trouble between myself, the Majeerteen, the Hawiya, and the Ogadeen by giving firearms to my enemies. I warned the Italian Government that I was offended with them on account of their ill-treatment, and that I had moved to the British side of the Border to avoid all fitna (quarrels). My intention then was to send you a letter with some of my elders and a caravan J, but, before this could be done, you attacked me without any cause or fault of mine, and I am oppressed. Further, the aero planes have oppressively attacked me, and this is a great abuse to a man in my position. You have also killed forty of my children who were infants and innocents, liable for their blood-money.

"I have heard that you are a good man and there are others who are my enemies. I am therefore, quite willing to undertake your settlement.

There are a lot to digest about the reply of the Sayid. Precisely, Sayid Mohamed said, "I know you are a trickery man and I cannot trust you. But, let us see if you can fulfill my conditions."

Unless we nullify his poems, as mentioned earlier, Sayid Mohammed was a badmouthed visionary. One more thing. We already stated that one of the worst sins human rights violations that people can commit is enslaving or killing another human being. In the reply to Geoffrey Archer, "my slaves" in his own words, Sayid Mohamed Abdulle Hassan was a slave owner. Across the board, Sayid Mohamed was not forgetful and was vengeful and forgive-full.

When the death of Sayid Mohamed is concerned, though it never reached the stage of Daraawiish headed by Sayid, the resistance did not die for good. 23 years after the death of the Darwiish, Sheekh Bashir tried to revive the struggle. Castagno Margaret, 141:

Sheekh Bashir who was a religious leader organized in 1945 an armed attack on British installations in the Northern region—British Somaliland. It is believed that the Sheekh was related to Sayid Mohamed and that, possibly he was attempting to carry on the Sayid's movement.

According to "Timelines of Somali History: 1400-2000, p. 77—81 by Farah Mohamed, Sheekh Bashir's father, Hagi Yusuf was a close and trusted adviser of the Sayid. A distrust got between Hagi Yusuf and the Sayid when Yusuf took part of a failed coup against the Sayid known as *Canjeel Talo-waa (The Tree-of-bad Counsel)*. Sheekh Bashir, perhaps grown up with Daraawiish fervor, wanted to carry on the torch when in his mid-30s. 1943—948, Gerald Thomas Fisher was the governor of British Somaliland, which can be a hint of tracing the footprints of Sheekh Bashir through the documents of Fisher's administration—most likely obtainable in British Libraries.

When the colonizers violated the terms of the treaties, traditional and religious leaders, or otherwise took a new approach of resistance. There are hundreds who stood to make their country free of occupation. Sheikh Bashir, Omar Samatar, Farah Oomaar, Sheikh Hassan Barsame and many more, and the next generation of SYL and SNL.

We can recall the well-written piece in "The Hunt for The Mad Mullah of Somaliland," by *Derek O'Connor,* for two decades prior World War 1, Mohammed Bin Abdulle Hassan, the self-proclaimed Mullah of Somaliland, was a persistent thorn in the side of British colonial authorities in the arid, sweltering East African protectorate."

To the British he was the "Mad Mullah," a quasi-religious bandit leader intent on plunder and disruption who imposed his will through savage execution and mutilations. To his adherents he was a messianic Sunny holy man, jihadist and freedom fighter. Regardless, the Mullah and his ferocious Islamic fundamentalist dervishes survived four major military expeditions sent against them by the British, in fighting so intense that no less nine Victoria Crosses (Medal of bravery (highest award of the United Kingdom honors systems)) were awarded. Although the Mullah was defeated in battle several times, **he was never captured**. The campaigns against the Daraawiish resistance, the British also used to call Somaliland campaigns, or the Anglo-Somali war, or Dervish war.

This is how one of the British authors concluded about the end of the Exile Government of Sayid Mohamed A. Hassan (Roy Irons 209), "The Sayid succumbed, on 23 Number 1920, after defying the devices of three powerful empires for over twenty years, to the deadly strain of influenza, the enemy of all and killer of so many, that had swept the world after the great war, killing many more than the war itself."

But the historians (Somalis) of Daraawiish state that "On 21 December 1920, Hassan died of influenza at the age of 64, his grave is believed to be somewhere close to limey town, but, the spot of the grave is unknown." That influenza is believed to be the Spanish Flu of 1918—1920, and we briefly show the link in the following Paragraphs. Most probably, that killer influenza is the same as the pandemic of 1918—1920 (Spanish Flu) which killed more than 70 million (2.5% of the world population) in all over the world. According to encyclopedia.1914.1918 phrasing as "When did the Spanish Flu of 1918-1920 reach Africa," the flu has reached East Africa by the sea at the Tanganyika in 1920, and killed many of King's African Rifles.

The infection also killed many people in North Africa and south Africa, and easily passed to East Africa also through the Red Sea towards the Gulf of Berbera. It is almost certain to say that the Second Wave of Spanish Flu killed Sayid Mohamed Abdulle Hassan and hundreds of his diehards who followed him up to limey (Shinily). The British used to move The King's African Rifles to all around the continent. As read earlier, the regiment took part in the last expedition against the Daraawiish, in 1920.

According to The Updating the Account: Global Mortality of the 1918—1920 "Spanish" Flu Pandemic, "Bulletin of the History of Medicine, February 2002, by Niall Philip Alan, Sean Johnson and Juergen Mueller "the flu Killed 25 persons in every 1,000 Somalis, 40 per 1000 in Kenya and 35/1000 in Madagascar. The epidemic swept the world in three waves.

Encyclopedia.org which cited Phillips, Black October (Spanish Flu) 1990, p. 47, "Indeed, in towns like Kimberley (South Africa), Addis Ababa, Port Louis (Mauritius), Windhoek, Ilorin (Nigeria), Secondi Ghana), Bloemfontein (South Africa) and Bathurst (South Africa), all of which lost over 4 percent of their populations to "Spanish" flu) such a cataclysmic outcome Must have seemed possible. With deaths topping 300 per day in Kimberley at the Height of the epidemic, a contemporary calculated that, at that rate, in sixteen months no one would be left alive in the city." The Golden Years of Somalia by Mohamed Ali Hamud, 45, "Said Mohamed Abdulle Hassan died of influenza at the age of 64 on May 1920."

www. Researchgate.net (the impact of the 1918—1919 Influenza Pandemic in Coastal Kenya: "After the First World War, all discharged soldiers were sent home back to their countries. Some soldiers and support staff were infected and introduced the pandemic influenza virus through seaports like Mombasa, Kenya in East Africa. On the northeastern, ships from Aden (Cadan), Yemen and India additionally have introduced the pandemic influenza virus to British Somaliland through Berbera and French Somaliland through Djibouti."

"Yes, Sayid Mohamed was the main founder and the leader, but the history of Daraawiish is much bigger than the Sayid himself. The history of Haji Suudi who was one of the founders of Daraawiish and sometimes was the Chief. Military Commander, Sultan Nuur who was also one of the founders, Ismaaciil Mire, battle strategist and poet, Bashir Yusuf and his son Sheekh Bashir who fought the British in Burco in 1945" should get pages of the pie of the history of the Daraawiish.

Chapter eight referenced notes

Note: An edited version of this article has appeared in a recent edition of the Journal of Anglo-Somali Society. Htto://www.anglosomalisociety.org.uk.home.php The article is based on:
__Moyse-Bartlett. H., The King's African Rifles. 1956, Gale and Bolden Ltd, Aldershot. Reprinted by the Naval and Military Press Ltd.
__Jardine, Douglas, The Mad Mullah of Somaliland. 1923, Hebert Jenkins Ltd., London.
The book is available in all amazon websites.
__Digest of History of Somaliland Camel Corps, KAR.
__3rd Battalion King's African Rifles Historical Record 1895-1928.
__ British Battles and Medals by Hayward, J., Birch. D., and Bishop, R.,
__ Magor, R.B., African general Service Medals. 1983, Naval and Military Press.

Chapter NINE

World War Two and The Rekindle of Somali Nationalism

The death of the Sayid of 1920 was not only the end of the freedom fighter but also a halt of the modern Somali nationalism. Until at the beginning of World War Two, the first stage of the Somali nationalist strife against the colonial states in the Horn of Africa had slowed down. The spread of Christianity which never gained strength in Somali societies during the Sayid did not go further. The public had in mind of the Sayid's warnings. However, the death of the Sayid gave relative tranquility to the colonial powers. That made them possible to extend their authority into the rural areas.

When WORLD WAR TWO broke out, Mussolini was an ally of Hitler. On 10 June 1940, he declared war on the Allies. About 3,000 well trained and equipped with an Abyssinian army with air support of Italy ran over British armies in Elwaq, Moyale, and then occupied British-Somaliland in August. Then, Italy installed a short-lived Italian East African Empire.

The whole Somali Peninsula with the exception of Djibouti became under an Italian rule. But in December 1940 to February 1941, Italy had been run over by British forces of African men from South Africa, Rhodesia, Nigeria and the Gold Coast (*Nine Faces of Kenya, page 153*). Britain launched its offensive from the same

110

location as Italy, namely Elwaq with three fronts. From the east through British-Somaliland which was on the first priority list, from the south from Kenya, and from the north through Sudan, and advanced into Italian-Somaliland. Nin Faces of Kenya by Elspeth Huxley, 157:

The overall British commander, Genera Wavell, planned pronged invasion of Abyssinia: From the east through British Somaliland which had first to be retaken; from the south from Kenya; and from the north through the Sudan. An East African, South African and a Nigerian brigade advanced at whirlwind speed into British-Somaliland and in February 1941, captured the capital Kismaayo, without a fight. They continued into an Italian-Somaliland and occupied the capital, Mogadishu.

Also, Despactches From the Front: The War in East Africa 1939-1943 by John Grehan & Martin Mace, p21: "There were thus three separate lines of operation against Italian East Africa: In the north from the Sudan by Kassala (town in Sudan) into Eritrea, in the center from the Sudan and later from East Africa into Abyssinia, and in the south from Kenya against Italian Somaliland."

Since the first priority list of defeating Italy in Somalia was to recapture British Somaliland, the following in another front that made for the British to recapture the protectorate. Grehan and Mace, p22: "A very skillful conducted operation from Aden under A. O. C. Air Vice-Marshal G. R. M. Reid, had resulted in the recapture of Berbera on 16th March, 1941. This was speedily followed by the reoccupation of the whole colony. The use of the port of Berbera and the road to Harar enabled general Cunningham greatly to shorten his line of communication."

Other than the front from Sudan to recapture Ethiopia, the capture of Berbera opened another front. The distance between Berbera and Harar is around 450 miles, while Mogadishu and Jigjiga are 740 miles apart. Grehan and mace, p26: "The conquest of Italian East Africa had been accomplished in four months, from the end of January to the beginning of June. All the Italian-East Africa colonies came under British rule with East African forces, South African battalion, and a Nigerian brigade."

Kismayo had fallen without a fight in February of 1941, then into Italian Somaliland were in the first time, the capital, Mogadishu became under British rule. It was taken on February 25 by a Nigerian brigade. Boosaaso was captured on 11th May and Hafun (Dante), one of the last places to capture came along on the 16th.

British generals had previously discussed to capture Kismayo before the rains broke in March with six brigade groups one being armored brigade. The option was to take the attack either before rains (March), or after rains (May). The plan worked with speed and skill. The area becomes muddy during the rains. The Somali Peninsula was united once under British military administration with the exception of French Somaliland, now the Republic of Djibouti. Some details of how the Italian-

Somaliland had fallen, The First to Be Freed: British Military Administration in Eritrea and Somalia, 1941-1943: page15:

The first Deputy Political Officer for Somalia was appointed on the 13th February 1941, while the armies were tearing their way through Jubbaland. Four days later he flew to Kismayo, the little Indian Ocean port. It had been captured only the day before. The northeastern and the central regions fell to the hands of the British Military in April at the latest. An aircraft was sent to drop pamphlets on Rocca Littorio (Gaalkacyo), the administrative Center of Mudug with instructions for surrender in early April. Bender Cassim (Boosaaso) and Dante (Xaafuun) fell as well. Italians regrouped themselves for a first and final stand near the Lighthouse of Guardafui but also fell short. The whole Somali peninsula with the exception of Djibouti under France stayed under the British Military Administration until the kingdom transferred the colony to Italy under the order of the United Nations on April 1, 1950.

The general population of the Italian-Somaliland welcomed the British Military Administration. It felt liberated from an enemy, fascist Italians who many of them were in Somaliland for employment opportunities. Fascist Italy did not allow the Somalis schooling beyond primary that knowing too much would be dangerous.

During the Italo-Ethiopian war, Italy still practiced slavery in the riverine parts in the south. "Italians began relocating men and women from their villages to the Italian plantations by force in 1935" (Besteman: 88). Furthermore, the occupation of the British Military Administration had also enlightened the vision of the Somali intellectuals. The takeover renewed their nationalistic views.

In May 1943, Somali Youth Club came into existence with great enthusiasm. Though warned not to be a political organization like told to SNL (Somali National League) in the north in 1935, British Military Administration was well aware of the formation. "With the approval of the British Military Administration, a group of young activists founded the
Somali political movement, the Somali Youth Club (Farer:64)."

The WORLD WAR TWO did not only stir the Somali nationalism, but the Italian Somaliland became one of those colonies which the Potsdam (German city, July 17-August 2, 1945 of Russia, Great Britain and USA) Conference decided not to return them to Italy (disposition of former Italian colonies).

In 1947, with a new name, Somali Youth League (SYL) with an anti-Italian attitude, and by a dynamic leadership of Abdullahi Isse, a real Somali nationalist, the movement took an independence agenda to the United Nations. The World body itself was founded in San Francisco, Californian of USA in October 1945 (Dhagar iyo Dhayalsi 1948 (back cover) by Cali M. Cabdigiir (Caliganay), SYL VS (USA, UK, France and Russia (Four Power Commission of the UN (The Big Four Commission is another name also known), ISBN: 9781985014732)):

The club had impressively raised its membership to more than 20,000 people. After the war in 1947, when the movement changed its name to the Somali Youth League (SYL), it registered over 25,000 members. People were enthusiastic to govern themselves. The independent-seeking political parties, especially SYL have taken one further step. They forwarded their determination of wanting to be an independent state to the newly founded World Body United Nations). Though not in its full merits, the UN had accepted to discuss the case.

Having investigated the Somalia issue, the UN proposed to make further studies of the ramifications of putting the Horn of African nation under trusteeship. The SYL started a campaign of educating the people about the prospects of self-rule in the country. Though Mogadishu always had the biggest demonstrations, other series ones took in the other major cities of the country. The UN sent an Evaluation Committee of the Four Powers to meet the Somali leaders and their people for the consultation of their future. The Four Power commission arrived in Mogadishu on January 6, 1948. Back to the head office of the UN, the commission reported its evaluation of more than about 14 political parties.

During the stay of the United Nations' Four Power Commission (United States, France, United Kingdom, and Russia) in Mogadishu, first, the Commission met the Chief Administrator of British Military Administration of Ex-Italian Somaliland. *Dhagar iyo Dhayalsi* by this author is a book written of what happened between the Commission and SYL.

In the following few questions and answers out of 180 questions and their answers between SYL and the Four Power Commission, we see how the British generals have spoken about the Somalis perhaps while there were no Somali representatives. The questions were between Brigadier General R. H. Smith, Chief Administrator of British Military Administration of Italian-Somaliland and the Head of British Government Delegation, Brigadier general Stafford, a member of the Four Power Commission. The interview took place on January 15, 1948, Mogadishu, Somaliland)). (Dhagar iyo Dhayalsi, Cali Cabdigiir, p70-74, ISBN: 9781985014732):

W7. Mr. Stafford: I should be very interested to know if before the events of the other day there was an armed conflict or serious trouble between the local Italians and the native population. I do not mean the ordinary sort of isolated incidents that occur anywhere, but anything on a scale sufficiently worthy of note?
A7. Brigadier Smith: No.
W8. Mr. Stafford: I seem to remember some months ago there was quite a lot of trouble in Mogadishu which people killed and so on?
A8. Brigadier Smith: Yes, there was some disturbance. That was between the Arabs and the Somalis.
W9. Mr. Stafford: Was their origin political or economic or just general rioting?   A9. Brigadier Smith: Both. Sometimes there had been resentment among the Somalis at the attempts by the Arabs to interfere with internal affairs and so on; also, on the economic side,

113

most of the export and import trade is in the hands of Arabs or Indians. There is a growing feeling among the Somalis they should have a greater part in the trade of their own country.
W10. Mr. Stafford: Brigadier, how long have you known the Somalis?
A10. Brigadier Smith: In Somaliland?
W11. Somalis as a race?
A11. Brigadier Smith: 29 years.
W12. Mr. Stafford: You would call them an excitable race, would you?   A12. Brigadier Smith: Very.

In 1948, even in British Somaliland, Indians traders owned and run most of the shops in Hargeysa. Nevertheless, the Somalia Conference, Patriotic Beneficence Union, Hisbia Dighil Mirifle (was to accept Italian proposal of 30 years trust ship), Union of Africans in
Somalia (5,000 members), Somali Young Abgaal Association, The War Veterans, The Edit (Ciidaha Islaamka) al Islam Shiidle and Moobileyn, The Bimal Union (300 members of Biyomaal tribe), Somalia Progressive Committee, which claimed by the Somalia Conference but about which only a little information was received, Seven Italian political parties affiliated to the corresponding parties in the homeland (Italy), The Arab community, The Indian Association, The association of Ethiopian Youths and the most important and the most powerful one, Somali Youth League were interviewed.

In the Commission's report, SYL with over 93,000 members and 79 branches outside Mogadishu, was the only one of clear political agenda towards independence.

The Goal of the SYL as the commission put it, was to unite all Somalis and eliminate all kinds of harmful prejudices among its citizens. When the UN reviewed the report of its Council in Somalia, it voted to go ahead with a trusteeship status.

After the UN discussed the decision of trusteeship, the SYL which hated Italy more than the British had been informed to live with only one of two options: Under British or under
Italian.

But, before WORLD WAR TWO which Italy was in the losing side, the administrative system which the Italians developed in Somalia was the style of Fascism, bureaucratic, highly centralized and which only the Italians directed. Since the SYL experienced that Italian fascism, the organization had complained that Italy would get a fifty percent chance of being a caretaker. And during the debates on the Trust territory in the General Assembly, SYL had raised its voice even to the point of threatening to use violence if the UN appoint Italy as the Administrative Authority.

When the Assembly granted oral hearing to the local political parties, the representative of the Somali Youth League, Abdullahi Issa's argument was:

Italy was temperamentally unsuited for the administration of the African people. During the fifty years of Italian rule, the population had been kept in a state of slavery, deprived of education, of commercial opportunities and of possibilities of social and political advancement. Our lands had been seized under the dreaded colonial system, our people had been forced into forced labor under conditions of almost incredible cruelty (Dhagar iyo Dhayalsi (SYL of 1948) by Ali Abdigir, 213).

Even the Ethiopian delegate, Aklilou, stated that "Ethiopia could neither admit nor tolerate Italy's return to Somaliland." Each of the colonial powers competed for further occupation and presented its case of why it had to be chosen as a trusted government to the security council. Though it was a WORLD WAR TWO loser, Italy wanted to be a caretaker.

But Britain which was one of the Four Big Powers of the UN, and a WORLD WAR TWO victorious proposed that it will unite the greater Somalia. That was an excellent offer from the Somali point of view. At that time, Italian-Somaliland, British-Somaliland, the Ogadeen, and the North Frontier District (NFD or Northern Frontier Province) were under the British Military Administration. That is more than ninety percent of the Somali peninsula.

From the Somali point of view, for reasons not fully pieced together in their merits, perhaps, the west did not want to create a strong Islamic state which would be an ever-existing threat to Ethiopia. The United States of America, the Soviet Union, and France opposed the British proposal.

However, further in-depth research is necessary if the British was honest of the Bevin plan. Somali piracy and Terrorism in the Horn of Africa, by Christopher L. Daniels, 4: "During the 1940s, British Foreign Secretary Earnest Bevin began to propose ways to unite all people of Somali descent under one flag. His plan, dubbed the Bevin plan, outlined this concept and gained wide spread acceptance amongst Somali intellectuals."

On page 6 of Christopher Daniels:

The British colonial authorities were burdened with task of juggling several conflicting interests iin the East African region and had to exercise the utmost amount of caution to avoid alienating its allies. One nation of particular concern to the British was Ethiopia, a longtime ally of many Western nations because of it being one of the world's oldest Christian states and its ability to remain independent throughout the colonial era. Having strong relation with Ethiopia provided Great Britain with a strategic stronghold in the predominantly Muslim Horn of Africa. Ethiopia was also considered to be a critical ally because of the Cold War rivalry between Western nations and the Soviet Union for control of East African region.

SYL presented cases of how Italy dealt with the public in general, pro-independence, unification parties, SYL and Hamar Youth Club in particular. And according to such accusations, SYL protested that Italy to be the caretaker. The UN

Council stationed in Mogadishu could not resolve that issue. But, despite the SYL's protest and the nation's best interest proposed by Britain—though we believe that the British had never been honest about its plan, unfortunately, what is considered one of the most crucial decisions ever made in the history of Somali peninsula or Somalis was finalized.

Regardless of Somalia's exuberant protest, Italy was chosen over the British. The trouble of the trusteeship did not stop in there either. Though both the Ogadeen inhabitants and all the Somali independent-seeking parties have vigorously protested about the move, the Somali politicians of the British Somaliland furiously fought with the British. A dynamic nationalist by the Michael Mariano of NUF (United National Front) lead a delegation to London and the UN, seeking to have Haud and Reserve issue before the world community. The following is an incredible witness of history for the above protest against of Britain's transfer of Haud and Reserve to Emperor Haile Selassie.

Michael Mariano, 1955
www.alamy.com

"**6,500 Sheep Price of UN Delegation Trip:** London (5 May 1955, Reuters)—a flock of 6,500 sheep were sold by nomadic tribesmen in British Somaliland to pay for a delegation of two who left by air for New York Tuesday night (05 May 1995) to attend United Nations Assembly. They are going to protest to the UN against the transfer of Britain of 25,000 square miles of their land to Ethiopia. An Arab League country to sponsor them. The two men, Suldaan Biixi Muumin and Michael Mariano, a Somali businessman want to take their protest to the International Court of Justice. Mariano said Tuesday: "By the time we have maintained ourselves at a modest Hotel in New York until the United nations ends in December; we shall have spent altogether $17,500. "This is an enormous figure for the humble tribesmen of our country. Many poor families have already given us a sheep." The British government maintains that the two territories concerned have been Ethiopia's since the Anglo—Ethiopian treaty of 1897."

Britain had defended her transfer of the land to Ethiopia with a counter attack of claiming the whole Somalia. Perhaps, as a further punishment, Britain transferred Ogadeen to Ethiopia of Emperor Haile Selassie in 1948. The territory had loudly raised its voice at the United Nations about the British handover, but nothing for the Somalis. During the Big Four Commission in Mogadishu, January 1948, the British delegation in the commission stated that Ogadeen will be returned to Ethiopia.

However, the British had never been honesty of the unifying Somali territories. *The Road to Zero by Mohamed Osman Omar.p18,* "All I want to do in this case is to give those poor nomads a chance to live. I do not want anything else. We are paying nearly one million
British pounds a year out of our budget to help to support them..."

When the British Government Just said that, though British could keep the Protectorate as long as it wanted, at the same time, it gave away immediately a part of the Ogadeen in 1948. As they were British predetermined decisions, it gave away the Haud, and Reserved in 1955. Dhagar iyo Dhayalsi by Ali Abdigir, page 71, Question 13:

Mr. Stafford: I would like to take you to one another thing concerning the map that you showed us on the wall. I have a map here on which the boundary between Italian Somaliland and the Ogaadeenya is a straight line, whereas yours is a wavy one. Supposing, as is presumably intended that territory is handed back to Ethiopia, which of these two boundaries would be followed?

The Head of British Government Delegation, Brigadier general Stafford, a member of the Four Power Commission asked the question Brigadier General R. H. Smith, Chief Administrator of British Military Administration of Italian-Somaliland. The answer of General Smith (*A13, page 97*):

That would have to be by agreement between Ethiopia and whatever power or whatever administration take over from the British Military Administration. I understand as far as treaty is concerned, it has never been clearly defined and I believe the only record which alleged to have existed is a map given by King Menelik. This was not published. Some Italian authorities quote the boundary as being one hundred eighty (180 km) from the coast; as others 180 miles. This was a very burning question and was presumably the excuse of the Italian-Ethiopian war.

The option of "Whatever Power or whatever administration" at that time was the British or a committee of the Four Big Commission for which the SYL was campaigning. Italy was not in the picture. General Smith showed a map which was different than the one Commission had. We can understand that the UK government did not update its administrator of Somaliland.

Finally, in late November 1949, the General Assembly of the United Nations had passed a resolution which made Italian Somaliland a Trust territory for ten years to Italian Administration under the United Nations. On resolution # 289 A (IV), part B and the draft Trusteeship agreement, it had also appointed an Advisory Council headed of three representatives, Amin Rostem Bey (selected as the first chairman of the council) of Egypt, Mr. E. De Holte Castello of Columbia and Mr. Manuel Escudero of the Philippines (Excerpts from the Resolution).

During the debates in the National Assembly of putting Italian Somaliland either under Italy or Great Britain, SYL declared the most violent anti-Italian emotions if the UN choose Italy as a caretaker. There was a good reason why SYL said that. Unlike the 700,000 of the Northern Somalis under the British, the 1.5 million (The First to be Freed, p49) of the Southern Somalis had hated the Italians. Because of the Italian Fascist treatment with the Somalis, "The Nomadic Somali still prefer to lead their life fine, free life, eating meat and milk, then to go in for such a laborious pursuit as agriculture." Tom Farer (71), "The protectorate (British-Somaliland) had no settlers, no investments, no wealth, and a port incomparably inferior to Aden and Mombasa." But "No wealth" is baseless characterization is an ocean of truth. Undeveloped yes, but the Somali peninsula in one of the resources-rich countries of this universe.

Rome, however, had always an interest in Southern Somalia for agricultural opportunities. Some 80 km from Mogadishu, Italy had a well-developed agricultural community called The Villaggio del Duca Abruzzi (Jowhar Now) run by the Societa Agricola Italo-Somalo. Nevertheless, The UN placed Italian-Somaliland under the Italian Administration for ten years from (1950-60).

In accordance with Annex XI, paragraph 3 of the Treaty of Peace with Italy, 1947, where the Powers concerned agreed to accept the recommendation of the General Assembly on the disposal of the former Italian colonies and to take appropriate measures for giving effect to it, with respect to Italian-Somaliland, recommends:

- That Italian-Somaliland shall be an independent sovereign state;
- That this independence shall become effective at the end of ten years from the date of the approved of a Trusteeship Agreement by the General Assembly;
- That during the period mentioned in paragraph 2, Italian Somaliland shall be placed under the International Trusteeship System with Italy as the Administrative Authority.
- An Advisory Council was stationed in Mogadishu as UN officers to monitor Trusteeship procedures set for Italy as a caretaker to follow. On Ist April 1950, British handed over the territory's administration to Italy. And on December 2, 1950, the UN approved the procedures that Italy as a Trust Government, had to follow for the territory. Hence, Italy became an Administrative Authority, and SYL was the most powerful political party in Somalia, the distrust between them grew. Such hostility did not end until Somalia became independent.

Though the trusteeship period was ten years (1950-60), to train Somalis for running a government when finally, the Italians handover the responsibility, still, there was an assumption that the Administrative Authority (Italian) could submit a proposal to the UN and recommend for more time to occupy. The Somali Youth League was well aware of that and ruled out for Italy to achieve that goal. To eliminate any possibility of that, throughout the trusteeship period, many clashes between the Italian rule and the public had taken place.

Though it is stated that 12 October 1954 was the first day that the Somali flag was raised, following the UN mandate, Italy had invited Somali officials to take part in the work of the Administration Committee as observers. Two years after, January 1956, Mr. Isse, well-liked young nationalist and energetic leader of the SYL was voted to be the first prime minister of the trusteeship.

May 7, 1956, Italian administration had asked Abdullahi Isse of SYL to form a government. The Prime Minister formed a Government of a Prime Minister and five cabinet ministers such as interior, industry and commercial, social affairs, justice, and religious affairs, and information (post and telecommunications).

In 1958, Municipal elections which women were allowed to vote were held. SYL got most of the seats. In that year, the British tried to purchase the Haud (Hawd), now part of Section 5 of Federal Ethiopia. That did not happen because of a counterproposal of Haile Selassie who claimed that the whole of Somalia was a part of Ethiopia which the European powers seized illegally. "You are by race, color, blood and customs, members of great Ethiopian family," were the words of Haile Selassie, but I would say same thing if would have been in that position.

However, this area was under the British Military Administration from the second World War on—and from the point of British interest kept it for Ethiopia. Page 29 of The Horn of Africa by John Buchholzer, "There are two parties, the National League (Somali National League) in the North and the League Youth (Somali Youth League. The latter is the larger with branches wherever there are Somalis, that is, not only in British and Italian Somaliland, but also in Northern Kenya and East Ethiopia." That popularity and recognition later blind-sided it from good leadership.

In British-Somaliland, also, there was an increasing desire to be independent and unite with the south (Italian-Somaliland). Serious political protests happened which forced the British government to accept the independence and the unification deal. The political parties, such as Somali National League in the north (SNL) like the SYL in the south, the National United Front (NUF) of Michael Mariano (1920—1986), and United Somali Party (USP), a late-comer had the same objectives as the Somali Youth League. At the end of the Trusteeship, because of the public support, most political parties in the whole Peninsula had been working with SYL. Finally, in February 1959, the British Government declared:

Her Majesty's Government is aware of the desire expressed by many Somalis of the Protectorate that there should be a closer association between the territory and Somalia. If, therefore. when Somalia had become independent, the Legislative Council of the protectorate finally resolves that negotiations with the Government of Somalia be instituted to determine the terms and conditions on which a closer association of the two tritones may be achieved, Her Majesty's Government in the United Kingdom would be ready to transmit this resolution to the Government of Somalia and enquire whether that Government would be willing to enter into negotiation. If so, Her Majesty's Government would arrange for negotiations of a suitable nature to take place.

On February 17, 1960, British parliament preapproved to grant Somaliland independence to permit union with Somalia (Italian- Somaliland). On April 6, 1960, the Legislative Council of British Somaliland finalized and set a date for independence and unification with the Italian-Somaliland as soon as it becomes independent. Having both territories had known the exact year of independence, very tiresome and intense negotiations of how to merge started.

In April of 1960, leaders of the political parties in the south and their counterparts in the north met in Mogadishu where they agreed to form one Republic Government under one flag, one president and a single parliament.

In May 1960, in reference to a UN Resolution #1418(XIV) of December 5, 1959, in which the UN approved to make the independence date of the Trust Territory on July 1, 1960, instead of December 2nd, 1960. Italy Complied with that resolution. Italian parliament passed a bill to let its colony become an independent country. From that date on, the political situation of the region entered into a new level.

Knowing that Somalia was going to be an independent state, Haile Selassie of Ethiopia offered full cooperation to Somalia when it becomes independent hoping for an early settlement of border dispute. When in 1950, the United Nations assured Somalia of going to be an independent state in 1960, people saw an image of Greater Somalia. The quick preoccupation with the Greater Somalia picture shadowed the real thinking of pursuing good governance. Many did not think over of the best way to proceed, and the next chapter, the New Republic covers the troubles of the unification.

Chapter nine referenced notes

Nine Faces of Kenya, Elspeth Huxley, 1991
Despactches From the Front: The War in East Africa 1939-1943 by John Grehan & Martin Mace
The First to Be Freed: British Military Administration in Eritrea and Somalia, 1941-1943
(Dhagar iyo Dhayalsi 1948 (back cover) by Cali M. Cabdigiir (Caliganay), SYL VS (USA, UK,
France and Russia (Four Power Commission of the UN (The Big Four Commission
The Road to Zero by Mohamed Osman Omar
resolution # 289 A (IV), part B and the draft Trusteeship agreement The Horn of Africa by
John Buchholzer the British Government declaration of February 1959
April 6, 1960, the Legislative Council of British Somaliland
UN Resolution #1418(XIV) of December 5, 1959

CHAPTER TEN

The New Republic

All means must be employed within the framework of legality and the pursuit of peace in order to obtain the union of all Somali territories, and their unification under the same flag. This constitutes for us not only a right but a duty which one cannot neglect because it is impossible to distinguish between Somali and Somali.
__Prime Minister, Abdullahi

Isse addressed the Legislative Assembly of the Trust Territory (Italian Somaliland). This is a portion of one of the Isse's patriotic and famous speeches, July 1959.

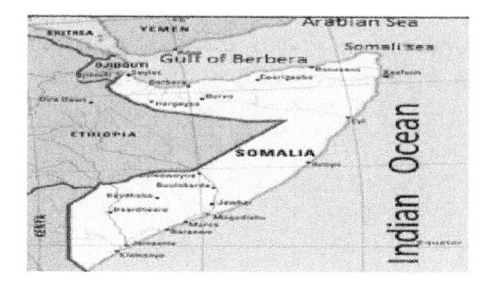

Somalia is situated in the Horn of Africa. It occupies the southeastern portion of northeast Africa. In the northwest, it lies 30 KMs off the Republic of Djibouti which is an independent state and partially considered a region of greater Somalia. Ethiopia is on the west and Kenya on the southwest.

The Gulf of Berbera is in the north. The Somali Sea also is below the Arabian Sea, the connection of Gulf of Berbera, Arabian Sea and the Indian Ocean. And the Indian Ocean is on the east of Somali peninsula. The region between the only two rivers of Somalia Jubba and Shabeelle, there is low agricultural land. The area that extends southwest of the Jubba river to the Kenya border is low-pressure land.

Both rivers originate from the Ethiopian highlands in the west and pour their waters into the Indian Ocean. They provide water for irrigation. Juba which is around 550 miles is only navigable in certain areas. Shabeelle which runs about 1, 244 miles dries up during some very drought seasons. Jubba brings more water to the Horn than Shabeelle.

Somalia has a tropical climate, and there is little seasonal change in temperature. In the low areas, the temperature ranges from about 76 degrees Fahrenheit 88 degrees Fahrenheit. The mean annual range is about 10 degrees.

The two hottest cities in Somalia are Berbera on the Gulf of Berbera and Luuq in the south. The southwest monsoon from June to September and the northeast monsoon from December to March influence the temperature and the rain. Heavy rains fall from March to May and the light rains from September to December. The average rainfall is less than 12 inches, irregular and the droughts are frequent.

In general, Somalia is described as a dry savanna. It has the longest coasts in the main land of Africa, on the Gulf of Berbera, the Somali Sea (below Arabian Sea, the corner of where the water Gulf of Berbera, Arabian and the Indian Ocean meet), and the Indian Ocean.

The waters of Somalia, Indian Ocean coast, in particular, are rich with tuna fish. The international communities define Somalia as a failed state, and since it could not protect its waters, foreign fishing vessels have no bars to come and make all kinds of illegal fishing practices. Puntland has many islands on all waters, uninhabited islands on the Gulf of Berbera, such as Sacaadadiin, and Ceebaad (Ebad), known as Saylac islands.

Geographically, Saylac islands are spoken of as:

The *Sacadadiin islands* are group of islands off the northern coast of Somaliland. They are situated near the ancient city of Saylac. The Saylac islands are made of six small islands all of which are low-lying and have sandy beaches. The largest of these islands are *Sacaadadiin* and Ceebaad which are six and nine miles off the coast of Saylac respectively. There is also a lighthouse at Ceebaad and the name for the archipelago comes from the Somali Sultan Sacaadadiin II who was killed by Emperor Yeshaq I/Dawit 1 of Abyssinia on the main island in 1415 (some notes make the date at 1410).

The Sacaadadiin Islands are well known for their splendid coral reefs similar to those found on the southern coast of Oman. These reefs are the most diverse and well-formed coral reefs on the coast of the Gulf of Berbera and possibly the largest in the region. From provincial counts, ninety-nine different species of coral from forty-three different genera have been found on the islands. There are also a hundred and thirty-two different species of coral fish found around the archipelago. Many of these species include those also found in the Red Sea, Gulf of Berbera, and the Indian Ocean.

The island of Sacaadadiin and *Ceebaad* both are sites of major bird colonies. On the island of
Sacaadadiin alone, there were more than 100,000 breeding pairs recorded. Following the 2004 Indian Ocean earthquake and tsunami, the International Union for Conservation of Nature (IUCN) and other NGO worked with local authorizes to establish protected areas and monitor fishers on the islands. The archipelago currently has no permanent residents and is uninhabited, though it is still occasionally visited by tourists, local fishermen, and those who wish to honor Sacaadadiin.

Somali researchers and writers always visit the islands, Sacaadadiin mostly. Still, it is not clear which island is bigger, Ceebaad or Sacaadadiin. However, according to the Gulf of Aden Pilot of Hydrographic Department of Great Britain, published in1887, 64-64 details:

Ceebaad island: is low and sandy, and 1.75 miles in length, by about a quarter of a mile (400 meters) in breath. Its south-west point is steep-to; there being 6 fathoms, about 11 meters within a short distance. On all other sides it is surrounded by a reef, dry in places at low water, and which extends in an easterly direction about 4 miles with a breadth of about three miles.

Sacaadadiin island: Forms the north side of saylac road. It is low and sandy, of coral foundation, and is for the most part covered with bushes, the tops of which are about 20 feet above the sea. It is surrounded by a bank of coral, mud and sand, which uncovers at low water. The bank extends about half a mile on the eastern side and from a half to one mile on the other sides. On the east side, a bank, with as little

There is another one on the same water, Maydh island or Rabshiga mountain, a bird sanctuary. It is just an isolated mountain in the water, about 20 Km off of Maydh town. Xaafuun on the Indian Ocean which is still attached to the mainland is sometimes called an island. It is the most populous of the islands. On the Jubbaland water (Indian Ocean), there are eight islands called Bajun islands. Koyama is the only inhabited one (detailed in Baadisooc, same author). Somalis share the Red Sea, the Gulf of Berbera, the Somali Sea (the corner of Raas Casayr, or the Cape of Guardafui), and the Indian Ocean with others on the opposite sides.

People

Both ethnically and culturally, the Somalis belong to the Hamitic group and Cushitic linguistically. Some people tried to question the homogeneity of the Somalis when the civil war broke out. However, over 99% of them share one common language, blackness and are Sunni Muslims. They follow the Shafie (Shaaficiya) School of Islam.

The only formal census ever was taken in 1975 which neither the world nor the general public accepted the outcome. The current (2020) population of Somali ethnic in the world is about 24 million, 0r 25 million at the maximum. 13 of which live in Somalia, 6.7 million or 6.2% of 110 million live in the Somali regions of Ethiopia, while 3 million or 6.5% of 50 million reside in the Somali regions of Kenya. The Republic of Djibouti has one million people which 60-65 % of that are Somalis, and 1.5 million are outside of East Africa. 2019, major cities such as Mogadishu (Muqdisho, Xamar), Hargeysa, Boosaaso, Burco, Berbera, Boorama, Kismaayo, Baydhabo, Beledweyne, Gaalkacyo, Marka and Baraawe host 4.2 million. Laascaano (Laas Caanood), Garoowe, Ceerigaabo, Baran, Galdogob, Guriceel, Cadaado, Caabudwaaq, Qardho, Jilib, Gebiley, Jowhar, Garbahaarrey, Buuloxaawo, Buulobarde, Luuq, Xuddur, Dhuusamareeb and Saylac host more than 1.2 million. In reference to those allocations, half of Somalia population is urban now. The life cycle is about 54 years and more than 40% of the populations is 14 years of age.

The Statehood and The Union

"Kaana siib Kanna Saar: Raise this instead," said Abdullahi SuldanTima-Cadde. He was a well-respected and famous Somali poet. An azure rectangular with a five-pointed white star emblazoned in its center, which Mohamed Awale designed it, is the national flag that Timo Cadde had gladly sung to be raised. Long-sought Somalia's independence aspirations became a reality at 12:01 A.M. on 26 June 1960, British-Somaliland got its independence. The following words are in farewell speeches of the British Empire.

Though it was the independence of British Somaliland in 1960, along with the famous "Wind of change" speech of UK prime minister of 1957—1963, Harold Macmillan (1920—1986) delivered to the South African parliament in Cape Town, on 3 February 1960, Sir Douglas Hall (1909—2004) was the last governor of British

Somaliland, 11 July 1959—26 June 1960, and he made a speech at a joint meeting of the Royal African Society and the Royal Commonwealth Society on December 1, 1960—in which time there was already an independent Somali government.

I have chosen as my title for this talk "Somaliland's Last Year as a protectorate"—I emphasize the words "Last Year" partly because I do not wish to join or appear to join the ranks of those who speak and write about Africa without the knowledge to do so.

Many of you who are here today know Somaliland better than I do, but for the sake of those who have not been there, I will give my impressions of my first few weeks in Somaliland during July of last year (1959). *I found a dry country much of which is aptly described as semi-desert. But in parts, particularly towards the east, I found some of the most magnificent scenery I have ever seen anywhere. I found great contrast; one can stand on the fringes of a cedar forest, over 6000 (Daalo mountains) feet above sea level; with a tendency to shiver, and look down through the clouds to the sea below; and one can drive down to that sea and, in a couple of hours, enjoy a bathe in water which is so warm as hardly to be true. I found a race of people who have most marked characteristics and physical endurance, good looks, pride and a tendency to flare up at what sometimes appears to be the smallest provocation. A tendency which is accompanied by a complete immunity from sulking, and a code of manners which is as attractive as it is strictly obeyed.*

With it all I found that desire for independence which is now almost universal throughout the continent, and which was supported by a deep-felt conviction, stemming from the pride which runs through the race, that they could go it alone. When I say "alone," of course, I do not exclude Somalis who live in other countries.

Those were some of the emotional words for the British to say good-bye to its physically dying empire while on the other hand, the populations of the independence-acquired nations were crying in jubilation to nominally rule themselves. I used the words "Physically and nominally" because colonialism did not die. After 1945 when the western empires started decaying, Europeans accelerated appropriate science, technology, and other aspects of western culture all over the world. They committed themselves to stay ahead to recolonize in another form. I, as an author, that is not to blame the Europeans but not to be mentally free, but a weakness of the newly independence—acquired nations.

The victorious nations of the WORLD WAR TWO needed secure control over their African colonies for resources to fight the Axis Powers (Rome—Berlin—Tokyo Axis), but the African wind of change for self-determination was indivertible.

Both education and technology, the western block was ahead of the rest where the other undeveloped nations had no many choices but to mimic the west. During the speech of the governor, Somalia had a spot on the world map, and was a member of the UN as an independent state, formed on July 1, 1960

However, it is a pleasure to read how frankly the governor Hall talked about the beauty of the Somaliland in his own natives' words.

The Horn of Africa, a sickle-shaped or seven shaped as Somalis call it was there. The public became triumphed, excited, overjoyed, and exploded with tears. They got their own free waving flag.

Political Path (1960-1969)

Italian-Somaliland and British-Somaliland formed the Somali Republic on July 1, 1960 Built on weak foundation. From that year on, specially, during 1960 to 2020 Somalia was many times traveling on a thorny path. Other than the unification issue, there were two other main points of discussion. Since the Somali dialect of Bay and Bakool (May) is different than the Maxay dialect, Hizbia Digil Mirifle wanted a federal system—where centralism finally won.

Somali Youth League, the most important party in the south took 90 seats of the parliament out of 123. Then, The National Assembly had chosen honorary Aden Abdulle Osman (1908—2007) of SYL as the official president of the Republic. Despite opposition from certain groups, he appointed Abdirashid Ali Sharmaarke as a prime minister. The national assembly had approved the nomination as well.

Though a government was born, there was no standard script of the Somali language. People spoke but could not write or read. The south used the Italian language and north English. Since the scramble of Africa, the British maintained a strategic presence in the North but showed limited interest to develop the colony economically.

We mentioned in previous chapters that one of the original interests of the British in northern Somalia were just a source of mutton and other livestock products for its naval port of Aden. "By 1886, a very few British authorities settled on the northern coast to ensure uninterrupted flow of livestock to Aden" (Besteman:195). Ethiopia and Sudan always seemed also more important for the British than Somaliland.

Before WORLD WAR TWO, Italy took advantage of the available resources of fertile soil, descent farmers, and ample waters. To mention some, a group from Torino Italy settled Jannaale in 1924 and made a developed district. In 1939, Riverine areas were fully Italianized. Italians fully undertook plantation projects for growing bananas, cotton, citrus and sugar. The district of Jowhar was named *Villaggio Duca deli Abruzzi (Villabruzzi)*. A railroad between Mogadishu and Jowhar were built (Ferro via Mogadishu—Villabruzzi (Xamar—Jowhar railroad)), and laid some other infrastructure. Various agricultural developments were concentrated in the triangular districts of Jowhar—Jannaale—Xamar.

In 1935, 30,000 (33%) out of 90,000 were Italians living in Mogadishu. Xamar got the name of The White Pearl of the Indian Ocean in 1940, and though the

Mogadishu's population came down to 50,000 because of WORLD WAR TWO, 22,000 (44%) out of
50,000 were Italians. More than 250 Italians were living in Marka, 150 in Baraawe, 120 in Kismaayo, 50 in Italo town (not sure its current name), 700 in Jannaale, 400 in Shalaanbood, and 3000 in Jowhar. One-time, the Italian population in Somaliland reached 50,000+. In 1960, there were about 50,000 Somalis who had at least one grandfather or great—grandfather Italian-born. There were inter—marriages between the Briton and the Somalis, but though it was much lower than the Somali—Italians, we could not secure the exact number of the Somali—Britons in British Somaliland in 1960.

Though I heard it existed, we could not find any clause in the British treaties with the Somali clans that outlawed that British moms deliver babies in Somaliland in order not to have British—Somali individuals. From beyond Beledweyne to Caluula, which was under the Italian control, less than 300 Italians lived, only in the major cities, such as Dhuusomareed, Gaalkacyo, Garoowe, and Boosaaso. British kept the protectorate of Somaliland from 1884 to 1960 just for a strategic sea route. The maximum number of Europeans ever lived one time in British Somaliland was around 7000.

As a refreshment, from 1860 to 1900, Europeans such as France, Italy, Germany, Britain and the African nation of Ethiopia (Ethiopia with help of the Europeans) were still competing among themselves to grab a piece of land of Somali peninsula. Europeans developed the systems for all of us as humans, and we were supposed to enhance the developments after they leave. We derive two main points from that history.

First, Water and fertile soil areas, and a world strategic route were a gold rush for the Europeans. when Somalia became an independent state, regardless of from what region, the best that the politicians and well—off could do was to selfishly grab what the Europeans left for personal greed. Those two groups practiced naked exploitation of the fertile and other resources.

Second, unfortunately, still today, we tend to blame the Europeans for our misfortunes, while we could not even maintain the systems they left behind.

Coming to the unification hurdles, though the two colonies became one homogenous nation, education, tax and legal systems, and currency were different. Administrative systems inherited from the colonial governments did proceeded without careful review. Emotions took over real thorn picking of the differences.

Opportunism is strong in the Somali personality, where it shadows nationalism and makes political decisions many times on emotions. Hizbia Digil Mirifle organization was formed in 1947 when SYC became SYL. HDM was formed to oppose SYL, and because of that, displayed open friendship with Ethiopia (A Pastoral Democracy of I. M. Lewis, 292).

The new government took one important step forward though. Being aware of the importance of the English language in the world, as a language of administration, Somalia chose the English language over Italian.

There was another system that the new republic preferred. The British administration in the north was extended to the rural areas while the Italian one in the south just used to focus on the main cities. After a study of the two systems, the protectorate system became the integrated law of the land in 1963.

Still, there were some misconceptions between the north and the south. During the trusteeship, British Somaliland continued to improve the judicial, educational and health system.

As mentioned earlier, still, in agriculture, economic infrastructure and middle-skilled labor, the south pretended to be better off than the north. And because of that, SYL believed that it gained administrative experiences far better than that of the north during the occupation including the trusteeship period. That conception itself had been one of the cradles of the political friction of the union.

Are the Somalis an example of those kinds of the world who are not comfortable to govern each other? If the majority of the people say yes, then I think the Somali scholars need to have a look into the subject.

SYL was also preoccupied with power and fought positions in clan alienations. But, in general, were the politicians and the intellectuals aware of the incompetence of the nation as a whole? According to John Buchholzer, the author of *The Horn of Africa: Travels in British-Somaliland* (First publication in 1959, 197—198) asked some Somali politicians around that time:

Are the Somalis mature enough to govern themselves? "No," say many Somalis. We cannot manage alone either economically and politically. "The day the Europeans leave, we shall start fighting. We shall assemble with our arrows and bows, spears, revolvers, rifles; and the result will be that every little village will try to win mastery over its immediate neighborhood. Everybody will want to rule everybody else; and nobody will want to let him be ruled. Everybody will want to be a king or a president. The Majeerteens of the north say that it is they who ought to rule, and we down here do not want to be ruled by them. They say that they are the obvious rulers because their country is an old kingdom from which future kings or presidents should be chosen, not from the inferior people of the south. Imagine those savage nomads having the impudence to call us inferior! And imagine what it should be like if we had one of them sitting here in Mogadishu with all his camels! A fine king or president he would make. "We are a wretched, ignorant people," one Somali District Commissioner out in the country said to me." And we are lazy. It is not a good outlook for us. We must learn self-Government by practicing it. We must learn it the hard way, and we must take the knocks we are bound to get. If it comes to civil war, then the Ethiopians will come and annex us. .... If there should be unrest in my country, as I fear there will be, and if we cannot find enough strong men to keep the country together—we never manage a democracy—then we shal have shown that we are not ready to govern ourselves.

I was so surprised when I was reading those statements about how that Somali District Commissioner spoke of Somalis' thinking, and how he predicted the civil war. Even today, 2020, not much has changed on the thinking of the Somalis. For sure, the Somalis are proud people, destructive though when it comes to nationhood.

But also, they are arrogant, individualistic, suspicious, each a king of his own, or irrespective of each other. And be mindful of that I was born and raised in Somalia, and authored more than 20 books about the peninsula and the people.

However, the sensitive, egalitarian, alert, and proud people were ready to have a government. The North also under estimated the south. Though many of the southern leaders were from the central and northeastern regions, still, a larger part of the population of the north mostly led by elders despised Banadir and riverine populations as unkeen, weak, pro-Italian and not real nationalists.

In 1962, Abdirazak H. Hussein (1924—2014) was the Interior Minister of the republic.

Regardless of his intentions of professionalism being famous for the Government of *Busta Rosa* (Red envelopes) to fight corruption and incompetence, in the north, he was not liked. Having decided to make an official visit to the ex-British-Somaliland, John Drysdale, a British politician advised him not to make the initiative. Drysdale pretended to be more familiar with the Northern public than their own interior Minister. The minister was infuriated that a foreigner tells him where he could go around his own country.

Clan sentiment was not that important for the public at that time. Northerners disliked the Interior Minister as SYLer. Though he was from the next region, Mudug and was as a nationalist, orator, and tough as those from Hargeysa, Burco, and Berbera, perhaps people thought he was from Walloweyn—an agricultural town near Mogadishu. "Allihii Walloweyn webi Ku furrow wasiirka gudaha wadnaha goo: Roughly as Almighty's gift of the river to Walloweyn give a heart-attack to the interior minister" were some of the words they were chanting during the visit in the region.

Though they gave him a bad reception as expected, he came back with some recognition. The northern public was too nationalist and regarded itself as a cradle for a greater Somalia.

About the Walloweyn town, during the referendum of 1961, more people than the whole population of the town voted. Though I heard that the Interior Minister fired the mayor, Walloweyn became the talk of the referendum. But having discussed "Allihii Walloweyn webi Ku furrow wasiirka gudaha wadnaha goo" with a prolific writer, Farah Saxarla (Farah Mohamud Mohamed), a good friend of mine, told me that there is another version of the composition: "Allihii Walloweyn webi Ku furrow Wajaale weerar soo geli." And it seems that the Walloweyn version is close being the first composed. And this is why Walloweyn version is older than the Wajaale version.

During the referendum scandal in Walloweyn in 1961, the river flooded into the community and created a big damage. The problem became a national level. The public translated the flood damage into a curse. The years that Italian-Somaliland was under the supervision of the United Nations, Italy kept some promise of preparing the Somalis to govern themselves.

The British being one of the victorious of WORLD WAR TWO, administered the North any way it liked. Britain was a veto-powered country and could keep northern Somalia for a long time. Therefore, the best it did for the protectorate was to be independent and unite with the south.

Though the Trust-ship period of 1950-1960, countries such as Egypt, China, and some others used to offer scholarships to the Somali Italian youth while British Somaliland stayed a somewhat neglected backwater. Somalia: A Country Study: 21, "In 1957 there were 2,000 students receiving secondary, technical, and university education in Italian-Somaliland and through scholarships programs in China, Egypt, and Italy." According to Somalia: Enchantment of the World, 91:

The Trust Territory of Somaliland established in 1950 under Italian administration had the advantage that a definite date had been set for independence. There was no such deadline for British-Somaliland. A territorial council (in the south) was set up in 1950 to serve as the base for the country's future self-government. It engaged in full-scale debate concerned proposed legislation to run the country.

Christopher Daniels, 9:

There was little economic investment and overall development in Somalia during the colonial era. In the minds of the British, Somalia's only value was the fact that the area could be used to protect its trade routes through the Gulf of Berbera to India and the cattle raised there could be used to ensure a steady supply of food to other colonies in the area. As a result of this low perceived value, little money was invested in making the colony function properly. The biggest investment made in the colony by the British government was defeating the Daraawiish.

In the south, in 1927 Banana was exported to Italy and became the backbone of the economy in 1929. The other important economic development was the creation of salaried employees while in the north, there was little literacy in English because of the nomadic community's resistance to missionary schools that led to the most of the civil service jobs to in norther Somalia being filled by Kenyans who had more exposure to education.

Further complicated the situation, SYL also exaggerated that as a big bargaining chip and used that as south vs north while the north did not see that as a big advantage. When the government chose the English language over the Italian, the youth from the North filled that gap. Most of the staff of the Ministry of education became northerners.

The central government was well aware of that. Though the south complained about it, the government stuck with the new policy. Historically, "of the colonial powers that had divided the Somalis, only Italy developed a comprehensive administrative plan for its colony (Sampson Jerry, 14)" because of the agricultural feasibility.

During the foundation of Somali Airlines in 1964, West Germany accepted to train the necessary staff for the new agency. It attached some conditions to the training, secondary education in the English language and to handle the process itself to be free of corruption. The government accepted the German conditions, and the Ministry of Interior of Somalia advertised the openings on the national radios and in the daily papers. The southerners raised the issue again about secondary education in the English language requirement. The Minister of Interior, Abdirazak Haji Hussein went ahead with the decision.

Abdullahi Ahmed Abdulle (Azhari) is an ex-pilot of Somali Airlines, a group of 1979 trained by Lufthansa, and an author of *Burburkii Bulshada iyo Barakicii Duuliyeyaasha* (The Crumbles of the Public and the Displacement of the Pilots, 25), 2019. Mr. Abdulle who is now a consultant of Seward Montessori School in Minneapolis confirmed me that 95% of the youth who passed the test of 1964 were from the north.

Though the new Republic proceeded with a stormy political atmosphere, one thing was never in question. The north was only fighting for the proportion of high government posts, fair distribution of the resources and development programs.

The Somali Youth League dominated the government which was what the north feared before the unification. But, one-time, SYL group led by Aden Abdulle Osman of SYL who later became the first president of suggested delaying the unification date for about a week for more thorn-picking.

But there was a bigger pressure than all groups, the public. The Somali public from Dante (Hafun (Xaafuun)) to Kaambooni, from Djibouti to the corners of NFP (Northern Frontier Province) was in full gear to finalize the unification.

The eagerness of merging to become Somalia also shadowed the problem of the national integration. The general election of the British Protectorate of February 1960, SNL got 20 seats, USP of **Dhulbahante, Warsangeli, Gudabuursi and Issa** 12 seats, and NUF one. Mohamed Ibrahim Egal who was one of the shrewd politicians the Somalis ever had was leading the 20 SNL members.

That election in the north, SYL was in the ballot but won no seat. Before merging with the south, the new Executive Council of the north consisted of the Governor, Chief Secretary, Attorney—General, Financial Secretary and four other ministers appointed from the elected members of the legislative council. "Following the election, Mohamed Ibrahim Egal was chosen as a prime minister to lead a four—man government from 26 June 1960 to 1 July 1960," —making the second shortest-lived nation in the world, first being Dubai and Abu Dubai (www.cntraveler.com), *The Golden Years of Somalia, 56.*

Though there were some hesitating questions, Egal wanted to go ahead with the merge and therefore rejected the delay. *The Cost of Dictatorship of Jama Mohamed Ghalib (ex-police commissioner and cabinet minister), 25*:

Both main parties committed themselves to early independence and union with Somalia to the South. While the NUF (National United Front) of Michael Mariano generally followed a moderate policy line—that of cautious negotiations for union and bargaining with the southern leaders for power sharing, the SNL (Somali National League) of Mohamed Ibrahim Egal with 20 seats of the 33 seats from the North capitalized on its rival's moderation and adopted a radical platform without any preconditions on the unity issue. This step would be long regretted, not for the union aspect itself, because that had been the longstanding wish of the overwhelming majority of the Somali people, but for neglecting to bargain and safeguard the North's rights.

Africa's First Democrats of Professor Abdi Ismail Samatar, another northerner says on page 98:

The break-up of the MPs into two political camps, one lead by Mohamed H. I. Egal that allied itself with Abdullahi Isse and his group and another group of at least 15 MPs including Jama Abdullahi Ghalib, Ahmed Haji Duale, Ali Hassan Booni, and Ali Garad Jama, who aligned themselves with the opposition made a unified northern position on the union moot (subject to debate) ... whatever the differences might have existed between the two union acts did not slow down the national momentum.

In any case, During the Somali debates, emotions take many times over the real substance of the subject. There is no misunderstanding that some southern politicians, Hizbia Digil Mirifle member advised the northern politicians to set and stick with their conditions for the union.

The government of Osman and Sharmaarke, Booni became the deputy prime minister, Ahmed H. Duale minister of Agriculture, Egal minister of defense, and Garaad minister of education. About the cabinet, the position which could have cooled down the temperature of the north perhaps was the Prime minister-ship. But there are other reasons not researched in their merits of why Egal was hasty for the unification.

Public Pressure

The ex-British-Somaliland raised the first free flag of Somalia on 26 June 1960. The population of the protectorate was a diehard nationalist and could not accept anything other than a strong independent Somali State. Also, northerners regarded themselves as the base of greater Somalia. Being aware of the demand, politicians could not afford to ignore that. Another point worth mentioning is that Egal was close to Abdullahi Isse who like Michael Mariano was one of the true dynamic Somali nationalists. Isse who was selected as the General Secretary in 1948 was in a position to may become the first president of Somalia.

Egal was a shrewd politician, and we can imagine some of his possible worries about nationhood. He was well aware of the opposing groups vying for power, and it is highly probable that he foresaw that fighting for high posts could jeopardize the national unification. Even just before his last days of life, the echoes of his speeches worth to be listened and listened again and again. He was a politician ahead of his people. Most of that generation is gone, but not too late to look back and make further researches.

In 1961, the government drafted the first Constitution of the land. The north and the Hiiraan region were unhappy with certain provisions in the constitution. They asked the government for modification, but Mogadishu refused to make any changes and sent it for a public vote.

Finally, despite the disagreements of former British Somaliland, the first constitution of Somalia as an independent state was approved by popular referendum on 20 June 1961. 90% of the voters approved it. But there was a catch. Although the majority in the south approved the constitution, in the north, even among the voters, less than 50% supported it. Hiiraan voted against it too. The grievance of those regions was down-played. According to Africa's First Democrats by Professor Abdi Ismail Samatar, the referendum for the new Constitution of 1961, 1.948 million of the 3 million voted. 40% of the population was under the age of 14— and also 75% of the 3 million was a pastoralist. About 80% of the public could not read and write any language.

And there was a corruption in the system of the referendum. Otherwise, there was no way that 1.948 million could have voted. Not only that. The record shows that 90% or 1.848 million out of two million of the south voted. The result stated that 10% (105,000 out of one million) of the north voted.

Another important factor that the referendum not only the north disapproved but also, in Hiran. The regions with strong politicians in favor of the referendum voted for it while the regions with likewise strong politicians campaigned against the referendum voted against it.

The northern and Hiiraan regions voted against the referendum but that was not in any way disapproval of the unification. They just wanted to be heard and their concerns are addressed. That was the general consensus of the public and the feedback of the notable northern figures such as Jirdeh Hussein. John Drysdale

(Whatever Happened to Somalia: 133), 1994, Haan Associates which also cited A Modern History of Somalia of I. M. Lewis: "The North had sacrificed more than the south. The south with the capital and the National assembly at Mogadishu was still the hub of affairs, but from its former position as the capital of a small state Hargeysa had declined to a mere provincial headquarters remote from the center of things, northern pride found it hard to stomach this reduction in prestige."

Being the opinion of the author, the Hiiraan's rejection of the referendum had no equivalent weight as Togdheer or Northwest region. Hargeysa and Burco came to Mogadishu with their own government regardless of the rivers through Beledweyne and Kismayo. As a remedy of the dissatisfaction of the constitution and the unification in general, the new Republic missed an opportunity. A deserved point which even today, 2020 or the coming years, if missed again there will be a further disaster.

Today, the public is well aware of the political consequences when the intellectuals, the elders and the politicians take very wrong steps. If Somalia becomes Somalia, there is no way that the headquarters of all the ministers, all the faculties of the national university, Federal Parliament Headquarter and foreign consulates will be in Mogadishu. Never the current Puntland state administration of Somalia and the Somaliland if it joins the union will accept governors sent from the capital.

Mogadishu paid a high price of being built by the negligence of the rest of the country. Again, it will pay a higher price as far as it sees itself as an untouchable capital. The current constitution is not based on sensible law, religion or otherwise.

According to the Islamic religion, you have to be 15 years old to be a mature person. For a punishable offense, the courts try you as an adult or as a mature person. Then, you cannot be a president in Somalia if you are under 40 years of age is an insult in the view of many. However, Article 1 of the Constitution of the Somali Republic   states (1965 version):

1. Somalia is an independent and fully sovereign State. It is a representative, democratic and unitary Republic. The Somali people is one and indivisible. Sovereignty belongs to the people who shall exercise it in the forms determined by the constitution and the laws. No part of the people nor any individual may claim sovereignty or as same the right to exercise it.
2. Islam shall be the religion of the State.
3. The National flag shall be azure(sky-blue) in color, rectangular, and shall have a white star with five equal points emblazoned in its center.
4. The Emblem of Somalia shall be composed of an azure escutcheon with a gold border and shall bear a silver five-pointed star. The escutcheon, surmounted by an embattlement with five points in moons stile, the two lateral points halved, shall be borne by two leopards

rampant in natural form facing each other resting on two lances crossing under the point of the escutcheon with two palm leaves in natural form interlaced with a white ribbon.

Regardless of how nicely the constitution was drafted and the majority approved it, the dispute and other problems of the political merger that made the north displeased created disgruntled officers. Although some concerns were heard, the northern grievance needed better attention than what the politicians in Mogadishu offered. The sanction of the constitution and a cabinet reshuffle were not enough to heal the wounds.

But as a matter of fact, the fundamental principles of the Somalis' politics are stirred on clan loyalties—a sickness that needs honest, visionary and able political doctors. To put ex-British Somaliland in a position to renegotiate the unification, in December of 1962, a group of young junior military officers from the north attempted a coup. The government captured the organizers and took them to justice, and later released. The administration valued individual rights and respected freedom of speech. In the constitution, every mature Somali citizen had the privilege to vote. Legal and peaceful means guided the Republic.

The union of the territories was always a priority and written in the constitution. The constitution also granted that "All ethnic Somalis, no matter where they reside in the world are citizens of the republic."

The discontent of the north which arose of mostly power sharing did not end up at the failed coup. Though it was never publicized, some northern politicians were aware of the coup preparations and did not end in there. High northern politicians attempted a more civilized one.

Two cabinet ministers Egal as one of the two, of Aden's government who were members of Somali National League (SNL) in the north like the SYL in the south resigned. Aden's new government had been shaken. Not only that. The defected cabinet ministers left SYL and have formed a new political party, Somali National Congress (SNC). The new party attracted many SNL members and a good number of southerners as well.

The high government officers became untouchable. A pursued phenomenon of acquiring wealth from government employment developed. Party politics was enlightened rather than building a viable economy to sustain as a nation. Politicians campaigned to unite their clans to support them elected to the parliament. Most of the times, Somalis view politics from a clan point of view. The most important part of political discussions is neglected.

Politicians mostly debate about who should sit on the top chairs. People do not usually see that fighting for a ministerial position is less important than to campaign for a project which will be beneficial for the region you represent for a long time, economic and employment wise.

When Somalia disintegrated into tribal regions during the 1990s, the regional Administration of Puntland state survived because of mainly of the Garowe-Boosaaso highway and the small port in Boosaaso. Likewise, Somaliland mainly survived because of the Berbera port which is the only sheltered port in Somalia, Burao-Berbera and Garowe-Burao highways.

The young generation has to be honest with the history and pursue in-depth researches about what went wrong during the unification of former British Somaliland and former Italian Somaliland. Even today, the debates do not go beyond who is supposed to sit on a what chair. The new government of 1960 neglected both the northern and central regions where Banaadir and riverine regions areas were a gold-rush.

The politicians' arguments about a well-functioning national administration were self-serving, and still are. It is true that Xamar got prime minister-ship, two-third of the senior cabinet post, two top posts in the military and police force, the headquarter of the parliament and all the ambassadorial residences. But where did the national projects go? Beledweyne—Burco highway, Burco—Berbera highway, Garoowe—Boosaaso highway and the port, Berbera cement factory, enlargement of Berbera port was all done by the military government.

Ali Garaad became the minister of education in 1960, and we have no record that he tried to build at least one faculty of the national university in one of the remote regional cities such as Burco, Gaalkacyo, Boorama, Hargeysa, Boosaaso, or Garoowe. Still, today, people are preoccupied with of who sits on where.

I wonder if Ali Garad would have given up the minister of education post for a branch of the National University in Laas-Caanood or Burco, or Hargeysa. If I can get a guaranteed signature from the government to build a Port in Hobyo and a connecting highway from Gaalkacyo, I would not fight for a ministerial position.

Personal greediness of the politicians is the real irony of Somali politics. When the politicians are vying for posts; they use the public and when they lose that they use the public. Either way, the public is the sufferer.

The public always sees what is wrong with the administration but do not take the right approaches to the problem. They line up into clan politics. Unless the public sees that the Somali politicians may do not sometimes represent for their common good, the public will be in a loop for a long time.

Going along with The Genesis of Somalia's Anarchy, at the end of 1963, the working relationship between the president and the prime minister got sore. And as a result, having the right to do so, the president dismissed the Prime Minister. *Before Blackhawk Down: A Look Inside Pre-Civil War Somalia by Abdurahman Sharif Mahamud, page 51* "The Prime minister felt that unification of all Somali populated territories should be the issue dominating Somali politics because of their borders disputes while the president felt that internal economic and social problems should first be attended to."

The president appointed Abdirazak H. Hussein in his place. That move was not without a cost. From March to early September of 1964, there was no federal government because of the opposition to the nomination of Abdirazak. Mar waa Risaaq mama waa Rashiid; inta kale ma rootiyaa (one term Rizak and the other Rashid; are the best bread!) is based on a Shirib (dancing poem) played in Mogadishu and surroundings.

Both Abdirashid and Abdirazak belonged to the same clan and regardless of their clan's well-played political games, and their nationalistic history, envy towards the Majeerteen had gradually spread.

But as far as Mr. Hussein's government is concerned, although he had wholeheartedly tried to create an atmosphere of professionalism and accountability in the government system, corruption had not slowed down either. Distributing unjustified economic favors to certain people for personal reasons became very noticeable.

Also, Somalis are an oral society in general. Sometimes they exaggerate stories. When the folktales are remembered, Siyad Barre was a top millionaire. In the early 1990s, I used to see some of his children in Canada who were struggling to get ends meet like the rest.

Referring to the Genesis of Somalia's Anarchy, to compete for the parliamentary post, the politicians formed many clan-based political parties. Some clans broke down into a subclass. Somalia held the municipal elections where SYL got seventy four percent. Women in the north voted in their first time while those in the south got that privilege in 1958. The British government allowed her women to vote in 1918 while it denied that same right to the Somali women under its rule, British-Somaliland.

In 1964, the Western Somali Liberation Front (WSLF) had also come into existence.

The birth of the new movement (WSLF) made Haile Selassie angry, the king of Ethiopia. Having renewed the old hostilities between Somalia and Ethiopia, further Somali uprising in the Ogadeen region had made the matter worse. Armed conflicts started along the Somali-Ethiopian border. The Somali republic hoped to seize Ogadeen, and therefore backed up the WSLF armed men with hit and run campaigns or guerilla warfare. The kingdom became aware of that. And after serious skirmishes by the liberation forces, as a result, a war broke out between the two countries.

Somalia founded the National Army from former British Somaliland Scouts and the former Italian Somaliland paramilitary police in 1960. But both training and military hardware, the Kingdom was superior to the new Republic. The national army of the Horn was weak and ill organized resulting in a quick cease-fire. Somalia became the retreated. The Organization of African Union brokered the cease-fire.

And since then, political frictions between the two countries over the Ogadeen, now Somali-Ethiopia of the Federal Democratic Republic of Ethiopia dispute had never been stable. As it is what is inside that counts, as I write these words, advocating for the unification of greater Somalia is very rooted in the hearts and minds of the Somali people. Just bad politicians are running the show and the public is not keen enough at the moment.

Which brings back to the course of Somalia's political journey, however, in March of 1964, Somalia held its first post-independence national elections. SYL got more than fifty percent of the 123 seats. Many illiterate elders who could afford to buy votes became parliamentarians.

1965 slipped away with no major events. Many educated and visionary people were not in Parliament. Rather, as a Hotel, uneducated elders used to gather in the headquarter of the National Assembly to practice their public speaking.

There is a joke I would like to tell. Two members of the National Assembly of Somalia disliked each other. In a tough debating day, one had a nap on the chair. When the discussions were concluded and were the time to cast the final vote, he woke up. He asked where his adversary voted. Then, without giving consideration to what was really at stake, he voted otherwise. Sadly, he voted against a project for his own constituents.

We share another joke with the reader. The public of a town in Bari (northeastern) region heard an announcement that XYZ won the parliamentary seat of the district. Also, the public did not witness any election held. So, two locals had a conversation about the matter. One said, "Who voted for the victorious of the seat (Ari boowe yaa doortay XZY?" And the other said, "You tell me brother (Boowe bal adba!)"

In his last day of an East African tour, August 29, De Gaulle stopped at Djibouti, French Somaliland, the last colony of France territory on the African continent, and which also became in 1977 one of the last European colonial rules in mainland Africa. Demanding their independence from France, the Somali nationalists gave him a grim boycott. Four people were killed during the first stop of the France president on August 26, 1966. People lined the streets and turned their backs when the president's motorcade passed through the town to the heavily guarded governor's palace, his overnight residence.

In Cairo, Egypt, Somalis mostly students demonstrated and stoned the French Embassy chanting independence slogans and denouncing De Gaulle's visit to Djibouti. The colonial authority in Djibouti arrested the leader of United Democratic Party, Mohamed Ahmed Issa, a pro- independence party in Djibouti.

According to Somali government, as a revenge of the bitter protests against De Gaulle, the French expelled between 12,000 and 18,000 Somalis from the territory (War Clouds on The Horn of Africa: A Crisis for Detente by Tom J. Farer, An American academic, author and former president of the university of New Mexico:

88, Making sense of Somali history by Abdurahman Baadiyow, 146). Many of those expelled left behind families, friends, jobs, homes and personal properties.

But that did not halt people taking to the streets still shouting for their independence from France. De Gaulle on the other hand, pursued his agenda of backing ties to Ethiopia. After days of talks between him and Emperor Haile Selassie, French offered help Ethiopia in Building a Railway between Ethiopia and Djibouti. To him (De Gaulle), every step that would relieve present or future pressures from Ethiopia against Djibouti, and help to direct that pressure against the unification of Somalia was a step worth the effort.

Even the New York Times Reporter, Lawrence Fellows biased against Somalia's stand for the independence. France offered to finance the construction of a new railway line deep into the interior of Ethiopia. President De Gaulle saw Djibouti as a growing rival to Aden in commercial and strategic importance in the Red Sea basin. Regardless of much-talked Pan-Africanism, Ethiopians kings never wanted a strong Somali government. BBC Somali, August 28, 1966 (Somali Government Publication of 1974: 66), King Haile Salasse said, "I would like France to stay in the French Somali coast forever."

"The Somali people are one and indivisible" is written in the constitution, and is a slogan of SYL to exercise its obligation of uniting their people under one flag, and some called it expansionist aims. A Columbia University professor answered that accusation of the Lawrence Fellows of New York Times with a "Somalia is not an Expansionist."

Whoever accused Somalia of an expansionist, that could not deter the will and the energy of the people. They were determined to fight for the freedom of their brothers and sisters. In all over the world, where Somalis could organize themselves to make a crowd, they held demonstrations against De Gaulle's East African tour. While the Republic was campaigning for the unification of its territories, the number of political parties was increasing in each election season.

Somalia also raised about the future of the Somali-Kenyans with the British government in 1961. The Osman Administration and the representatives from the Northern Frontier Province (NFP) demanded that Britain would pre-arrange for the separation of NFP from the colony before it would become an independent state in 1963. British government reviewed the case, and it became known that the Somalis did not want to be part of Kenya.

This coming piece of information is a new avenue for research. Author Christopher L. Daniels is professor of political science at Florida A$M University with PHD in African studies. (Christopher Daniels, 7:

Kenya proposed the creation of an East African federation that would include Kenya, Somalia and Ethiopa. According to this plan, all Somalis residing within this entity would be united under one government. Somali representatives were also in favor of this proposal, but the major sticking point came on the timing of the unification of Somali territories. Kenya wanted the unification to take place prior to the formation. This proved to be a significant obstacle, ultimately causing the negotiations to collapse.

The proposal was backed by Britain which as you read was never honest about the unification of Somali territories. It was a delaying tactic that the UK played with the Somalis. Mr. Duncan Sandys, who since Churchill was a high level British politician put in writing "That there could be no session of Kenyan territory so long as the British Government was responsible for Kenya" (www.nation.co.ke).

The British administered many portions of Somaliland for 80 years and never stopped betraying the Somalis to even comply with its treaty obligation. The Kingdom signed many treaties like the one coming with the Somali tribes and see how carefully it is drafted. "We, the undersigned Elders of the Issa tribe, are desirous of entering into an Agreement with the British Government for the maintenance of our independence, the preservation of order, and other good and sufficient reasons. Now it is hereby agreed and covenanted as follows: -

1. The Issa tribe do hereby declare that they are pledged and bound never to cede, sell, mortgage, or otherwise give for occupation, save to the British Government, any portion of the territory presently inhabited by them, or being under their control.
2. All vessels under the British flag shall have free permission to trade at all ports and places within the territories of the Issa tribe.
3. All British subjects residing in or visiting the territories of the Issa tribe shall enjoy perfect safety and protection, and shall be entitled to travel all over the said limits under the safe-conduct of the Elders of the tribe.......In token of the conclusion of this lawful and honorable bond, Ali Geri done, ...and Major Frederick Mercer Hunter, Assistant Political Resident at Aden, the former for themselves, their heirs and successors, and the latter on behalf of the British Government, do each and all, in the presence of witnesses, affix their signatures, marks, and seals, at Zaila, on the31st day of December, 1884, corresponding with the13th Rabual-Awal,1302."

In 1967, Somali-Kenyans made movements to secede from Kenya and unite with Somalia. Border hostilities between Kenya and Somalia increased, and the Somali government renewed the issue. The Kenyan government claimed that from 1963 (its year of independence) to 1967 its security forces killed over 2,000 Shifta (Farer:89). Those Kenya called Shifta were all Somalis fighting for their separation from Kenya. In 1964 Rasna Warah, 132), the president of Kenya, Jomo Kenyatta said in front of the parliament: "To the people who live in Northeastern region, I have to say this: We know that many of you are herdsmen during the day and Shiftas (bandits (shufto in Somali)) during the night." In 1962, British colonial administrator, Sir Charles Eliot advised the British government that to declare that the districts of Wajeer, Mandheera and Gaarisa as part of Kenya (Rasna Warah, 130).

Furthermore, according to declassified documents recently, the British made a secret commitment to defend Kenya in case of an invasion by Somalia ("Bamburi Memorandum of Understanding" (www.nation.co.ke)). That led to the Arusha Memorandum of Understanding between Kenya and Somalia to end the border hostilities in which the prime minister, Egal gained a lot of heat and blame domestically. Though he defended that move very well, many non-politicians did see that treaty as a give-up. *Pan-nationalism issue lost some of its intensity in the Somali society.*

June of 1967, also the term of the Somalia presidentship had to expire. In the south, the presidential election had turned into a fierce clannish battle more than an ideological. Though in the name of SYL, it was campaigned as a fight between Hawiye and Darood.

In any case, in the final count of the federal election, the former Prime minister, Abdirashid Ali Sharmaarke defeated his former boss and became the second president of Somalia by a secret poll of the National Assembly members. He appointed Mohamed H. I. Egal, the prominent politician from the north to be the prime minister. Mr. Egal formed a new government.

However, the new administration did not cure the cancer of corruption, nepotism, and favoritism but rather became widespread. The intellectuals and the members of the armed forces were the most critical of the civilian administration. One of the most important jobs of any state is to protect the interests of its citizens. Government officials are elected and nominated to make sure that their citizens are not ripped off.

Since the statehood, some posts were ill-fatedly and not deservedly assigned
according to a clan. Lavish houses, cars and going on vacation to Europe and North America became something of a norm for cabinet ministers, and other high-paid Government employees at the expense of the public treasury. Certain ministers looted the budget of their ministers. One of the folktales stated that one cabinet minister had accumulated as much millions of dollars as his age.

Whether that was true or not, there is not a known trial for that one or a similar one. The Road to Zero, 69: "After a relatively short period in the Government, a 31-yearold politician of the time was said to have amassed 31 million Somali shillings, around 5 million US dollars. God knows if it was true, but it was the talk of the town."

I never heard if any branch of the administration had launched an investigation. While the public treasury was being dried up, the majority of the population was unemployed including many college graduates—though foreign trained graduates from different schools of ideology used to public confusion.

This was a Somali folklore story. One day, a man ran to a crowd of people. People became scared and asked him why. He said, "I ran away from a moral disaster taking in an unexpected place." The crowd listened to the man, understood the problem, and get terrified too. Then, they said, "let us take refuge in the Mosque." And he said, "No! No! We cannot do that. The disaster is happening in the Mosque."

The public elected the Parliamentarians to safeguard their interests but rather watched, or perhaps many waited for a chance to do the same. Since Somalia became an independent nation in 1960, many people used to come to the Capital for employment, or some expected monetary favors from their relatives in the government. Many men bought votes on government money, and it became a habit that someone would come to Mogadishu to ask money someone whom he empowered with a ballot.

To get a job, having an elected official of your clan in the parliament was as important as having a college degree. Somalia was very democratic and very rooted in corruption. In the first post-independence elections of 1964, eighteen political parties participated.

The last election of March 1969, the eligible voters of about one million had to choose over 1,000 candidates representing more than 62 political parties have competed for only 123 seats in the National Assembly. Remember that the referendum of 1961 was so corrupted that the government registered almost 2 million votes.

In any case, though the election process was too fraudulent, SYL had got more than ninety percent of the seats. The following can be one of the clues of how SYL rigged the election. The government advised Mohamed Abshir Muse, the police commissioner of Somalia, to get instructions from the interior minister. Though he was a political ally of the former president, Mr. Osman, the commissioner resigned. That resignation did not hurt Sharmaarke and Cigaal (Egal), the candidates for the posts of president and prime minister. The next move was to call Jama Mohamed Ghalib, the police Commander of the northern regions, and a close confidant of Mr. Abshir into Mogadishu. Those two moves, which many believe were what Egal and Sharmaarke wanted to open the doors for vote-rigging.

Farer, page 91, "With Abshir temporarily out of the way, Sharmaarke and Egal
shuffled senior police officials, apparently to assure the presence of pliable commanders in key elections districts. The commander of the northern region, Col. Jama Mohamed Ghalib, a man noted for his integrity, efficiency and political neutrality, was recalled to administrative tasks in Mogadishu."

The primary motivation was always the language of power into wealth, and the public was very much aware of what was going inside the government offices and in the bank transactions? It is not a controversy to say that in some instances candidates openly offered cash for votes. The rule of law was not rightfully dictating the election process of the nation.

The citizens voted out over seventy percent of the incumbents in the last election of 1969. That was some kind of exercised democracy, but there are no enough researches, however, if the public balloted-out the incumbents because of fighting corruption, or if the incumbents were over-spent.

It reached a point that the public calls the government the biggest thief and many thieves in the country, but the public itself had never been an innocent bystander. It neglected its rights and responsibilities. Clannism is a cancer and highly polarized by all. And there is a question if any administration had ever introduced a system of accountability? There is another problem with this. The most academics and professionals, yet today, don't address the core of the nation's troubled nationalistic views in their worthiness.

Rather, they use tribalism as a scapegoat from the main topic. The public finally got the perception that their government in Mogadishu no longer looked after their welfare. Some even viewed the president and the prime minister as tribal leaders. For unclear and not well-researched reasons, when Mr. Egal, a Northerner became the Prime Minister, the unhappiness of the north with the government got worse.

1968 passed while still, people were wondering what a national government meant. I love that year. As a camel herder from the rural, that year, a good uncle of mine, Diiriye warsame put me into a school. We make a very important assertion in this chapter. Mogadishu did not swallow

only the pride of the north, but the government in the capital abandoned the responsibility of developing the rest of the country. *Kadeedkii Xamar iyo Kalaguur* (Disintegration and the Escape from Mogadishu (back cover)), Ali Abdigir, 2018, Amazon, ISBN: 97817296734540 is one of Thy books to read about the Somali Civil war.

The book highlights how the central government neglected the British-Somaliland as well the other regions with no watering rivers, fertile soils, and great vegetations. There are thousands of examples of the consequences of how the previous governments and what came after them neglected their responsibilities.

Qaranbila, a girl who was born and raised in Boosaaso finished her National Service of teaching one academic year in the elementary and junior schools in 1980. She did not want to live anywhere else in the world, but Boosaaso. She had one single condition, university education. She was from a poor family and knew no one in Mogadishu.

With no other choice, Qaranbila went to Mogadishu to enter the National University of Somalia which was the biggest higher education institution in the country, and only in the Capital. She became a medical doctor of general medicine and diagnosis in late 1987. She went to the United States of America for an extra training of War Trauma.

1990, ready to go back to Boosaaso, Somalia disintegrated into clannish regions. She lost some loved ones in the civil war. The two dreams, one achieved and the other destroyed is excellent reading.

The assassination of The President

The second president of Somalia, Abdirashid Ali Sharmaarke was assassinated in Laas Caanood in northern Somalia on October 15, 1969. He was touring drought-stricken area while the Prime Minister, Mr. Egal was somewhere in the United States of America vacating after an official visit (The Road to Zero, 87).

About the murder of the president, the feeling was like that the nation was recolonized. The Republic faced the political assassination of its most important figure, the first highest murder in the nation's history left the whole country in shock. People were in tears.

In the aftermath, people seemed to be asking themselves, where are we going to go from here? In a country with matters of corrupted administrations and tribal confrontations, the murder of its only second president, a nation of being less than ten years old as an independent state, was largely an unexamined possibility. Among all groups, the reaction to the murder of Sharmaarke made the public nervous and unstable in general, and politicians in particular.

The president died at the hands of a government employee, a police officer, Mr. A. K. Abdi. The killing of the president, Abdirashid Ali Sharmaarke is still a subject worth an investigation. As a matter of responsibility, it is very important for young scholars to look back and pursue independent investigations of their own. There is no doubt in my mind that new information will come out. If Mr. Abdi, a bodyguard of the president was a lone assassin, let it go into the history books as such. But somebody have to do the job.

The government curbed all political activities and banned all meetings of more than 5 persons. After the burial of the president, the parliament held an emergency session and debated fiercely about a replacement. There were only two issues of whether to select a new president for the remainder of the term or set up a transitional government and then hold elections for a new government.

Discussions did not make any progress that some even suggested to be nominated as a transitional president just because of being from the clan of the murdered President. Nonetheless, there is a Somali saying of a question and its answer. It states:
"Question: What is the value of death? Answer: It creates an opportunity for another."

The defeat of Italy, Germany, and Japan in WORLD WAR TWO helped many nations of the world to govern themselves, which the Italian-Somaliland was one of them. The transfer of Haud—and—Reserve and Ogadeen to Ethiopia put the British into a very embarrassing position by what they saw as Britain's betrayal of the treaties with the Somali clans against raids, Ethiopians in particular. We recall "*have left them at the mercy of raiding Abyssinians who have no other employment than that of making raids on Oromos and Somalis."*

When it became apparent that Italian-Somaliland was going to get its independence from Italy in 1960, the northern public increased political protests demanding its freedom to govern. Britain thought over the future of the Protectorate and made some preparations. It introduced a representative government and accepted to merge with the Italian-Somaliland. There is one more citation before we proceed with the next matter.

A Master's Degree professional thesis (Rethinking the Somali State) by Aman H. D. Obsiye, The University of Minnesota, May 2017:

Britain did not have a policy of granting the Protectorate independence until December 1958. This is the reason why the Protectorate's Somalization programs were initiated much later than Italian Somaliland, whose independence was decided in 1949. "According to John Hugh Adam Watson (British Foreign Office), it was impossible to maintain British rule over Somaliland once Somalia became independent. There was an urgent need, he argued, for a rapid devolution of power to the Protectorate . . . Somaliland was to be granted its independence in 1960, which would coincide with the date of independence of the Trusteeship Territory, Italian—Somaliland."

The disparity between the ex-British Somaliland and the Italian Somaliland in economic development and political experience is somewhat very misleading. Like the British, the Italians neglected the central and the northeastern regions. The politicians of the northern and central Somalia themselves abandoned the regions of their constituents and put all their eggs in Banaadir and riverine areas.

Chapter ten referenced notes

The forgotten Front 1914-1918: The East African Campaign by Ross Anderson
Nine Faces of Kenya, page 153
The First to Be Freed: British Military Administration in Eritrea and Somalia, 19411943, 15
Dhagar iyo Dhayalsi 1948 by Cali M. Cabdigiir (Caliganay), SYL VS (USA, UK, France and Russia, Four Power Commission of the UN, 70-74
The Four-Power Commission Report
The First to be Freed, p49
UN Resolution #1418(XIV) of December 5, 1959,

Despactches From the Front: The War in East Africa 1939-1943 by John Grehan and Martin Mace
Somalia: History, Origins, Migrations, settlement, Sampson Jerry
Allihii Walloweyn webi Ku furrow wasiirka gudaha wadnaha goo, Allihii   Walloweyn webi Ku furrow Wajaale weerar soo geli
Somalia: A Country Study, 21
Enchantment of the World, 91
Burburkii Bulshada iyo Barakicii Duuliyeyaasha (The Crumbles of the
Public and the Displacement of the Pilots), 2019 by Mr. Abdullahi Ahmed Abdulle (Azhari), page 25
The Cost of Dictatorship of Jama Mohamed Ghalib (ex-police commissioner and cabinet minister), 25
Africa's First Democrats of Professor Abdi Ismail Samatar, 98
John Drysdale of Whatever Happened to Somalia, 133
Article 1 of the Constitution of the Somali Republic states (1965 version)
The Tree on The Moon of Mohamed Urdoh, 210
The New York Times
BBC, August 28, 1966 (Government Publication of 1974, 66
(www.nation.co.ke) *"Bamburi   Memorandum   of   Understanding"* (www.nation.co.ke)
__Making Sense of Somali History, Abdurahman Abdullahi Baadiyow, 2017

CHAPTER ELEVEN (1969-1977)

Military Government

Because certain things have changed not necessarily mean that anything was corrected. __Ali Abdigir

The bloodless Coup D'état of 1969

The assassination of Dr. Abdirashid, the second president of Somalia gave an opportunity to a power-hungry institution, the military.

In general, there was a wind of military takeover blowing in the African continent and other under-developing countries from 1960s—1970s. The national army was infested with that disease. It had been increasingly critical of the political direction and the accountability of the civilian officials. It thought over to topple the government. It waited for a chance. "The value of death" arrived at the right time.

While the parliamentarians were still debating to select a president and form a new government, a group of mostly military officers seized the power of the nation in October of 1969. They selected General Mohamed Siyad Barre (1919—1995), the highest-ranking officer of the armed forces as a head of the group.

Though the slaying of the president came unexpectedly, when they heard that the military overthrew the corrupted administration, the population started celebrating. The general public had the feeling that the things will get better and welcomed the revolution with green leaves. Unfortunately, it was the wrong government at the right time.

The coup architects of over 100 (Dawn from the Civilization to the Modern Times by Mohamed Farah Aideed and Satya Pal) officers selected a Supreme Revolutionary Council (SRC) of 25 men as the ultimate decision-makers engineered. And after some political maneuvers, on October 23, 1969, General Mohamed Siyad Barre became the chairman of the SRC and the head of state.

The revolutionary group immediately suspended the constitution of the land, imposed dawn-to-dusk curfews. It did not stop there, but also annulled the national assembly, abolished all national parties, dismantled the Professional Associations, installed the death penalty and put all the civic organizations under its mandate. Crime in urban life was almost none existence while in the rural though, there existed clan fighting.

The public welcomed the coup but, some educators and experienced elders
raised eyebrows when the military restricted the freedom of expression. After a couple of months, the Peace Corps (Americans) were asked to leave the country. Many Somalis were not annoyed for the expulsion of the Peace Corps having had a perception of being Christian missionaries and American spies. But the internal power struggles inside the regime had surfaced quicker than many thoughts.

Failed Coups and the Consequences

In less than a year, an unpleasant window of the new military rule appeared.
When the military took over, Somalia was defined as a neutral state but not long after Barre welcomed the communist Soviet Union. General Jama Ali Qorshel (Qoorsheel), the vice president of the new Revolutionary government and the head of the police force questioned the move. From the beginning, the police were not very involved in the preparation of the coup but could not resist the outcome.
In April of 1970, General Ali had been accused of the planning of a coup and
arrested. It was not difficult for academics and good thinkers to understand that Militant Barre took care of one of his first political challengers. General Qorshel had not been executed but sentenced to a prison term. Perhaps reacting to the failed coup, or a suspicion of it, the government abolished the right of Habeas Corpus. Clannish verbal conversations (tribalism) were publicly prohibited.

In October of 1970, the first anniversary of the revolution, the new government adopted scientific socialism, created National Security Courts to handle all political cases and the National Security Service (NSS). The regime gave the NSS a decree of monitoring the professional and private activities of civil servants. The NSS later became too famous for terrorizing mainly for tracking down the potential dissidents. It had a training relationship with East Germany, a communist state, and it developed a pervasive climate of fear and suspicion. Even the high-ranking military personnel who kept eyes on the Barre's chair also became under the NSS surveillance.

Barre had trusted no one including his children with the power to become a lone ruler. He obligated himself to be on top by any means necessary. Other officers who were hungry for power, general Aynanshe, general Gabayre and colonel Dheel (high ranked military officers) attempted a real coup in 1971. They were not spared like Qorshel. A high military court sentenced them to death and a firing squad made the execution. Some did see that as a double standard.

Nonetheless, from that day on, not many educators of good conscious have doubted seeing enough about the Regime. Barre also realized that his government was vulnerable. The challenging questions of General Qorshel and the coup of the Caynaanshe group affected the stability of the Regime.

A new era of political instability had begun. The school of the goals and the objectives of the Revolution became the sole acceptable Political School of Thought in the country. Security forces started seizing political dissidents without warrant, explanation or reference to any central authority. Many of those detained had been held under harsh conditions. Torture was used to be done but not a wide spread.

For more than ten years, the previous democratic governments could not finalize to choose a script of the Somali language. The military government speeded up the process and nominated a Commission. Within three years, the committee recommended the Latin alphabet with some modifications. The administration announced the official script of the Somali language in 1972. That was one of the best achievements that the totalitarian Regime had ever reached.

There were reasons that the Commission recommended Latin over other scripts such as Arabic. The new writing suited best to represent the phonetic **structure** of the Somali language and is also flexible enough to be adjusted for the dialect. Another advantage that Latin was preferred over others was that modern printing equipment would be cost effective. In the same year, the regime created the victory pioneers or uniformed militia "Guulwadeyaal" to spy on the people. They were trained to infiltrate the public and arrest anybody who speaks of a tribal word.

In Gaalkacyo, the capital city of Mudug region, even one Victory Pioneer accused his mother of clannism. The regime set up a Special Tribunal, the National Security Courts (NSC) as a judicial system and tried the most political cases. New more laws were introduced, and any person accused of harming the nation's unity, peace, spread propaganda against the military rule, or the sovereignty had to face a death penalty.

The government started to adopt a self-help program known as the Crash Program. The regional or the municipal leaders had the authority to mobilize the public to participate in construction, and cleaning projects without their consent and without pay. It was not a fully voluntary program but somewhat forced mobilizations. In some places of the country, people demonstrated against the forced mobilizations.

Tom J. Farer (page 95) states "In October, 1973, residents of Burco (Burao) in the north and of the surrounding area rioted in response to demands that they undertake a self-help exercise in street cleaning and they pay taxes. The army intervened and, in suppressing the outburst, reportedly killed eight people." That is the only or one of few worth researching that the public revolted about the crash program. Interestingly, according to Historical Dictionary by Margaret Castagno, the Somali police and the American Corps were active in initiating some of the Self-help projects.

Though the good expectations that people had with the new government did not fully materialize still, the acceptance or believing of the military rule as a means of solving some political and social problems of the country did not all disappoint. Also, the keen people got more distrusts of the regime, but they dared not to raise their voices either. Being realized that the biggest threats to the military administration might have been coming from the educators and the well off, perhaps as a lesson, private institutions such as schools and the banks were nationalized.

And consequently, a flow of brain drain-out had started. Whenever the opportunity knocked on their doors, many educated people took advantage of it leaving the country. Some educated and professional people became hopeless of the military administration and left the country.

Oil producing Arab countries have utilized their education and muscles as well. Realizing that in the long run, the brain drain-out would backfire, the role of the NSS, the official principle intelligence agency of Somalia, had obtained an unlimited "practice as you like" power to detain people for an indefinite period. Having given the go-ahead of the decree, it launched a campaign to stop the flow of professionals, students, dissidents and the youth in general out of the country.

People still managed to leave by all means. The regime established a one-party, state and the situation almost reached a stage of hopeless. The last hope of re-installing democratic administration disappeared and the establishment of a ruling by gunpoint became a reality. The academics and the professionals lost trust in the system and started deserting.

The Regime became well aware of the brain-drain and took extra measures to crack down the flow of the elites, and the opposition activities. The public became scared of the most feared of all the government employees, the NSS. The agency routinely monitored the movements of individuals who held important positions in the government. High government and sensitive posts went only to entrusted men. And the trusted officers had no fear of using public funds for private uses.

Since an anti-revolution became the worst crime to be accused of anybody and was punishable by death, General Barre uniquely mastered and drove Somalia by murdering those who tried to challenge him. He imposed a reign of terror so pervasive and profound that most politicians actually believed the president watched them by the hour.

People were witnessing the misuse of the public treasures all those years, an echo of the civilian administration. The public saw as a fool of any high post-holding person who did not abuse the public responsibility entrusted with him. Scholars did not do enough researches of this ill-phenomenon. Eastern Hornites behave most of the times in a way that the country is not theirs. People experienced food shortages throughout the Somali peninsula. In the simplest living terms, people used to queue for rationings, such as sugar and cooking oil.

The Literacy and the Census campaign

The year 1974 was unique in Somalia. Five major events that each came with its circumstances took place, Organization of African Union (OAU) Meeting, becoming the first Sub-Saharan African nation to sign a treaty of friendship and cooperation with Soviet Union (Losing Mogadishu: 19), Joining the Arab League, Literacy Campaign, and Dabodheer (long-tailed famine).

Somalia became a member of the Arab league February 1974 (The Road to Zero, 126)). It became the only non-Arabic speaking member. The linkage of Puntland to the Arabs is not by blood. It is rather of the proximity, religion and a matter of economic interests. Some non-Arab African nations further distanced themselves from Somalia. The alliance created a confusion of whether the Somalis see themselves as Arabs or black Africans.

The African Union Meeting helped the economy with just a temporary face-lifting for the administration. According to Margaret Castagno of Historical Dictionary of Somalia, the year of 1974, Mogadishu residents were not more than 250,000.

The military rule went further than the introduction of the Somali script of 1972. The literacy campaign of 1974 was one of the best remembered of the military regime. When the military toppled the democratic administration in October of 1969, more than seventy-five percent (not many disputes this number) of the population were nomads and illiterate.

Before the operation, the literacy rate was less than twenty percent while after the campaign it jumped to over 50 percent (not verified, but some government documents showed). As a heart of the matter, the operation was of two types; literacy campaign and the General census. Teenage students (up to grade 11) were sent to the countryside and used to move with the nomadic families. Each student was assigned to a group of families to teach the writing and reading of their mother tongue. Those students who were placed in agricultural communities and small villages were very fortunate.

As I was one of the students, it was a challenging and testing job to have undertaken. During the last two months of the campaign, while performing our duties, we were trained to learn how to conduct a national census. More than 20,000 of intermediate, high school students and teachers participated in the operation. According to (Adan Mohamed Ali (Maalmihii Noloshayda (Days of my Life, 64))), more than 28,000 personnel including the students and the teachers took part in the overall operation. The census which was the most difficult and the second part of the campaign was done in 1975.

The Somalis are always very curious and questioning people by nature. Therefore, it was hard to convince them of why their number and the number of their animals were being investigated.

The nomads knew what communism meant, and they could easily relate that to the census. Many breathed to us that the reason for the census was to take their animals away from them and the government would force them to leave in the cities. Other than the 8th and 12th grades, intermediate and high schools were closed for a year.

Bar ama baro (teach or learn) became a motto from the inception of the script. The year of the operation was recovered within the next couple of years shortening the academic year vacations, and the breaks until the gap was filled.

Both the world and the Somalis were anxious to know the population of the nation. The result of the census was not publicly published, but there was a rumor of about 7 Million. In 1988, also certain government records showed 8 million which is not in agreement with the current (2020) estimation of 12-13 million. The rate of Somalia population increase per year is 2% to 2.2%. Even if we take a 7million and 2.2% rate of increase, that cannot go with the present best estimate of about 12-13 million. Above 42% of the population is under 14.

In 1960, Somalia had a population of about 3 million, 2 in the south and one in the north. Though 600,000+ perished during the civil war, and almost one million live outsides, a 2.2% increase for 58 years can give us more than the current estimation. Mathematically, 3 million of 2.2% (though you may see various percentages) of rate of increase per year for 58 years is in close agreement with the current estimation of 12-13 million.

The census was not wrapped up smoothly. We recall that the average rainfall is estimated at 10-12 inches, and at the same time, irregular, droughts are frequent, in the Northern and central regions in particular. Another drought had badly hit the central and northern regions killing around 20,000 people.

Within a few months, more than 250,000 people were drawn into refugee camps. Most camps were run by the students and officials. The operation was expanded. The military administration tried to educate the public and develop a market for Ocean produce of the longest coast in Africa.

With the help of the Soviet Union, financially, and technically, over 100,000 people who lost their animals were airlifted to the riverine areas in the south. The planes were airlifting the people with their belongings from Caynabo town of Sool region and the Hobyo town of Mudug region. Around another 20,000 were settled along the coast to be trained as fishermen. That whole operation was another intellectual thinking of the revolutionary government.

Techniques of future urbanization of the airlifted people started in all scales. People were trained for all sorts of middle skills, fishing, farming, carpentry, small business and so on. Many of the resettled people went back to their pastoral areas.

In the education sector, the military government did a good job. Almost in every little town in Somalia, a school was built. Many parents who have never dreamed of sending their children to school during democratic governments have seen their dreams come true.

In general, the quality of primary education had somewhat deteriorated not because of the introduction of the Somali script as some perhaps short-sighted scholars claim, but because of the brain drain-out and the lack of motivation of those remained to teach.

Even today, there are people of Somali origins in the west who feel ashamed to write or read books written in Somali. About the higher education, both quantitatively and qualitatively, the military regime did very well. The National University was enlarged. It produced needed, able and respected graduates accordingly. However, it stayed in the capital, and the high school graduates from far away towns and cities like Hafun and Saylac were to travel to Mogadishu or forget about higher education at all.

There is an important event in the Horn we have to mention before we leave this chapter. In September of 1974, military officers overthrew Emperor Haile Selassie, the ruling king of Ethiopia. The coup did not stop there. Another political contest, Mengistu Haile Mariam came to the top. Until early of 1975, the totalitarian government of General Siyad still enjoyed some degree of popular support.

In January of 1975, the government introduced a new law. Since British Somaliland and Italian-Somaliland created Somalia, the Republic had a hard task to make a unified law out of the legislation and judicial structures drawn from Italian, British, customary and Islamic legal traditions. The government unified the three legal systems of Secular, Sharia and the Customary into one main legal system.

The application of Islamic law was left to handle marriage, divorces, family disputes, and inheritance. The socialist system of Barre administration took one step further. In early to mid-1970s, a commission was appointed to reform the family law. The president and the Secretary of State for Justice and Religious Affairs modified the draft which a selected Commission recommended.

The code aimed to abolish customary laws, and repealed previous British and Italian era legislation relating to family law. Article 1 of the Family Code of 1975 provides that the leading doctrines of Shafia school and general principles of Islamic Law and social justice are to serve as residual sources of law.

In contrary to the Islamic religion, the new law gave women the right to inheritance on an equal basis with men. The law harmed the military rule more than it was would have helped. The public in general and the men in particular, the new law was silently rejected. Some religious people had daringly demonstrated against the new bill.

The government rounded many of those who peacefully expressed their rightful grief with the legislation. A special military court heard their case. Certain Muslim countries appealed to the Regime not to execute them. The fate of Siyad Barre as a ruler was on the line.

On January 15, of 1975, the regime executed ten religious' men, the ringleaders of the demonstration by a firing squad. People were in shock of the first mass execution, and the death sentence was too quick and unexpected as well. People were speechless and stunned. The country mourned silently.

Two Somali fighter planes collided on that day and killed more than thirty people including the two pilots. Some of the religious men who organized the demonstration escaped unharmed.

Until they became power-hungry groups like Al-Ittihad which formed during the 1980s with the goal of creating an Islamic government in Somalia or Al-Shabab, people always had a lot of respect for the religious people and institutions. Another important piece of history has taken in the capital of Somalia, Mogadishu. Four men have kidnapped the French ambassador to Somalia.

The coming below of the New York Times is not readable, but that was how the world reacted to the kidnapping of France ambassador to Somalia.

French Envoy in Somalia Held by Anti-Paris Group

MARCH 25, 1975 (New York Times Archives)

MOGADISHU, Somalia, Tuesday, March 25 (Reuters)—Four armed men kidnapped the French Ambassador to Somalia over the weekend and took him to a suburban villa. Negotiations for his release have proceeded since then, with the building surrounded by Somali troops and policemen. The kidnappers, who said they belonged to an organization seeking to end French rule over the neighboring Territory of Afars and Issas, demanded the release of two guerrillas from that territory now imprisoned in France. The two men who were in life terms were Omar Osman Rabeh and Osman   Elmi Kareih of "Front for the Liberation of the Somali French Coast."

According to the Somali press agency, they also demanded a ransom of $100,000 in gold for the
Ambassador, Jean Gueury, and a plane to fly them across the Gulf of Aden (gulf of Berbera) to Southern Yemen. The Italian Ambassador, Giorgio Jacomeili, who has been conducting the negotiations with the kidnappers, said they had not threatened Mr. Gueury's life but had imposed a 36hour deadline for his release. The deadline passed without incident. [In Algiers, a man describing himself as representative thereof the kidnappers' organization, said Mr. Gueury would be "liquidated" if the demands were not met.

Mid 1976, Western Somali Liberation Front (a pro-independence movement born in 1964 for the Somali territory under Ethiopia) conducted guerilla warfare unapproved by the Somali government. Barre had cracked down the insurgents and arrested some of the men. However, at the end of the year, the conflict between Ethiopia and Somalia increased. In that year, surprisingly, the Supreme Revolutionary Council (SRC) was disbanded.

The regime created the Somali Revolutionary Party (SRP) as the sole party of the country. During the party meetings, the president used to propose the goals and the policies of the Party. Those who did not raise their hands in favor of what the chairman (Barre) recommended could have invited their death penalties or other punitive measures.

In the year of 1976, another big event took place in Somalia. Ethiopia and Yemen became an important military strategic area for the superpowers. Being Somalia and Ethiopia were already military Governments, Russia saw an opening and pursued it.

The new leader of Ethiopia, Mengistu Haile Mariam got an invitation from the Kremlin. Discussions between the two countries developed a new relationship. Ethiopia was convinced to choose socialism. Moscow wanted to keep south Yemen, Ethiopia, and Somalia under its influence. Since all the three concerned states were socialists, Moscow won the first phase of the marathon.
Unfortunately, in the second phase of the campaign, Somalia raised the question

of Ogadeen. That was a touchy issue which the Soviets did not want to bother the colonial made border disputes in that delicate moment. Abdurahman Sh. Mahamud, 64 (Newsweek, May 1977), harsh Soviets conditions include:

- Withdrawal of all regular Somali military units from the Ogadeen.
- A promise by Somalia to respect Ethiopia's internationally recognized boundaries.
- A formal renunciation of Somalia's claims to Djibouti and Kenya's NFD.
- Regranting of Soviets rights to Somali Naval facilities.
- Somalia's participation in a political grouping with Ethiopia and South Yemen.

when all Russian diplomats failed to sell the idea of postponing Ogadeen issue, Fidel Castro of Cuba was sent to Somalia to recant its position. The president of Cuba had failed too. The only colonial demarcated border that Somalis did not complain about is the one between Somalia and the republic of DiJabuuti. It is known as Anglo—French Treaty of 1888.

No matter the channel used, Somalia could not be convinced to stay with the new coalition and pend the Ogadeen question for a while. As a result, the political atmosphere of the region got worse. As the only choice left from the regime's point of view, in November of 1977, Somalia immediately expelled Russian military experts. Most of the expelled advisers did not go back straight to the Soviet Union. Instead, they went to Addis Ababa, the capital of Ethiopia.

Somalia had never legally signed the artificial boundaries that the colonial powers marked. Whenever the issue is raised at African Union meetings, the black African states sided with Kenya and Ethiopia. Before British-Somaliland and Italian-Somaliland became an independent state, the Somali officials of the British-Somaliland protectorate unyieldingly used to talk to the British government that they would not be bound by the 1897 agreement between Ethiopia and Britain. From there on, that had been always the statement of any Somali Administration.

"It is the position of the Somali Democratic Republic as she had always maintained in the past, that she cannot be bound by colonial agreements which she had formally denounced on her attainment of independence. 1977, Barre played a unity card to cut off the Somali-Ethiopian regions from Ethiopian into Somalia. A war broke out, and after Somalia was the defeated, Barre's popularity started to go down until USC ousted him from the capital on January 27, 1991."

It became clear to the Somali government that supporting WSLF groups alone would not be enough the capture the Somali-Ethiopian region. The regime made some calculations to seize Ogadeen which the British transferred to Ethiopia in 1948. Having that in mind, financially and militarily, the Barre government supported the Western Somali Liberation Front. WSLs and certain elite units from the Somali army carried hit-and-run campaign against Ethiopia, especially Somali inhabited villages.

When that was not enough either, Somalia mobilized all the national security forces in a short period to participate in the war. The October revolution launched a massive attack on Ethiopia before Russia could modernize the Ethiopian army. The war went into full scale.

Though it somewhat seems to be swelled, the number of military personnel of Somalia was over 65,000. Furthermore, the total number of the security forces (police, Dervishes, NSS, the militia combined) was roughly 100,000, A Handbook (Somalia: Area handbook by the Department of the U.S. Army, Headquarters 101st Airborne Division and Fort Campbell Fort, Kentucky, 42223-5000), stated as follows: (a) Army = 61, 300, (b) Navy = 1,200, (c) Airforce 2,500. Up to a pistol, the little book had full details of the Somali National Army.

According to War Clouds on The Horn of Africa by Tom J. Farer (page 3, which also quoted International Institute of Strategic Studies "Somalia deployed approximately 23,000 men, 250 tanks and over 300 armored personnel carriers, and, by African standards, a respectively modern little air force."

Also, *Somalia: The New barbary by Martin Murphy, page 44*, states the foreign aids from the Arabian countries, Soviet Union and United States increased the Somalia army to 120,000 members in the mid of 1970s.

Somalia almost captured all the Somali inhabited areas. Nationalistic songs were simultaneously airing both from radio Hargeysa and Mogadishu. There were only two radio stations in the country. From Tyranny to Anarchy: The Somali Experience by Hussein M. Adam, p. 237:

By the end of 1977 most of the Ogaadeen had been liberated. The city of Jigjiga was in Somali hands, Dire Dawe was controlled by both sides with Somalis gaining the upper hand, and the ancient Islamic city of Harar was under siege surrounded by Somali troops and WSLF guerrillas. Siyad, who had hoped to make a historic contribution to the perennial problem of Somali liberation and unification, lost the war, his sense of direction and his ideological bearings." JIJIGA, Ethiopia, Sept. 27,1977 (The New York Times) — Somali forces fully control this strategically important town and a vital mountain pass nearby that cuts through the Kara Marda range into the central highlands of Ethiopia.

The public became happy with quick military success. And as a result, the popularity of the October administration got some life. Eritrean liberation fronts also took advantage of the situation and put more pressure on the Ethiopian army. Somali army repeatedly captured Cuban soldiers in fighting for Ethiopian defense since 15,000 Cubans were with the Ethiopian armed forces (Christopher Daniels,

19). The Golden Years of Somali by Mohamed Ali Hamud put the numbers of Cubans in the fight 20,000.

On the Somalia side, both morally and financially, some Arab countries Aided Somalia while Israel and most black African nations sided with Ethiopia. An Egyptian airplane carrying artillery shields and explosives to Somalia was forced to land in Kenya by Kenyan jet fighters forces. Knowing that the Kenyan army could not deter them, units of the Somali army went through the Kenyan border towards Ethiopia to fight in the Oromo regions. Nairobi constantly protested while Somalia never stopped of denying.

At the end of 1977 and in the early months of 1978, the Somali Ethiopian war reached its climax. That was difficult for the Mengistu administration to handle two strong and determined fronts at the same time. The military government of Ethiopia came to its knees. But it was not the first time that Ethiopia was in a bad situation and somebody came for its defense.

While Ethiopia and Somalia were fighting each other, a jubilated event took place in the Horn on 27 June 1977. After with the help of Arabian countries, Somalia and the people of Djibouti bitterly fought for the independence of Ex-French Somaliland. That became a reality on 27 June 1977. At that time, the political situation of Eastern Africa was rather volatile. As mentioned earlier, the Red Sea of Somalia, newly independent state (Djibouti), Ethiopia and Yemen, became an important military strategic area for the superpowers.

Chapter eleven referenced notes

Kadeedkii Xamar iyo Kalaguur, Ali Abdigir, 2018, Amazon
John Buchholzer, the author of *The Horn of Africa: Travels in British Somaliland* (First publication in 1959)
Maalmihii Noloshayda (Days of my Life) by Ex-education Minister, Aden M. Ali, page 63-65
Article 1 of the Family Code of 1975
The New York Times, MARCH 25, 1975
A Handbook (Somalia: Area handbook by the Department of the U.S. Army

CHAPTER TWELEVE (1978-1987)

Clan Exploitation

Somalia is a nation of clans in search of a state, and clan system can be used negatively or positively in nation-building. __ Abdurahman Abdullahi (Baadiyow)

Lust of power took over citizens' interest. __Unknown

In my life, I will firmly remain curious and may be distrustful about the logic of a point of view that says, "The only way to lead a nation is to do it my way" __
Ali Abdigir.

The aftermath of The War

In early 1978, the Ethiopian leader called his friends for help. Regrouped Ethiopian army with more than 15,000 Cubans (Warriors by Gerald Hanley, 224, 2004 edition, afterword done by another author) 3,000 of the people's Democratic Republic of Yemen, 1,500 Soviet advisers and also with some North Korea advisors, trained Ethiopian army (page 77 of The Golden Years of Somalia by Mohamed Hamud) overwhelmed the Somali forces. Barre turned to the other superpower, the United States. Carter Administration rejected Somalia's plea.

The superpowers termed the military government of Somalia as a noisy and uncooperative third world poor nation which expelled the American Peace Corps at the born of the regime, and the Russians in 1977.

Soviets, on the other hand, decided to teach a lesson its former client. Tasting the consequences of being uncooperative, in April of 1978, Somali National Army and Western Somali Liberation Front (SNA—WSLF) were defeated in humiliation.

That was a major blow to the Barre's government, and to the pan-Somalism as well. And as a result, the moral of the army forces went down.

Despite the defeat, Somali National Army showed that it made the best use out of the equipment and the training acquired. More than that, provided with the right resources, Somalis never doubted that they could fight until the last drop of blood.

Before it was over, the war also created a huge influx of refugees which became a burden on the rest.

Since Somalia lost the war, an already wounded public support for the authoritarian government dwindled further. Even the loyalty of the national forces for their commander in chief came to its lowest point. There are no concrete figures, but some put the numbers of the people displaced by the war in both sides into about three million. The refugees to Somalia, 1 million to 1.2 million, mostly women, children and elderly.

There are times the chance is on your side. The longer you delay taking advantage of it, the harder and the longer to accomplish something good historical to accomplish for the sake of your people. The president realized that he failed with that political calculation.

Many intellectuals believe that president Barre missed the opportunity of his life. Instead of stepping aside as a head of state, he obligated himself to remain in power. He stuck with "My way is the only way." Somalia did not deliver because not only of the technology and the manpower used against it during the final stage of the game, but also the timing was not ripe.

There was a circulating rumor among the Somalis that Barre suggested to step down. There had never been a real debate of that subject at the highest level. Every intellectual or ex-high-level official asked, nothing materialized. If there was any talk at all, we believe that was just a bluff of testing his adversaries.

In all high level tribal or other political games played against him, cunningly, Barre used to come at the top because that was one of his fields of expertise.

Somalis usually being labeled as clannish people, please just hold the horses for a second. Unless one thing is first done, I firmly disagree with whoever believes that the Somalis are too tribal minded. With or without governments, clan alliances were the principal source of individual and family security. Hence, people have to see a better way of life then what they had been through in their existence, then ask which one they would choose.

The president had been quoted a couple of times as: "Our nation is too clannish. If all Somalis are to go to hell, tribalism will be their vehicle to reach there." His administration did not show a better road either.

The national army was always one of the most respected institutions in the country. Since it was defeated, it too became distrustful of the government. There developed a rebel group almost in every battalion.

A Somewhat-organized group of military officers tried to overthrow Barre's government after the war. The revolt was quickly crushed by loyal troops. Such a quick attempt while still, the public was in the healing process from the defeat, further infuriated the Regime and made it very nervous.

Another thing we have to mention is that the majority of the coup organizers were almost from one clan, Majeerteen. And because of that, it did not take Barre long to convince the nation that Majeerteen were greedy political opportunists.

Finally, the administration executed 17 men of the organizers on October 1978 where 12 of them were from the same clan. Colonel Abdullahi Yusuf (1934—2004), the architect of the coup, escaped to Ethiopia. Barre institutionalized despotic rule but he could not silence all the antirevolutionary activities.

Colonel Yusuf with the help of other men mainly from his clan formed an opposition movement known as the Somali Salvation Front (SSF) in Ethiopia. In the beginning, SSF was formed as a multi-clan-based movement but shortly moved to a single clan opposition group. Having a base in Ethiopia, the enemy of Somalia, at least we were raised to see it that way, resentments towards SSF developed. And from there on, just to stay on the top chair, Barre started naked clan exploitation.

The National Security Service concentrated its efforts on watching the activities of the dissidents, opposition sympathizers, and other government opponents.

Until the total collapse of the regime, the agency was one of the elite organizations that sustained the dictatorship. Hangash, a military security agency was created. It was given a surveillance power even over the NSS. Mohamed Siyad Barre strongly believed only an ideology of political survival, a quotation we will see later.

The NSS having power over the Hangash (Military Security Agency) or the military and vice versa is somewhat confusing. To make it easy, the power control of the Regime periodically shifted to the organizations headed by trusted individuals such as family members.

1979 started while there was a known anti-regime organization, Somali Salvation Front. Perhaps, the Somalis have a problem of differentiating political opportunists and the public—especially between fighters and others who are not part of the hostilities.

The state launched a harassing campaign against the Majeerteens in central regions, specially Mudug and Nugaal. Some water holes and reservoirs were broken down to leak water to the ground forcing many innocent people to run for their homes.

Reliable sources later confirmed that on some occasions, some people were thrown into wells alive and left them to die inside as it happened in Gebiley town a decade later (March 1988 (The nation, 25 June 1988, page 884)). Barracks and houses were burned. The whole country was watching and did nothing significant.

SSF was never an innocent abroad-based bystander either. It used to thrust the blood of innocent civilians in the same area where their clan partially inhabited. Such attacks backlashed and increased animosities towards the SSF. If Siyaad Barre might have a point when he labeled the Somali nation as a clannish, then, there was a consensus that he too was an expert clan manipulator.

The chairman of the October revolution persuaded the public to perceive the SSF as a clan which did see itself as the sole ruler of Somalia. Magically, he rallied the public to have disliked the SSF. On August of 1979, the regime had passed a new constitution.

Then, on January 24, 1980, the People's Assembly (171 members with few women) held its first session to elect a president. As designed, Barre was reconfirmed to be the president. On the other hand, however, until another clan, the Isaaq in that case, had filled the place, the harassment of the Majeerteen did not stop. The individual rights of the SSFs civilians got worse than the rest.

Still, some clans who were neither sympathizers of Majeerteen nor supporters of the government felt that Barre always preferred to deal with the challengers.

The civilians were punished for crimes they did not commit. Koofiyadcas, red-hatted (Red Berets or military police) used to go to the areas where the clan (s) of certain dissidents inhabited. In certain occasions, they raped women and illegally confiscated public trucks. When opportunity knocked, SSDF (1978) militia did the same.

Naively, other clans kept silent. The government and the renegade organizations were acting shows and the rest were the audience. Certain clans were even narrow-mindedly clapping for such ill-fated public silencing methods. People downplayed that such moves were punishing whoever dared to speak. Because of such naïve thinking, Barre succeeded to mobilize the whole public against one clan at a time. It never stopped, just the name of the game had been changing.

In the international arena, strategically, Somalia was still very important. In early October of 1980, to use the airfields and ports of Berbera on the Gulf of Berbera (Gulf of Berbera before 1839) and at Mogadishu, the capital on the Indian Ocean coast, Reagan Administration authorized arms sales to Somalia.

To enhance U.S. military access to the Indian Ocean and the Persian Gulf, the Pentagon convinced the oppositions such as the then Appropriation subcommittee's chairman, Representative Clarence D. Long (Democrat from Maryland).

In the same year, at the anniversary of the revolution, the SRC was reinstated. In the 1980s, the dream of greater Somalia was wounded badly and a good example is this. The Road to Zero: Somalia's Self-destruction by Mohamed Osman Omar, 170-171:

The security network of the Ethiopian Embassy in Khartoum, Sudan was led by the counselor of the Embassy, a Somali origin who later became Ethiopia's ambassador to Libya. His brother was Djibouti's ambassador to Saudi Arabia. Another brother of his was the Somalia's director general in the ministry of Foreign Affairs, and later was appointed as an ambassador to Lagos, Nigeria.

Northern Uprising

The defeat of the Somali-Ethiopian war, shortage of the food pipeline and the Somali-Ethiopian refugees settled in Hargeisa further contributed to the problem.

In 1981, the University entrance examination became too tainted with nepotism and clannism. Students could not go to the faculty of their choice in accordance with their preferences and marks started leaving the country. Passports were sold in the black-market and expensive. That did not stop them leaving by sea, air, and on transport trucks, and on foot to the neighboring countries, especially to Kenya and Djibouti.

Some youth got lost to get to Djibouti at night by foot, and mistakenly entered a French military base patrols and airport runways. In the same year, the new uprising started in the north.

Encouraged by the voice of SSF which existed since 1978, and the bravery of the people in the north to organize public demonstrations which were forbidden under the code of the Regime, a group of men exclusively from the north (Isaaq) formed Somali National Movement (SNM) in London, United Kingdom, 1981. Two more political opposition groups, Somali Workers Party (SWP) and Somali Liberation Democratic Front also joined the Somali Salvation Front (SSF).

In that regard, the SSF became the Somali Salvation Democratic Front (SSDF). Colonel Qadaafi politically supported the SSDF. That annoyed president Barre very much.

Having been immediately informed about the move, the renewed opposition and challenging initiatives taking place both outside and inside the country forced the Regime to take different politically survivable measures. More complicating the situation also was, the masses in both Burao and Hargeisa have increased riots. Adding to the ongoing upheavals, Qadaafi also kept supporting SSDF.

The case of Qadaafi greatly damaged the relationship between the dictatorial states and went from bad to worse. On August 25, 1981, Somalia cut off diplomatic relations with Libya and ordered the Libyan embassy staff in Mogadishu to leave within 24 hours.

Economically, the purchasing power of the Somali shilling went down to 12.46 to the U.S. dollar from 6.23 while more than 700,000 people were still in refugee camps inside the country.

In 1982, the government created the Mobile Military Court (MMC) and the Regional Security Council (RSC). Whenever the security of the revolution was on the line, the RSC was superior to all other security branches. More laws which put the civilians under a strict jurisdiction of the military tribunal were passed and gave a mandate the government security forces.

A couple of times, the MMC authorized pursued execution. The main job of the Hangash (Military Security Agency) was to maintain surveillance over the military, the NSS as well as the civilians.

Barre got into a panic mode of who was loyal and who was not. The government banned public gatherings of greater than a small group and emphasized searching public houses without warranties. The NSS, Hangash, RSC and other trusted national security branches increased to crack down underground movements.

The incoming mail including foreign magazine, Newspapers, tapes, and books became under the subject of censorship while it was a common practice to check or open the mails of anti-revolutionary known families and suspected dissidents.

In some occasions, as I have stated earlier, the internal struggle of which security agency should oversee what and which, took place between the Hangash and the NSS. Such confusion never ended until the complete collapse of the military administration in early 1991.

As far as human rights are concerned, regardless of the international human rights groups' appeal to the head of the government, the systematic torture and harsh detention conditions of political prisoners had been an ongoing secret procedure growing up with the deterioration of the dictatorial rule. People were afraid to speak up.

Since getting a passport was very difficult and costly, certain government officials who had access to the passport section of the immigration made extra income straight to their pockets of selling passports in the black-market. The regular fee of the passport which was less than 300 Somali shillings skyrocketed reaching more than 5,000 Somali Shilling each in the black-market.

Many people especially the youth, who could neither get the faculty of their choice in the National University nor a modest job to rely on desperately continued to leave their homeland, mostly to the oil producing Arab states and to the United States. Certain public institutions carried after the names of the clans to which the head of the institution belonged.

In the mid-1980s, in the United States, there were a couple of thousands of Somali youth. More than 90% was male under the age of 30 years. New York,

Massachusetts, Pennsylvania, District of Columbia, Maryland and California had the biggest communities.

The corruption inside the country traveled with the youth to the well-off countries. The children of those cabinet ministers and productive agencies used to go to universities in North America and Europe in full time or with less hassle. Those determined to have an education with no luxury of financial backup, on the other hand just used to register for the courses they could pay for the semester.

In the country, socially, consumption of Khat (Qaad (a green leave Somalis to chew for its mild feeling)) was also seen as a disease infested in the government system and paralyzed the national economy.

The government realized that Khat had rotted the core of the workforce, and characterized it as an addictive drug. Men worked hard in the morning until they settled the Khat for the day, and chewed it in the afternoon. Arab News, Monday, March 21, 1983, *"The Government of Somalia has decided to outlaw Khat, a mild narcotic leaf chewed by thousands of people in the Horn of Africa."*

The state tried to ban it with strong public support. The campaign turned out to be fruitless because the techniques used to fight against it were questionable and ineffective. The consumption did not go away just the price went up.

The political relationship between Ethiopia and Somalia worsened. Ethiopian armed forces with SSDF armed men invaded Somalia in the middle capturing Galdogob and Balamballe of Mudug and Galguduud regions respectively. Somalia protested while Mengistu warned to split Somalia into two. Barre administration could not retaliate but further degenerated into a brutal dictatorship. The troubles in the north also escalated.

A group of junior military officers headed by Captain Cawil Cadnaan Burhan hijacked one of the country's airlines on November 24, 1984, and ordered to land in Ethiopia. That was another slap on the face to the dictatorial administration. After an intense negotiation and fulfilling certain demands of the hijackers, later at the end of the month, Ethiopia released 120 of the 130 original passengers and the plane.

That detente opened the way for later talks between Addis Ababa and Mogadishu which lead to a peace treaty which we will see it at the end of the chapter.

Sometime of 1986, according to Minister of State of Foreign Affairs of Somalia from 1982—1990, Mohamed Ali Hamud (The Golden Years of Somalia, 2014, page 79), Mohamed Siyaad Barre wanted to seal a deal with Mengistu Haile Mariam in Djibouti. Mengistu said, "I have no mandate to sign this agreement until I consult with my people in Addis Ababa." Then, Barre said to Mengistu, "I am a dictator and I do not consult with anybody and, so are you, so let us sign the agreement." According to Mohamed Hamud, the Somali delegation consisted of president

Mohamed Siyaad Barre, permanent secretary of foreign affairs Ahmed Mohamed qaybe and Hamud.

The hijacking incident created a big problem for the regime. The loyalty of some fighter pilots became under suspicion. We will see some details during the bombardments of the northern cities. According to *Timelines of Somali History by Farah Mohamud Mohamed,* 26 men from the north, especially from the Isaaq clan, have been executed by the military government. Some of them were:

1. Ibrahim Sheekh Ibrahim
2. Yusuf Abdi Suleyman -Student
3. Mahadi Haji Ishaal
4. Abdi Warsame Said
5. Daoud Daahir
6. Abdullahi Abdi God.

Rounding men suspected of anti-government activities became the norm. People did not stop or slow down showing their anger towards the merciless government which was at war with its people, especially in the north.

In late May 1986, there was a fatal car crash where Barre survived in a narrow margin. Assumed that he could not make it, the leadership of the country went into a wild chase.

One group with the Barre's family wanted to take over while another group stuck to follow the written procedures. Though fragmented, more clan solidarity of Dhulbahante Ogaadeen and Marehan who Barre mostly trusted to the high posts strengthened.

In that respect, many believed that the inside power struggle finally paved the way for later massacres. The political atmosphere of the country became wait and see. The public voice or opinion did not count.

The educators, elders, and known nationalist business people who expressed their political views different than those of the revolution fell into different scenarios. Some slipped out of the country or sent their families out while those remaining went to jail, became under house arrest, under surveillance and some get executed without questions and due process.

Those who had not fallen into any of the categories mentioned were as corrupted as Barre. Some dared to speak up against the Regime, but only after they missed preferential treatment from their former boss and realized that the regime ran out of teeth to bite.

Both the demonstrators and the organizers were well aware of the consequences, the death penalty. The pressure from the outside world about

Somalia and Ethiopia was mounting. People's Liberation Front of Eritrea and other Ethiopian opposition movements, such as Tigre had offices in Mogadishu.

Still, the SSDF, the SNM and other dissident political figures against the Somali government were also in Ethiopia. It was tit for tat. Both administrations cared much about their own political survivals, and as a result, committed gross human rights violations.

The rebel organizations based in Ethiopia, SSDF and SNM, in particular, did not keep their hands off from the blood either. They used to attack innocent villagers and water wells while each had an ongoing power struggle inside. The oral society of the Somali nation did not write much about that subject, but each organization eliminated some of his members for political reasons.

Chapter twelve referenced notes

The nation, June 25 of 1988, page 884
Appropriation subcommittee's chairman, Representative Clarence D. Long (Democrat from Maryland)
Timelines of Somali History by Farah Mohamed Mohamed, page
Wolfgang Weber of Die Zeit, 1988
Understanding the Somalia conflagration, 18
The Cost of Dictatorship, 253
Somalia in Pictures, 62
The Nation, June 25 of 1988, page 884
The Missed Opportunities by Sahnoun, 8
The Cost of Dictatorship, 255
Time Magazine
__Making Sense of Somali History, Abdurahman Abdullahi Baadiyow, 2017

CHAPTER THIRTEEN (1985-1990)

Wide spread Revolts

You cannot appreciate the value of government until you are forced to live without it. __Unknown

Wolfgang Weber of Die Zeit:

After ten years of the Somali-Ethiopian war, there were 40 refugee camps in Somalia. More than 800, 000 people needed help. Most of the people in the camps were women and children where their dependence on international aid became debilitating. The men were either killed, marginalized or went to the cities for work.

The Somali civil war of the late 1980s and early 1990s, the government carried many massacres, but with different magnitudes. We liked to look at some of them and evaluate if we can characterize as genocides. Most agreeable definitions

Massacre: Is an intent to kill more spontaneous. In a massacre, not every individual need to be hunted down. Example: in a massacre, a pregnant woman is killed by chance while during a genocide, the fetus has to be killed too because he/she is the potential enemy.   Genocide: Is the intent to completely eradicate a particular group/groups of people (be it religious, ethnic, tribal etc.). It is more often than not performed/sponsored/backed by a government/military body and will commonly see multiple events of violence as a result of historic/political/religious tensions. A very clear and defined example can be found when reading into the Rwandan Genocide.

Then, we came to a point to characterize the level of the killings as a massacre, but we declined to call them genocides. There were clan cleansings in the Somali Civil War, and even non-Somalis wrote about them, but that is different than genocide. It is not right to generalize any community, and the Somalis are far from being angels. But, when good people neglect their responsibilities of standing against the bad, then that community is doomed to chaos.

However, that does not mean that genocides never happened in the Somali peninsula. The word "Uurdoox (vulgar caesarean)" is in the Somali language in a violent term. Known atrocities defined as genocides perhaps happened during certain clan war-fares in the history of the Somalis.

In April 1988, the Somali and Ethiopian head of states signed a political survival peace treaty. They agreed that each had to stop harboring opposition movements of the other in his country. That peace accord had greatly wounded the operations and the future of the opposition movements of both Regimes.

In the Somalia case, at that time, the SSDF was already in a breakdown process, and could not continue fighting. Even some higher ranks of the opposition went back to the government and get named for important posts.

SNM on the other hand was still intact. There were no many options left for it, and as a result decided to attack the main northern cities with force, instead of disbanding its forces and asking forgiveness from the Regime. It is commonly agreed that the real civil war started in 1988. The last three years (1988-1990) of the regime, people have suffered severely and was getting worse since then.

1988 was the landmark as Wolfgang Weber of Die Zeit wrote, "After ten years of the Somali-Ethiopian war, there were 40 refugee camps in Somalia and more than 800, 000 people needed help. Most of the people in the camps were women and children, the men were killed or have gone to the cities to work and their dependence on international aid had become debilitating."

Northern Massacre

The effects of the defeat of the Somali-Ethiopian war a decade ago did not ease. The shortage of the food pipeline which started in the early 1980s and the Somali-Ethiopian refugees settled in Hargeisa further spoiled the situation.

The Hargeysians got a feeling that Siyad Barre played a game of planting his mother-side ancestral refugees from Ethiopia (Somali Ethiopians) into Hargeysa to dilute the exclusiveness of the Isaaq population for future political implications.

The military rule of Ethiopia ordered the SNM to leave the country because of the April peace treaty he signed with Barre. SNM took a very calculated decision of do or die. In late May 1988, SNM attacked the main northern cities with force and seized some towns including both part of Hargeisa and Burao. That was the first time that Somali opposition forces challenged the government militarily. The revolution had only two options: To accept defeat and deal with the SNM or put two Somali armies against each other.

As the history of dictatorship reveals, the military government later preferred the last. Since it had the opportunity and the will, responding with heavy weaponry of war, the state committed atrocities.

In a move to deprive the SNM of a civilian base of support, government troops, security forces, and curfew patrols unleashed a campaign of indiscriminate killings. The magnitude of the rape, extortion, and looting is somewhat disputed, but they were done. The October administration also mercilessly bombarded Burao and Hargeisa.

The air force of the nation and hired mercenaries with Hunter Fighter (manufacturing company) planes participated in the aerial attacks. One Somali fighter pilot who finally settled in Luxemburg landed in Djibouti instead of bombing his own people.

The Regime tried to silence the massive uprising in the north before it would spread to the rest of the country. The Government forces killed thousands of civilians instead of protecting them. Depends on which book you read and who you talk to, but for sure in the thousands.

Some documents such as "Understanding the Somalia conflagration by Afyare, 18," *"The Tree on The Moon of Mohamed Urdoh,* Somalia," "The Untold Story, Judith Gardner: 45," "The Timelines of Somali History by Farah Mohamed: 154," and Enchantments of The World (Somalia by Marry Virginia Fox, page 99, put the number to more than 50,000. "Government at War with Its Own People" of Human Rights Watch has more details of personal experiences.

The security forces destroyed and burned houses, and looted as well. There are some accounts that people get drowned in wells.

How Marry Virginia Fox put it is an example (page 101). Frustrated at its failure to defeat guerilla rebels of the Somali National Movement, the army turned to indiscriminate bombing and shelling of areas containing civilians suspected of sympathizing with the guerillas. Land mines were laid across wide areas. Water reservoirs and livestock were destroyed. Members of the Isaaq clan, the major ethnic group of northern Somalia, were systematically persecuted. The fighting forced nearly half a million Somalis to leave the country, most of them becoming refugees in Ethiopian. ....., an estimated 50,000—-60,000 civilians were killed within a two-year period. The major city of Hargeysa was left in rubble.

SNM was not watching innocently. Though not clear when and by who, the northern public came up with a new name known as Faqash (Barre remnants/loyalists) for the regime's security services such as Hangash (Military Security Agency), ill-used National Army, NSS, and Red Berets. People popularized the name until it became synonymous for a Darood individual, the major clan to which people say Barre belonged.

SNMs committed atrocities against also the civilians in the northwest region, mostly on the none-Isaaq clans previously suspected of siding with the ousted regime, or neutral. The group did not spare Isaaq people suspected of collaborating with the Regime, and I am not sure if the people created a name for that. However, all the later administrations of Somaliland got a different name from the public.

About the mercenaries and the Hunter Fighter planes mentioned in previous paragraphs, first, the government purchased the hardware from South Africa. The regime which lost trust with some of its air-force pilots was not happy to send them abroad for short training of the new fighter planes.

Therefore, the military administration hired South African and Rhodesian (The Cost of Dictatorship, 253) mercenary pilots to train the Somalis inside.

When a Somali fighter pilot landed at Djibouti instead of shelling his own people and cities, the hired mercenary pilots took part in the operations. Till late of 1990, they were in the payroll of Somalia.

Staying on the road to final disintegration, SNM executed some government officials knowingly by virtue of being government loyalists. Some individuals just recognized as Darood were also killed, not for historical hatreds but the periodical political polarizations. The civilians of all clans were also sandwiched and suffered in between. The marathon was on.

Up to that moment, the worst and the biggest massacre took place and did not happen only in Hargeisa and Burao but also, in Berbera, Sheikh, and Gebiley. More seriously, 400,000—600,000 People had run for their lives. They fled from the battlegrounds. Anywhere. Hundreds of thousands took refuge in Ethiopia while others joined their relatives in the countryside. There were others who went to the capital, Mogadishu.

Names such as xabbadi-keentay (bullet-brought) seemed to enrich the Somali language followed by the perfect name for the rest Xabbadi-sugtay (bullet waited) which later became a reality. But that was not the first time which the term "Bullet-brought or bullet-fetched" enriched the Somali language.

In 1967, Southern Yemen was committed to getting its independence from the British, which the public separated into pro-independent seekers and Pro-British. The Somalis who were the third number of the population, over 20,000 in southern Yemen, mostly in Aden (Cadan: Somali) would want to be neutral. But they could not, and because of that, they went to Somalia where they got the name of 'bullet-brought' people.

Aden, the biggest of Yemen had been a home for many Somalis for a century or more. According to *"Early Days in Somaliland and other Tales by H. Swayne: 223:*

In 1884, Aden (Cadan in Somali) was interested, as about half the native inhabitants of this town are Somalis and many supplies for the town are drawn from Somaliland including about 60,000 sheep each year. The British-Indian government therefore appointed Residents in Somaliland and sent small detachments of troops and police to occupy the coast ports of Berbera, Bullaxaar (Bullaxaar) and Saylac.

Because Somalia was still an important strategic asset for the superpowers with a good working relationship, the United States of America was supporting the Regime. The port of Berbera on the Gulf of Berbera was important for the U.S., particularly because of the renewed tensions in the Persian Gulf and the middle east. In exchange of $41.9 million for fiscal 1988, the Regime granted the United States the access to use Berbera port for military use.

The water of Berbera is the deepest on the Gulf of Berbera coast (Somalia in Pictures: 62). In general, when it comes to looking after the American goals and objectives, the human rights of other countries are not that important. Hence, since the U.S. vital interests were on the line, the Reagan administration pretended blindfolded from the human rights violations in the north. But his administration could not ignore the problem when the media reported, and the American public became aware of it.

The World pretended to be blind about Somalia, and the regime liked that way. And furthermore, the foreign aid helped the military government to prolong.

According to the Executive director of Human Rights Watch, a scheduled meeting between president Barre and president Reagan of June 13-16 was called off because of the fighting between the government troops and the SNM troops in the northern regions (The Nation, 25 June 1988, page 884). Journalists have been denied visas to enter the country.

Much of the world was either ignoring the civil war or was indifferent to what was going on in Somalia. Then, July 1988, the military assistance to Somalia had been cut off by the State Department of the United States under the pressure from the House Foreign Affairs Committee (Sahnoun, 8).

The failure of the public to take the right approaches when the government used to harass innocent Majeeteenis encouraged the regime to commit more massacres. Every level of the government also started crumbling step-by-step.

Mogadishu Friday Massacre

The capital tasted the main dose of medicine. Bandits and insurgent groups set up roadblocks and checkpoints everywhere in the nation. Mogadishu itself became very unsafe. Security forces increased watching the Political figures and respected business people suspected of antirevolutionary activities. Secret executions of political prisoners and dissidents were never retired.

Some Foreign NGOs and Christian organizations had been recruiting young Somalis to Christianize. Religious intellectuals warned the Regime. Mohamed Alidahir, an ex-pilot, governor, a metal factory director and a Colonel in military rank had written extensively about the religious interference of the country. Barre on the other never liked to be told what to do. And though he verbally promised that he would look into the matter, nothing materialized.

Though the Western-based NGOs are the most famous, richest and the biggest of all, are too big to be independent. They are in no way immune of corruption though. Aids to the developing countries is a double sword edge. Being a human to help is a universal belief but politically, it also slows down the developing of the receivers. *A January 12, 2017 title of "*Why Corruption in The NGO World Alienate Donors*" by www.miro.medium.com states:*

In third world countries, NGO corruption is a word not uttered in front of donors. In countries like Uganda, it has been accepted as part of charity organizations. Globally, war-torn Somalia and North Korea are perceived to be the world's most corrupt countries with a shocking score of 1.0 (highest).

In armed conflicts charity organizations will choose to pay bribes or what is commonly called "illegal taxes" to access people in need. In 2008, 11 out of 17 of France's largest NGOs refused to participate in a confidential 'Médecins du Monde' corruption study. This on its own reveals how uncomfortable organizations are to admit that they have a problem. Charity organizations are known to be reluctant to report crimes such as fraud and corruption. When a corrupt employee is caught, the matter becomes confidential. It is believed that publicizing corruption damages the image of the NGO.

On July 9, 1989, an Italian Bishop (Monsignor Colombo) with the title of "The Bishop of Mogadishu" was killed in Mogadishu. He was in Somalia from 1943 until he was killed. In those 46 years, perhaps few, but there are no known people he converted. Warriors by Gerald Hanley, 29:

I knew an Italian priest who had spent over 30 years among the Somalis, and he made two converts, and it amazed me that he got even those two. The prophet has no more fervent, an ignorant, followers, but it is not their fault that they are ignorant. Their natural intelligence is second to none and when the educations start works among them, they should surprise Africa, and themselves.

But that natural intelligence Hanley mentioned resulted in the formation of tribal-based opposition groups and the other three Somali-inhabited regions were losing the hope to see a greater Somalia. Killings became a norm, and though too late, people became fearless to speak up in the capital. There was a rumor that the self-appointed military administration was trying to accuse and arrest religious figures for the killing of Bishop Colombo.

To rightfully shift the blame away, Religious groups got together and decided to have a peaceful demonstration after the Friday prayers.

On Friday afternoon, after the Friday prayer, July 14, 1989, the people from Sheikh Ali Sufi Mosque of Hodon Village in the Capital had started rioting shouting with God Is Great. The crowd got larger and larger. Armed security forces wanted to stop the march, but were overwhelmed.

The merciless security forces called for reinforcement and opened fire on the demonstrators. That was another ugly massacre in the hands of their own government. Some documents including Hospitals' reports put the number killed into hundreds, some in the thousands. *The Cost of Dictatorship, 255 writes,* "The regime responded with its usual brutality," killing over a thousand people on the first day alone."

Anybody who could tell Barre any trick to stay on the chair for some more time was his friend. Human Rights International made some documentation and informed to the world. International communities were watching that the Regime was on its way to a total breakdown but waited until it became too late, for reasons, not well known, perhaps intended that Somalia disintegrate before Ethiopia.

A Time Magazine reporter said, "Instability is threatening the rulers of Sudan, Ethiopia, and Somalia." The political survival agreement between the Ethiopian and Somali Regimes which relied increasingly on terror for their survival

174

put all the previously stated groups in a do or die situation. Clans with no opposition groups (Jabhad) had debated at least once to have one. Barre fully realized that he run out of any more tricks other than to stay in power by massacring anyone in his way.

Jazeera Massacre

On July 16, 1989, another massacre took place in the capital. It is known as a Jazeera massacre or a Mogadishu Isaaq massacre. Some people state that rounding up the men started before midnight which makes the date July 16. However, a well-known Somali author, Farah Mohamud Mohamed puts the morning of the killing on July 17, 1989. In his book of Timelines of Somali History (1400-2000: 159), 59 names are listed, but could be more. The first 20 of them are:

1. Ibrahim Hassan Gelle, US-OMC-Somalia
2. Ibrahim H. Abdullahi Dirie -Businessman
3. Mohamed Ismail Ahmed -Businessman
4. Yusuf Mohamed Handulle -US Aid
5. Said Mohamed Mumin -Assistant professor, Lafoole
6. Musa Abdi Gaas   -Businessman
7. Hussein Ali Aden -Businessman
8. Said Nur Musa -Businessman
9. Abdirahman Mohamed Bihi -Businessman
10. Abdiwahab Farah Ahmed -student
11. Abdifatah Ahmed Jiir -Student
12. Mataan Abdi Habashi -Student
13. Mohamed Mohamud Abdi -Businessman
14. Ali Mohamed Abdi -Student
15. Hassan Awnur Barud -Businessman
16. Abdi Mohamed Abdi -Technician
17. Ahmed Yasin Omar Jama -Businessman
18. Mohamed Abdi Hassan -Businessman
19. Ibrahim Hassan Ege -Technician

A man who was one of the rounded was left as dead survived. He later gave details of the ordeal. Human Rights groups and others wrote many of his accounts. The Tree on The Moon by Mohamed Urdoh, p54, recounting his nightmare to Amnesty International, he says:

There were loud cries as the firing started. I lay down with my chest pressed against the ground during the shooting. One bullet hit me below the left shoulder. After a short time, the shooting stopped. The soldiers checked the bodies to see if there were any survivors. Then they began burying us with their own hands. There was a lot of blood on me from myself and from others. As I could not stop shaking because of fear, a soldier shouted, 'This one is alive, get some more bullets.' But another soldier told him that it was the convulsions after death. I was not buried completely because they were in a hurry. The soldiers mounted their vehicles and left. I came out and looked around to see if there was anyone alive. There was no one. I went to the sea to wash off the blood and sand.

There are at least two stories why northern notables were rounded up. One tale is just silencing the northern uprising. Another says it was a naked vendetta because northerners instigated or played the biggest role of the protests of the Friday before.

About the massacres of Friday, July 14, 1989 and Jazeera of 16-17, 1989, Kenneth Rutherford, 2008: 7:

Anti-Barre protests started to occur in Mogadishu, where on July 14, 1989, during Friday prayers, the Islamic Somali Ulema Council in Mogadishu encouraged people to take to the streets to protest the continued national economic decline and government human rights violations. After leaving the mosque, protesters jammed the streets protesting governmental policies and then clashing with police, resulting in many casualties. Two days later, on governmental orders, Isaaqs tied to anti-government activities were executed on Jazeera Beach south of Mogadishu.

All the opposition groups were also in search of peace with a gun. It was too late to sustain any form of a new administration which, still Barre was the president. A Distinguished Professor of history at Rutgers University in New Jersey and one of the premier scholars of Somalia Said S. Samatar put in his book (Somalia: a nation in Search of a state, 1987).

In the early 1980s, the president entrusted his sole political ideology with a close friend. Somehow, his friend told the secret to Dr. Samatar who then put it in his book. Other than knowing that his friend betrayed him, Barre got irritated. As a retaliation, on behalf of the president, unprofessional comments which offended not only the professor but his clan as well, were aired from the national radio (Mogadishu National Radio). What Barre told his political friend as Professor Said Samatar put:

According to a rare confession breathed in the ear of an intimate political confidant, jaalle Barre is alleged to have declared: "I believe neither in Islam, nor socialism, nor tribalism, nor Somali nationalism, nor pan-Africanism. The only ideology to which I am finally committed, " the president reportedly said 'is the ideology of political survival. In a similar vein, a wealthy Dhulbahante businessman said of the president: "All he wants is power. He has no family life and no bank account.

Other clans formed United Somali Congress (USC) in Rome and Somali Patriotic Movement (SPM of Jees) inside the country, 1981. Both were clan-based opposition movements. At least, six more clan-based opposition groups vying for power-sharing came into existence in 1989. The civil order went out of hand all over the country including the capital.

Mogadishu became the main center of the attention while all other main cities such as Gaalkacyo, Hargeisa, Burao, Bossaso, and Beledweyn were almost deserted and became ghost-like cities, or under some control of insurgent groups.

Sometimes exaggerated, urban riots, widespread banditry, and interclan fighting became unafraid.

In the north, the SNM was a force on the way of capturing major northern cities. With a very uncertain future, 1989 ended with still Barre somewhat in charge for about two decades.

Chapter thirteen referenced notes

Timelines of Somali History (1400-2000, 159
The Tree on The Moon by Mohamed Urdoh, p54
Somalia: a nation in Search of a state, 1987

CHAPTER FOURTEEN (1990)

The Major Turmoil: Intensification of The Insurgents

"Those who do not learn from history are doomed to repeat it" is inherited from George Santayana.

The quotation purely defines the Somalis. They have learned from history in the wrong way. They urbanized clan warfare with modern weapons and more hatred.

Around November of 1990, "Let first Barre go" said to me by a close friend of mine in New York. I, too supported that judgement. We did not know much about civil war. We had neither been smart nor experienced. We have been living in New York since early of 1980s.

Since I left Somalia in 1981, Puntland has moved from bad to worse. If I would have read horrible stories about civil wars, even American civil war, I would not even said anything like that. Emotions got ahead of the logic.

The government kept repressing its population and resulted in nothing but further mass killings. Mogadishu got separated into small communities of clan and sub clans.

In 1990, clans were founding opposition groups one after the other. Being one of the founders, Somali National Democratic Union (SNDU) of Leelkase came into existence in New York. The organization modified its objectives later in Somalia, but like the others, we formed it on the vision of clan politics.

Mid of 990, USC (1981) formed an alliance with the SNM, and shortly afterward Somali Patriotic Movement (SPM) of Ahmed Omar Jees joined the group. They agreed to oust Barre first; form a transitional government and hold elections on October 2, 1990 (Timelines of Somali History (Xusuusqor: 167, Current History of May 1994, page 233)). At that time, some top members of SNM had a succession agenda in mind.

The revolution of 1969 promised that it would hold elections, and the result became a clan-exploiting and massacres. After more than two decades, people had no more trust with another military rule and was not ready to listen to another military general.

The disintegration process went into full gear. Both self-proclaimed organized men and Barre's armed guards robbed people at gun points inside the capital. Organized groups who were not helping the public either realized that the regime was too vulnerable and ineffective. The president's signature became invalid in most places. Yes-men friends who probably realized that regime became too weak to do anything against them, ill-trained, and poor-advised close relatives were partially running something of a show-like.

State armed guards, the NSS, Hangash (Military Security Agency) or the pioneers had no command of anything except being government uniformed bandits. They were not getting paid either and were disorienting speedily.

The courage of the people in the north in the mid-1980s finally paid off. The cancer which Siyad feared so long to spread extended its infection into the capital. The strong man, Mohamed Siyad Barre, the military General, the untouchable, the man who ruled Somalia for more than two decades became a nominal president.

Stadium Massacre

On July 10, 1990, at a soccer match in Mogadishu, people took advantage of an opportunity. They exercised some of their rights. They yelled at Barre who wanted to make a "Nothing is wrong with my system show-up like" speech in the stadium. "Liar, liar, the system crumbled" they shouted. "You have failed us." The noise got bigger and bigger. The whole situation went out of control a little bit. People also started throwing anything at reach at the soldiers.

The ill-fated so-called security forces of the president turned out a disaster, and the government tried to minimize the massacre. It reported that only three people killed (Abdullahi Farah Barre at the Somali Embassy in Rome) while even the hospitals confirmed the number of deaths.

In November of 1990, over a hundred respected elders and intellectuals from all clans, known as Manifesto intervened. They wanted to save the country from further chaos. Although some of them were weighing on of how to acquire power, however, they showed him that it was time for him step aside. That was the only foreseeable solution. He heard their concerns but shrugged off. He just wanted to buy more time.

Even Italy and Egypt offered mediation between the opposition movements and the government. Barre ignored everything other than holding on to the chair until removed by gunpoint.

There are two versions of this. Barre rejected to sit with oppositions is one version while the other option is the opposite. The exact date that the elders took a unified position is not a clear-cut.

However, it is believed that the Manifesto itself did not speak in one language. A group of mostly USCs which Dr. Hussein Hagi Bood was one of them wanted only one outcome, Barre out of office by any means necessary. Barre was aware of that and arrested some of the elders.

Also, two honorary civilian politicians, Muse Boqor and Hashi Weheliye lost their lives. A rocket-propelled grenade landed on their seating, and it is not clear who was behind. Majority of the public accused the regime while others blamed the rebels.

Some leaders and elders armed the public up to the teeth to fight the Villa Somalia, but also turned to each other where the regime armed certain clans as well. Government employees could not be paid since public treasury had already been dried up, and many members of the armed forces started selling ammunition without fear of repercussions to anybody who could pay for.

The relatives of the innocent Somalis whose loved ones were tortured or killed by the government were waiting to see justice done. But that did not come the way they would have liked.

Wisil and Colguula Massacre

Mudug is one of the regions that the clan fighting is a habit and There was a mass execution, a unique one, in Wisil, Wargalo, and Colguula, towns on Gaalkacyo-Hobyo road.

Majeerteen, Leelkase and perhaps with other clan militia with the help of the regime militia killed about 70 Sacad men, most of them known elders. When I went to the region in the mid-1990s after I had been out of Somalia for more than 15 years, I got some details that some of the killings took place in a Mosque. This incident paved the way for another bigger massacre in Gaalkacyo when the civil war was at worst. We will see it later. During the closing months of 1990, people just crossed their fingers and had no idea where the political direction of the country as a health one headed.

The story of a lion and three bulls is well known in most Somali inhabitants. Three bulls, white, black and brown/red and a lion lived in an area. The lion could not face the bulls together. He convinced the brown/red and the black that the white one was very dangerous to their safety because of its colour that could attract enemies. Then, after sometime, the lion convinced the brown/red with the same reason used against the white bull. We know the end of the story. We mentioned earlier that certain clans were even narrow-mindedly clapping for the government when it was harassing civilians of certain regions.

The Chaotic Capital

There was no peace and no one had the charisma, the will, the courage and the luck to install. It was "Nabadda ceelkaan Ku rido haddii cidi ka soo saarto," a portion of a poem roughly if anyone pulls the peace out from the hole I may put!" There were known quotations of the president. "I myself built Mogadishu and I myself will destroy it," and "I will leave the land and people behind but not infrastructure" were some.

According to *The Mayor of Mogadishu: A story of Chaos and Redemption in the Ruins of Somalia by Andrew Harding:122,* one of the president's nephews, an army colonel said, "We are a royal family meaning Marehan clan. We are like the royals in Saudi Arabia. And if we lose this fight, all of Somalia will be destroyed." Remember that a Somali intellectual in 1959 said, *"Everybody will want to rule everybody else, and nobody will want to let him be ruled. Everybody will want to be a king or a president."*

The elders of the nation always play a big part in the general stability. They regularly influence uneducated rural youth to fight or not to for various reasons.

Finally, in December 1990, massive uprising got intensified in Mogadishu. "I would be surprised if there wasn't be the mightiest slaughter, "said by Rakiya Omaar of Africa Watch in London.

Socially, financially and politically, the system ceased to function. Neither the elders nor the opposition leaders succeeded to prevent civil war and further bloodshed. People were coming to the capital for over 30 years for opportunities such as employment, education, visas, etc.

Those who left the capital before 1990 were lucky. That whole year people were sitting on an active volcano which started exposing its lava, and the neighbors run for their lives. The public get sorted in tribal alienations in the capital.

One more unfortunate thing to this was that those whose grandfathers and grandfathers came from other regions, especially from northern and the central regions could not get safe passages. Every major highway in the country was under the control of an insurgent or more.

The insurgents were well aware of that and had no other agenda except to oust the president at gunpoint and what happens afterwards. The safety of the unarmed public was not very much on their priority list. Or they did not know how. What was the primary motivation one may ask? Lust of power and perhaps personal vendettas against Barre plus brain-washed young gunmen.

The capital became a slaughterhouse while on the other hand, the opposition leaders kept their eyes only on the chair. Having realized that Barre could not stand against their forces, some warlords portrayed themselves as future presidents. There was a power struggle even in the inner circle of Barre, his clan in particular.

The intellectuals (elders, other respected public figures, the majority of the public) were well aware that ousting one General from power and empowering another was like "from a frying pan into a fire." Tensions escalated faster than in a way many could not predict. Daylight ambushing of both public and private cars and trucks picked up, regardless of where in the capital.

Qabtii (explosion) came. The most famous day of the Qabtii (eruption), the battle for Mogadishu is December 30, 1990. The already swollen volcano finally erupted. The opposition leaders who agreed to force the president out of power quickly found blood in their hands. They could not formulate a consensus administration. Mengistu Haile Mariam of Ethiopia left Addis Ababa peacefully instead of watching his capital be turned into rubble when opposition forces advanced.

In Somalia, opposite took place. Siyad Barre, on the other hand, was not done with Somalia yet. In his last days, his armed guards shelled the city from the presidential palace. The USC forces shelled the presidential palace in retaliation. The young gunmen fired aimlessly. Their bullets did not hit only Barre's armed loyalists, but many innocent people. In the Somali communities, political loyalty is synonymous with clan loyalty

All foreign Embassies and most NGOs evacuated their personnel from Somalia in early January—an evacuation that sped up the Somalia crisis. Including some international communities, many predicted that Barre would either be killed, captured or would flee the Capital. USC gunmen started singling out people recognized as Darood including intellectuals who were antirevolutionary government even from the beginning.

Some elders and intellectuals campaigned against killing the elites of certain clans, but the militia overwhelmed them—while some with same titles were doing opposite. International communities were watching the Somalia crisis. "The situation looks sickeningly similar to Liberia," said a U.S. congressional aide.

At that time, the civil war already claimed more than 60,000 lives. People were waiting to see for a specific day, a day which Barre was not a president of Somalia anymore. He was still in Mogadishu being hostage of the situation, in an underground bunker at a military base south of the city.

Chapter fourteen referenced notes

Author was one of the founders
Timelines of Somali History
Current History of May 1994
Documented Massacre

CHAPTER FIFTEEN

The Last Day of the President in the Capital

Clannism shadowed nationalism. Through war, does peace always come? Some justify war by saying that it brings peace. Somalis tried, but the outcomes were not mostly pleasant. Therefore, peace should be a race against violence.

Mohamed Siyad Barre fled Mogadishu on January 27 (Sunday), 1991. Both the U.S. and the Italian forces lifted foreigners from Mogadishu by separate air and sea operations at the beginning of the month. The ouster of the civilian administration was ousted. But this time, the ousters (later named warlords) were many vying for a single chair. In a time of uncertainty and crisis, people look for a leader who stands up for the challenge to solve problems, and takes the necessary steps to do so.

Those who stood for that challenge and people lined behind could not go above clan mentality and egoism. After that, the road is the present (2020) Tiih (meehanaw (Jaahwareer (loop of chaos))).

Somalia is ethnically homogenous that 99% are Somalis—so there are no significant clan hatreds. And though there is some clan resentment, Somalis do not want to talk about it because nobody wants to tell the truth. How long can this culture go on? It is not too late to overcome the clan bridge and act as a unit.

Mohamed Siyad Barre temporarily remained in the southwestern Gedo region of the country, which was the stronghold for his clan. From there, he twice launched a military campaign to retake Mogadishu. He met the final blow in April May 1992 when the forces of General Mohamed Farrah Aideed who was a highly qualified Military general overwhelmed him into exile.

The general also crushed the Al-Ittihad as well when it refused to be allied with him as a group. The Al-Ittihad group tried hard to be intact as an organization in a nation that is deeply rooted in the clan system. Nothing but failure after failure until the worst came, Al-Shabaab.

Coming back to the exile of the president, he initially moved to Nairobi, Kenya. Friends and foes made movements which became a big burden for the government of Kenya to handle. It is not clear, however, whether the Kenyan government advised him to relocate to somewhere else which is not very likely or it was his own decision to fly to Nigeria.

That stay was only for two weeks. He died on January 2, 1995, in Lagos from a heart attack and he was put to rest in Garbahaarrey District in the Gedo region of Somalia. One time, Mengistu wanted Siyaad Barre to sign off the Somali-Ethiopian regions. Barre said to Somali advisers (The Golden Years of Somalia, 2014, Mohamed Ali Hamud, 80), *"They are not going to write in the history that Mohamed Siyaad Barre gave up one inch of Somaliland and therefore I am not going to stand in the way of the future generation, let them fulfill what we could not have achieved."*

It is also so unfortunate that all Somali mass killers get buried in the strongholds of their clans. The children, mothers and the widows who the deceased and honorably buried warlords by their clan elders killed their loved are still mourning. In Mogadishu, one warlord shelled a village in the city. Some young journalist aired about the damage and the type of the weapons used. It is internationally recorded that the warlord confirmed the shelling, and said, "Young wrong guys (journalists)! The weapon used is not what you called."

From 1895 to 1921, Sayid Mohamed Abdulle Hassan had fought bitterly against Ethiopian kingdom, Italy and Britain over the future of his homeland. In search of peace and free his country from foreign domination, he was accused of killing thousands (around 200,000) of Somalis to follow his directions during the campaign. We mentioned earlier that the burden of the blame should not be directly on the Daraawiish, but on the colonial powers.

Finally, other than the aerial bombardment of colonialist Britain, he was also defeated because of sticking with his way of "My way or no way." Though he is the greatest Somali nationalist hero ever lived in according to his ideology and the length of the struggle, he could not achieve his goal with a gun through "*My way or no way.*"

On January 14, 1991, a Newsweek reporter wrote, "Now, even his (Siyad Barre) death or resignation would probably do nothing to end the brutal ethnic bloodshed in the Horn of Africa."

When president General Mohamed Siyad Barre fled Mogadishu, many had cheered and expected better governing. The course of the Somali history of searching peace and stability with bullets had not changed. The forces of the Somali United Congress (USC) controlled Mogadishu.

No one lost time capitalizing in the wrong way on the removal of the head of state. How Siyaad Barre and his family left Mogadishu had many versions, but *The Mayor of Mogadishu: A story of Chaos and Redemption in the Ruins of Somalia by Andrew Harding:124-125*:

On the night of January 25, 1991, President Siyad Barre's family was taken in an armed convoy up to Villa Somalia. The show was nearly over. 24 hours later the president and his entourage would drive out of Mogadishu, never to return.

But for now, the first family needed a loyal escort, and Loyan volunteered to accompany them through the streets of Mogadishu. An armored car led the convoy. Loyan came next in his Nissan, followed by the president's family. Half way along the still-elegant, tree-lined Somalia Avenue, near the Jubba hotel and the main post office, the Nissan stalled. Loyan jumped out, abandoning his car and leapt onto the running board of the vehicle behind. The convoy raced off again, but with a gun in one hand, Loyan struggled to keep his footing.

By now the convoy had nearly reached the foot of the hill below Villa Somalia, but it seems ambushers were hiding in trees on either side of the road and opened fire on the convoy. One bullet hit the drivers of the vehicle carrying the president's family and a swaying Loyan. For a few seconds the driver lost the control and, as the car swerved violently, Loyan was hurled on to the road. The convoy raced on, up the hill toward Villa Somalia. Loyan's body was found the next day. The country was now in free fall.

People held victory parties in Mogadishu, Hargeisa and other major cities—same way in 1960 when Somalia got its independence from Britain and Italy and united—and also when Barre toppled the civilian administration. But at what cost? Even the minimum human rights standards protecting those who took no active parts in the hostilities have not been respected. The north was already in the hands of the SNM where some of the members had a succession idea in mind. That was not a done deal. The organization was still weighing its options.

It became the second time that the destiny of the public fell into the hands of a power-hungry mostly military generals later identified as Warlords. First, it was the military junta headed by Barre in 1969. The second group was the military generals, graduates of Barre's clan-exploitation university. For the first time in more than 30 years, Somalia ceased to exist as a unitary state.

More seriously, for somehow, the chaos in Somalia failed to attract the world's attention. More than 40,000 pieces of ammunition from M16 rifles, fighter planes, AK47 rifles, 122mm D30 howitzer, 89mm LRAC antitank rocket launchers, 120mm M-43 Mortars capable of firing 15kg shell for 5.7 km, tanks, artillery, mobile guns, mines, armored personnel carriers, surface-to-surface missiles, antiaircraft weapons, and many more fell into the wrong hands at the wrong time. Some of the artillery requires a crew of 11 men, but Somalia had not been short of trained artillerymen.

Even in late 1993, there were approximately 400 of them in Mogadishu alone (an American report).

The Xabbadi-sugtay "bullet-waited," the Mogadishu residents ran for their lives, same as in the north in 1988 while some experienced cruel killings. Somalis suffered more than they could take. Even those who somehow held on to make paid a very heavy price which today, 2020, the nation is paying higher than any wild imagination.

The international communities saw it as a private war until it was too late. People endured and accepted abuses each assumed that he would be spared and that was the harvest of their cultivation. Singling out certain clans was not a preorganized campaign, but the circumstances created the banditry.

The removal of the president was not enough to restore law and order. It was different than what the warlords brainwashed with the illiterate youths mostly from the rural. They told them that there would be a better government. Perhaps, some had an idea that there was a gold in the presidential palace. Some of the outcomes, The Mayor of Mogadishu: 130 put:

Before long, bloated corpses littered Mogadishu's streets, a frenzy of looting erupted, and tens of thousands of civilians— above all, the Daarood, who bore the brunt of the invading militia's fury—began to flee. It became known as "clan cleansing," as the legitimate opposition to president Siyad Barre curled into a battle for supremacy between the Hawiye and Daarood. Some of the displaced-on foot, and some clambered on the trucks heading first inland to the market town of Afgooye and then onto their clan strongholds and beyond to neighboring Kenya and Ethiopia."

The young gunmen raped women without protection and looted their properties where the Daroods suffered most. The United Somali Congress (USC), the most powerful opposition group which forced out the president to leave was not in full control to stop the mayhem. Also, there were no well-organized religious groups who could collect and bury the decaying bodies on the streets.

A full-scale clan cleansing took place in the capital, and neither the international communities nor the Somali scholars did write about the subject in its merits. Young gunmen knowingly captured Daarood scholars, businessmen, and politicians, and killed them. We have many proofs and will make the record straight.

The only fully written about is the northern massacre, where today, 2020, Boorama, Hargeysa, Berbera, and Burco (Burao), young people try to excel and saturate the market of authorship and researches—which a sensible and fair person should be proud of.

When all the walls of the administration completely collapsed, USC forces captured the presidential palace. There was no gold but just unopened mail— some of them dated two years back.

One of the motivating factors for the young nomadic men was that there was wealth in Mogadishu—in the houses of government officials and businesspeople. One of the main targets were Daarood houses—some later marked with D.

Somalia: The New Barbary by Martin N. Murphy, page 67:

With the Barre regime in the final stages of collapse the Habar-Gidir under Aideed's leadership, attacked Mogadishu in December 1990. There they took their revenge of those clan they saw as Barre's supporters, mainly Daarood. Tens of thousands were displaced from the city and Lower Shabeelle valley suffering torture, mutilation, rape and execution without burial. The bulk of Mogadishu's Daroods inhabitants followed in April 1991 and headed south pursued by Aideed's forces.

Self-Proclaimed Interim Government

Without discussing the future of the country with any other opposition group, on January 29, two days after Barre fled the capital, USC appointed a prominent businessman, Ali Mahdi Mohamed as an interim president. The nomination created an uproar even among the USC ranks, General Aideed in particular.

January 27, of 1991 was the last time that Somalia had a recognized functioning central government and a national financial authority. Regardless of having a spot on the world map as a sovereign state, when it can no longer function in the best interest of its citizens, it is a failed state.

However, according to (A Memoir: The Struggle and Conspiracy by Abdullahi Yusuf Ahmed: 156), the chairman of SNM, Ahmed Mohamed Mohamud (Siilaanyo), a long-time minister of Siyad Barre mentioned that it was a discussed policy of SNM to renegotiate of a new unification.

Also, a PDF retrieved Wardheernews news clip of May 12, 2012, Siilaanyo proposed a power sharing Framework in March 1991 between the SNM and USC under a New Transitional Government. When some Manifesto members and USC leaders nominated Ali Mahdi as an interim president, immediately, the other groups rejected.

Though SNMs always had an appetite of opening up the unification wounds of 1960 though SNL, USP and NUF (33 seats) led by Mohamed Ibrahim Egal refused to delay to unification process, still wanted to see how things could go. We wiil set the records even from the point of northern politicians.

However, the USC's announcement of an interim president in February 1991 without consulting any other group made SNM think twice.

Many books show that Ahmed Mohamed Mohamud (Siilaanyo) who became the president of Somaliland in 2010 spoke against clan cleansing. He was quoted saying, "The enemy is the Barre government, not the clan."

In February of 1991, Mr. Mahdi invited all factions to a national reconciliation conference in Mogadishu. Some feared for their safety while others declined to attend for other reasons. The period from January 1991 to February 1992, the civil war reached its peak.

Thousands had already died of gun-fight and gun-shot wounds. Ammunition was always available. "More than 40 distinct armed groups were operating in Mogadishu in 1991," *The New barbary,1.*

The Isaaq rebellion did not come to power and soon controlled the countryside in the north only because of the collapse of the regime's security forces and merely its attacks. The success was matched by the Ogadeeni clan, which launched the Somali Patriotic Movement and gradually took over the country's southern region, Bay and Bakool. Ousting the president was a concerted effort by the opposition groups but not on common page of national agenda.

The area controlled by SNM had its own internal conflicts. Amnesty International August 1992:

Clashes between different Isaaq sub-clans in Burco and other towns in January 1992 left hundreds of combatant's dead. Further conflicts flared up in later months and led to outbreaks of fighting between Isaaq sub-clans and disputes between the SNM and non Isaaq clan groupings, each with its own armed group controlling its territory with far less extensive than the slaughter in Mogadishu. That has just proved the culture of camel looting which Somalis say, "Camels are among all men or belong who can keep them."

However, Current history of May 1994, 234:

The hostilities between and among politicians and former army officers who had defected to the SNM escalated into a tense political standoff. In January 1992 the rivalry erupted into open warfare in Burao (Burco) between the militias of Habar Toljeclo (Habar Jeclo) and the Habar-Yoonis, two Isaaq clans, civilians fled Burao. The conflict spread to Sheikh, and to Berbera where armed confrontations between the militias of Isse Muse and Habar-Yoonis for the control of Berbera port.

"The enemy is the Barre government, not the clan" was a repeated warning of the Long-time minister of the military government before he joined SNM and a former president of Somaliland (2010-2017), Ahmed Mohamed Mohamud (Siilaanyo).

Without considering the advice of Siilaanyo, reprisals against former Barre remnants took place as an act of revenge in the northern regions. Killing civilians of certain clans have been documented, but there was no clan cleansing reported in the north.

The city of Slaughter

by Amnesty International, August 1992:

In the first three months after Barre's overthrow, hundreds of Daarood clan members were killed and Daarood women raped in Mogadishu and their property looted, mainly by troops loyal to General Aideed. The USC' hostility to the whole Daarood clan-family extended as the SSDF, a Majeerteen-based force formerly based in Ethiopia and involved in fighting Siad Barre's troops in the early 1980s, was organized in 1991 to oppose USC, ...

In Mogadishu, USC, the opposition group which the major credit of forcing Barre to flee went to it, could not control its army. Clan cleansing practiced in Mogadishu mentioned earlier has many backings. This is a concrete example. Hussein Kulmiye Afrah (1920-1993), the famous right-hand man of Barre for 21 years became a member of USC, Dr. Hussein Bood, Ali Mahdi, general Galaal, ex-minister Abdiqasim Salad Hassan, general Alihashi, General Mohamed Abdi, Former Finance Minister Mohamed Sh. Osman and other well-known figures remained peacefully in the capital.

Unfortunately, Somalis put down those who restrained from killing and gave more weight to general stability. Hussein Kulmiye Afrax who was known for his honest straight-talking, did not take part in the civil war. He many times said, *"USC as a clan militia is incapable of uniting Somalia. If it is a national upheaval overthrowing an oppressive government, then, I should be under arrest by this time instead of living in Mogadishu freely."*

On the other hand, USC militia knowingly killed lawyer Abdirahman Sh. Hassan (Isfiilito) who had been an antirevolutionary government since from the beginning, general Abdalla Fadil who also used to be a defense minister, Dr. Hassan Hashi Fiqi, former Director of the National Insurance Agency and, Professor Abyan as well.

How Professor Ibrahim Abyan was knowingly killed is nothing but a piece of genocide. The details of the director of SIDAM (the Somali Institute of Administration), professor Abyan are in the Clan Cleansing by Lidwien Kapteijns, 2013: 139-140.

Colonel and the author of Ignorance is The Enemy of Love (Aqoondarro waa u nacab jacayl) 1976, the Shackle of Colonialism (Gardaduubkii Gumeysiga)

1978, the Unknown Victim (Dhibbanaha aan Dhalan) 1989, Farah Mohamed Jama "Farah Awl," along three of his children were intentionally killed in the town of Beledweyne in 1991.

Hussein Hassan, an Ex-director-general of the Ministry of Foreign Affairs was also one of those captured, killed and his body left on the street. Clan cleansing was never only between government against Majeerteen or Isaaq civilians, between Hawiye against Daarood, but there were one SPM did in Kismayo against Harti clans.

Another ugly one was that in the first week of February 1991, USC attacked Jees-SPM militia at Afgooye having suspected of siding with Daarood. None Daarood officials could stay in the capital—while also more than 400,000— mostly Daarood crossed to the Kenyan border.

Timelines of Somali History by Farah Mohamud, 168 "The Darood in the capital was cleansed at the end of February 1991. Approximately 15% of the Mogadishu population was Daaroods, and less than 10% Isaaq. Daaroods took refuge in Kismayo, Gedo regions, central and northwestern regions taking various routes, and many of them to Kenya." There are more vivid and eyewitness details of the clan cleansing in various forms but not fully written about them.

In retaliation of the previous massacre in Wisil, Wargalo, and Colguula (about 20 km, southeast of Galkaio) in 89/90, in the first week of March 1991, USC (mostly Habar-Gidir) armed men went to Galkaio, the capital city of Mudug region. They committed atrocities. People dispute about the number, but in the neighborhood of 900 persons of Daarood, mostly Majeerteen.

Though that was the biggest public execution in the city, it is unfortunate that today,2020, after almost 30 years from that massacre, Gaalkacyo communities are not in harmony. The worst fights had not taken between Darood and Hawiye, but between Darood clans and between Hawiye clans.

Note: The dates of Gaalkacyo massacre are not agreed on 100%. It took place in the time frame of February 26, 1991, to March 3 of 1991.

The political spectrum of the ex-Italian-Somaliland completely shifted to Hawiye versus Darood. Appeals to Darood unity further encouraged the indiscriminate revenge killings of people of this clan family. Hawiye people who happened to be in the Daarood inhabited areas had not enjoyed peace. Human rights abuse became widespread, especially in southern Somalia. As of today, 2020, the whereabouts of many is still a mystery.

The camel-boys whom the USC brought to the city to oust the president killed 20,000 in a period of six weeks. According to Amnesty International August 1992, An Index: AFR 52/01/92 writes "Between mid-November 1991 and April 1992 some 10,000 unarmed civilians, including many children, were killed in Mogadishu. Most were victims of medium-range tank, artillery and mortar exchanges between the two USC rival groups, and a substantial number were deliberately and arbitrarily killed by gunmen, some of whom belonged to one or other of USC groups."

USC held a video-documented meeting in Lafweyn Hotel in Mogadishu in February 1991. SNM observers were present and did not like what was going on. Also, there was no other opposition group. We already mentioned that during the first week of May, Aideed militia forced Barre to cross the border to Kenya where he asked for political asylum.

The exact date that Mohamed Siyad Barre crossed the border to Kenya is sometimes disputed. It is either early May of 1992, or very late of April.

Timelines of Somali History by Farah Mohamed, 180, makes it April 29, 1992. Around at the age of 74, Siyad Barre died in Nigeria January 2nd, 1995. However, before he crossed the border to Kenya, even as a nominal and as a matter of technicality, Barre was the president of Somalia.

On May 18, 1991, SNM declared independence. The Pan-nationalism and the hope of greater Somalia which Somalia fought for years wounded.

The unilateral decision of USC to form a new government without even consulting the SNM is neither the first or the last. However, that was one of the last unfortunates turning point that pushed SNM to leave the Union. Current history of May 1994, page 234 puts:

The unilateral decision by Ali Mahdi Mohamed of the USC to form a government, without consulting the SNM, was the last draw. The SNM leadership, anxious not to antagonize the other anti-fallen military administration forces and the international community, waffled until popular opinion forced a showdown at an SNM conference in Burco in May 1991."

Dead or alive, there are many clannist quotations from the mouths of many so-called Somali leaders. Some of the reasons that why they are not widely spoken of are: Clan politics and clan loyalty outweigh more than nationhood. Somaliland declared independence from the rest of Somalia without consulting with the other numerous political factions of Somalia. Some Somalilanders claim that the session was a pragmatic move to distance from the factional fighting in the south. But that is not strong enough to leave the union. The most logic of breaking away, possibly are:

-
- USC formed a transitional administration without consulting with any other opposition group. Even, all USC leaders were not in agreement of the formation.
- SNM never hid to re-open the old wounds of the 1960 unification.

- You always belong to the clan of your father which does not change when you marry, for either a man or a woman. The northerners, Isaaq in particular have no territorial claims in the south. For many of the northerners, most Isaaqs, emotions took over what was at stake as a nation. And as a result, they blamed the northern massacres for Daaroods rather than for a dictatorial administration.

However, regardless of the SNM's secession, a relentless power struggle created new political faces in the south, inside USC leaders. But aside from the lust of power and the polarization of clannism themselves, Somalia did not run out of honest and able leaders.

Instead, by the circumstances, people immediately recognized as leaders and lined up behind with those who acquired effective weapons and enough young gunmen.

In February of 1992, USC members selected Aideed as the chairman of the organization. Regardless of the selection, Ali Mahdi took office in August. He appointed Omar Arteh Ghalib as a prime minister. Almost all the factions accepted but SNA of Aideed.

Daarood factions wanted Mohamed H. I. Egal to be the prime minister having in mind to drag the north again into the union and denying Hawiye of the presidentship. Informal Daarood conversations circulate another rumor. When Daarood politicians could not get supports for their proposal, they rallied to backup Ali Mahdi as an interim president to create a great rift between USC leaders.

While still, that was going on, a new rumor circulated that Ali Mahdi amended the constitution of the land before Barre took over to acquire more executive powers. That further annoyed the other factions including the SNA of Aideed. The other USC factions also accused Ali Mahdi of being very preoccupied with power rather than the stability of the country.

Although immediate cease-fire of all parties was one of the Djibouti accords, the clan-based fighting picked up.

In September, the factions agreed that Omar Arteh to stay as a Prime Minister. Mr. Ghalib who was always as a shrewd politician and a real Somali nationalist could not form an agreeable government. He reached a hopeless stage and started looking for a way out.

In mid-1993, Omar Arte went to Saudi Arabia. From there, he went to Hargeysa, the second capital of Somalia where he ran for president in Somaliland and lost.

In April 1992, the Somali National Front militia, consisted mostly of Marehan and other members of Daarood tried to recapture Mogadishu. They fought back within 50 km of the capital.

On their way to Mogadishu, they killed civilians, burnt houses and raped women. SNFs forces singled out non-Daarood clans whom they suspected of supporting the USC.

At the outskirts of Mogadishu, fierce fighting took place. The better equipped and determined forces of General Aideed had enabled to fight back with weapons from SNM. They pushed back the militia of SNF which branched from SPM in 1991 through Bay region. The SNFs had retreated into Gedo Region. *Whatever Happened to Somalia, by John Drysdale,30-31:*

Seven days later (8 April 1991), some 2000 of Barre's regular army had reached Afgooye, 30 KMs west of Mogadishu. Aideed was short of Ammunition. He sent to Abdirahman Tuur, his SNM ally in the north-west region. Plane-loads of ammunition, captured when Barre's huge standing army in the region fled at the end of January, were flown by the SNM to Mogadishu in support of the USC. Aideed's militia and Barre's regular troops clashed at Afgooye on 8 April 1991. Barre's troops withdrew to Jannaale. Two days later, Morgan had retreated with his forces to an area between Baraawe and Jilib, pursed by Aideed's militia.

All non-Hawiye inhabitants fled from the Capital to their traditional clan territory. Southern Somalia further fragmented into clan and sub-section rivalries. When Siad Barre mobilized his forces from Kismayo in early of 1991, they abused the peasants along the way. They Killed, looted and raped, took rations and slaughtered the camels, cattle, sheep, and goats. The whole population of Baidao (Baydhabo) tried to flee for Mogadishu while the nomads of Bay region split into factions in the countryside.

The revenging forces of the former president reached the town of Daafeed near Afgooye [heading for Mogadishu]. The USC forces prepared an attack that drove them back to Buurdhuubo, Bay region.

While USC forces were driving back Said's army both groups plundered whatever property they came across [Somalia: The Untold Story, Judith Gardner: 45]. But not only Barre's army and USC forces made the abuses. On their way back, in retaliation of what had been done to them by the Barre's soldiers, the Rahanweyn savagely tortured the captured Daaroods or Barre loyalists.

The 1992 military campaigns in southern Somalia led by Mohamed Said Hirsi "Morgan," the son—in—law of Mohamed Siyad Barre, was also one of the main causes of the famine (Somalia: Fourteenth Time lucky by Richard Cornwell, Institute for Security Studies). Amnesty International August 1992 states, "Once in control of the border town of Buulo-Hawo (Beled-Hawo) from April 28, 1992, General Aideed's forces proceeded systematically to round up members of the Daarood clan."

First Political Reconciliations

First political reconciliation which is known as Djibouti One Conference backed by Italy, Egypt and Saudi Arabia took place in Djibouti in March of 1991 (though the official one was on June). Various faction leaders tried to stop any further bloodshed and the cannibalism of the infrastructure.

USC split into two factions, Somali National Alliance (SNA) of Aideed and the regular USC of Ali Mahdi. Most Daaroods felt relief over the division of the USC, not for the common good of the country but for more troubles of USC.

Regardless of what each group would have liked, the Djibouti government called Somali factions for reconciliation. They could not settle their disputes. Too many warlords, either organized or an organized militia, and the abundance of ammunition as well further spoiled the leadership.

The Somali National Movement (SNM) had boycotted that reconciliation conference. Having made decisions on emotional pleas, most of the agreed points did not materialize. There are some reasons why the faction leaders have failed to reconcile for the sake of their motherland.

First, Barre was still in the country, and though powerless, technically, by name, Barre was the president of Somalia.

Second, USC believed that only USC drove Barre out of office, and as a result, it had every right to rule the country. A videotaped conference of USC took in Djibouti hotel before the reconciliation meeting started. During the discussion, some members said, "If Daarood wants to live in the country peacefully, it is fine, but they have to forget to participate in the new government."

Third, Daarood factions did not want Barre to be captured and brought to justice while Hussein Kulmiye was in Mogadishu peacefully. That indifference of the Daarood factions also further infuriated the USC.

Fourth, Daarood factions did not want to fight against Barre's regrouped army. Still, he had a formidable army that all other factions combined were not ready to face. The main battles shaped between Barre and Aideed.

And when the international communities had started to give some attention to the Somalia case, in mid-1992, drought contributed to the chaos. At that time, 300,000 people already lost their lives, though it seems somewhat exaggerated, around 3,000 (Somalia Diary: 4 (ABC World News, 3 September 1992, Kenneth Rutherford, 38) were dying in a day, more than 500,000 fled to the neighboring countries and further while more than 70% of the livestock in southern Somalia were gone.

1991—1993, 250,000 to 300,000 died from the fighting or from famine (Somalia: The Enchantment of The World, page 106, Abdurahman Abdullahi Baadiyow, 156) which quoted the UN. That was the same as the total population of British Somaliland in 1900.

World Broadcasting Companies started airing images of people dying for starvation. The pressure was mounting on the factions, Intellectuals, and elders as well to reach some consensus.

Hassan Gouled Abtidoon (1916-2006), a proud Somali, the president of the Republic of Djibouti (1977-1999) gave another chance to political reconciliation of the Somali factions. Djibouti II Political Reconciliation Conference which Italy and Egypt backed took place in Djibouti in July-1991. The USC factions and the SNM refused to attend, and whatever agreed could not be implemented.

There is another piece of history need mentioning before going to the next chapter. Halima Khalif "Magool" played a role of the clan cleansing. She sang a song "Eryaay eryaay (roughly: Chase chase)" which used to be aired both from the Radios of Mogadishu and Hargeysa 1977-1978 war against Ethiopia.

Chapter fifteen referenced notes

Newsweek, January 14, 1991
The Mayor of Mogadishu: A story of Chaos and Redemption in the Ruins of Somalia by
Andrew Harding:124-125, 130
A Memoir: The Struggle and Conspiracy by Abdullahi Yusuf Ahmed, 156
Amnesty International August 1992
Current history of May 1994, 234
Amnesty International August 1992
Clan Cleansing by Lidwien Kapteijns, 139-140
Timelines of Somali History, 168
Gaalkacyo Massacre
Amnesty International August 1992, An Index: AFR 52/01/92
Current history of May 1994, page 234
Somalia: The Untold Story, Judith Gardner, 45
Whatever happened to Somalia by John Drysdale, 30-31

CHAPTER SIXTEEN (1991-1992)

Further Disintegration

Egotism painted on good leadership. During the last quarter of 1991, the history of the Somali civil war expanded to another disastrous level. A Somali saying states: "Do not dig a hole to trap your brother: and if you do, don't make it deep; you may never know whether you will trap yourself."

People neglected their rights a long time ago, and as a result, they had no good alternatives to choose from except that each tribe lined after its group leaders. Unfortunately, the rebel groups perceived as a blessing for their clans before Barre was ousted turned out to be cursing.

The nation ravaged by wars was no nearer to peace or stability. Each clan became a government without portfolio in its area regardless of the size. The question is: How many quasi-states were there? But somebody had to count the clans first.

The SNM which formed because of the government's dealings towards the northern population broke down into tribal alienations. Each clan lined behind a power-hungry warlord fighting for the presidency, and for the port of Berbera and not restrained until 1996.

Current regions under Puntland administration, supporters of the Islamic group, Al—Ittihad (religion-based on multi-clans which had no trust with any other system other than Islam, and existed until 1975) and militia of SSDF which showed no better Somalism than the rest fought over for control of the Boosaaso port, the capital of Bari region.

In between, they killed more than 200 including one of the leaders of the Islamic organization, Abdelaziz Farah, a religious scholar.

At last, the SSDF maintained control in the area. New fighting broke out between Habar-Gidir of Aideed and Abgaal alliance of Ali Mahdi in November of 1991 in the capital

The militia fired mobile rockets to both directions for more than four months. The middlemen were busy selling weapons to both sides which increased the casualties. There was clan fighting each other in almost every region of the country.

One of the Somali writers, Afyare Abdi (Understanding the Somalia conflagration: 19) states "The fighting between Habar-Gidir and Abgaal destroyed what was left of the city putting back into Stone Age with the nation's weapons.

There were also fights between Habar-Gidir and Murursade, between Habar-Gidir clans, between Absame and Hart clans for control of Kismayo, and between Marehan and Harti sub-clans."

Nonetheless, leaving the new political faces as I may develop, the two warlords, Aideed and Mahdi demarcated Mogadishu into two zones of influence, north, and south. It is beyond belief they made The Pearl of Indian Ocean, Mogadishu into a ghost capital. Before the new clan warfare in Mogadishu, from November 1991 to March 1992, the death toll reached 30,000 and over 100,000 wounded.

The agony of the conflicts is that small groups can easily term their fight into clan warfare. The awful and unfortunate of the Somali civil war is also that the elites melted into clan militias and then progressed into organizers. I believe, however, the elitism in the Somali societies is either a misunderstood one or a lost one. Most of the Somali elites could not go beyond clan ideology.

Regardless of what happened to Somalia, as a matter of fact, there are no deep-rooted animosities between Hawiye Against Daarood, or Daarood Against Isaaq, or Rahanweyn against any of the above, but the masses have been misled and divided by those who are supposed to unite them.

No single faction ever overpowered another, and unfortunately, that increased the death toll. Dead or alive, many Somali so-called leaders can never wash their hands out of blood.

There is a very painful memory of the Somali warlords. Many passed away without even paid any heavy price. Still, some live peacefully in Hargeysa, Garoowe, Baydhabo, Kismayo, Mogadishu, and in other cities. As Osman Ato (caato) put it, USC members characterized Aideed as a political savior of Hawiye.
But to find out how many agree with him is another subject. Not only that. Osman Ato was the one who convinced Aideed to accept the American troops to come to Mogadishu.

Later, when he had political friction with Aideed, Osman Hassan Ali "Caato" said, "He (Aideed) wants to be as much of a dictator as Siyaad Barre. I don't want to see any more suffering for nothing." Osman Ato militia bitterly fought with Aideed militia at the Mogadishu airport where at least 5 men killed (The Economist, March 4, 1995).

But General Mohamed Farah Aideed (1934-1996) succeeded to force the US-led coalitions to withdraw from Somalia in 1995. He declared himself the president of Somalia afterwards and died in the 1996. His presidency worked not even in Mogadishu. However, we have to mention one good piece of Aideed's history. Before his death, the charcoal trade was forbidden in the areas of his influence.

The game kept changing for the same old wrong direction and Osman Ato who used to call Aideed the savior of Hawiye developed political differences with Aideed and reached a boiling point in 1996. The militia of Ato (Caato: Somali) is the one bitterly fought against the militia of Aideed, those of former boss of Ato. Not only that. According to the April 27, 1996 and 4 May issues of the Indian Ocean Newsletter, Mr. Osman who was once the second-in-command of Aideed masterminded the killing of Aideed.

While the new tribal fighting and alliances unfolded, the western media jumped on the wagons with full speed. It wasted no time to report the new warfare between USC factions. There was also a partially manmade tragedy which increased the speed of the death rate.

Due to a delay of rains, historically, from 1918, documents reflect that the nation frequently subjected to famines, the north and central regions in particular. The worst ones have happened in 1964 to 1965, 1974—75, 1991—93.

But during the last one, the north and central regions which mostly depend on livestock products still had their usual trades with the neighboring countries such as Yemen, United Arab Emirates, Saudi Arabia, Djibouti, and Ethiopia. And in that sense, they were somewhat better off while in the southern, the case was different.

During the first year (1991) of the main turmoil, the agricultural communities of Rahanweyn, Digil, and smaller clans in the interreference areas, people especially men, were in hiding for a year both From Daarood's regrouped troops and the USC troops of Aideed. The peasants had no chance of cultivating their farms and whatever they had stored for the dry season, was previously looted by both troops.

And mainly for that reason, they had suffered immensely and the international NGOs which went back to Somalia when Barre was ousted and later comers could not do enough. The situation overwhelmed them. They warned to the world that they had a crisis of great magnitude in their hands, but not in time.

The Role of Mohamed Sahnoun

Finally, though many thinks that it was intentionally delayed, in early 1992, when the SNA of Aideed and the USC of Mahdi just had a ceasefire, the UN looked into the matter. The Secretary-General, Mr. Boutros-Ghali asked Mohamed Sahnoun of Algeria, a brilliant politician, and internationally known dynamic mediator, especially in the diplomatic world to go to Somalia for a fact-finding mission. Not only Mr. Sahnoun accepted the mission, but he had the sympathy and the will to take that challenging responsibility. He stated (The Missed Opportunities, Vii):

When the Secretary-General of the United Nations, Boutros Ghali, asked me if I would be willing to undertake a factfinding mission in Somalia in March 1992, I accepted without hesitation. I had already been informed by some friends in the region about the humanitarian tragedy that was unfolding in parts of the country. Therefore, I was eager to find out for myself the extent of the tragedy and to assess how the international community should respond.

I lived in the Horn of Africa, or more precisely in Addis Ababa, Ethiopia for almost a decade, in the late 1960s, and early 1970s, and I am very attached to the region. I was the deputy secretary General of the Organization of African Unity, in charge of political affairs, and therefore oversaw some of the conflict situations in the continent and particularly in the Horn.

The UN appointed Mr. Sahnoun of Algeria as a Special Envoy to Somalia. Though some Somalis jumped on the wagons accusing him of partiality, the international communities and many Somalis felt his presence immediately. The extensive knowledge of the Sahnoun of the area and the people paid off and created an atmosphere of some accountability to the United Nations in warlords. After negotiations, almost all warlords except Aideed approved some kind of foreign forces involvement. Those warlords who wanted UN peacekeeping forces were not more nationalists than Aideed, but they were inferior to him in terms of arms that each mobilized.

The UNOSOM director, Mr. Sahnoun negotiated with the warlords, mainly Aideed and Ali Mahdi to allow 500 UN forces to come to Somalia. He convinced them that they were obligated to ease the lines of the relief supply and renew political reconciliations for the sake of their country.

But you can ask: What country and what people? Still, there was some fighting in the southern regions. Kismayo fell into the hands of opposing factions back and forth from early of 1991 to late of 1992. Baardheere (Bardera) is one example where heavy fighting took place.

In October of 1992, the militia of General Mohamed Said Hersi (Morgan), the son in-law of the former president, Barre, captured Kismayo from Aideed. However, food without balanced spices does not taste optimum. The media was adding spices to the Somalia crisis.

Airing the images of fleshless limbs and bloated bellies of dying children, women and old men from Somalia by the western media did not slow down.

Though it is naive to suggest that all of them were self-serving, western media heavily involved in the crisis.

By July of 1992, Jane Pere from The New York Time reported that at Baidao (Baydhabo) area, people were walking skeletons dying every few minutes. Despite the famine and the fighting which were taking heavy tolls, too many interests were involved. Even the UN Envoy, Sahnoun and his boss in New York had two different settlement approaches about the Horn.

The first African Secretary-General of the United Nations liked to do something about Somalia, but the organization he was leading needed a new direction. The UN weighed its reputation more than the interest of the Somali people. In one angle, the political solution of Somalia was seen as too complicated while too feasible in another without defining the problem.

The Relief Organizations, Foreign NGOs plus the media which Boutros-Ghali said, "The Security Council is 16, 15 plus the media (CNN)," magnified the famine and the anarchy in Somalia.

The state which did not collapse all of a sudden on January 27, 1991, but rather of a built up of prolonged systematic political persecution, internal clan conflict, social distress, dried up public funds, looting of the public and private properties, further faced wide starvation.

Media Campaign

Philip Johnston, Ph.D. was the president of CARE which had been in Somalia since 1981. Page three of the Somalia Diary he authored 1994 says, "In the summer of 1992, the emerging famine in Somalia seemed almost incomprehensible.

In September, Seattle times reported that since the 1991 civil war, an estimated 100, 000 people had perished. Of that number, 40-45,000 Somalis had died of starvation and related diseases in the seven months since January' and the situation was worsening."

The Care president was in Somalia before the troops arrived and also was the UN Appointed Chief Coordinator of Humanitarian Assistance (Somalia Diary: 4). He went to Mogadishu, Baydhabo (Baidoa), Baardheere, Kismaayo and other cities. He documented a very powerful life experience. He quoted both Seattle Post-Intelligencer and the Seattle times as follows, "Some 200 children a day were losing their lives in Mogadishu. In Baidao (Baydhabo), 200-300 bodies were being gathered daily, according to Muslim crescent.

An estimated 1.5 million people, one-third of the country's population, faced imminent starvation."

Aiden Hartley who wrote The Afterword to the 2004 edition of Warriors (Gerald Hanley who passed away 30 years before that) said on page 226, "The situation became so appalling that in the town of Baidoa (Baydhabo) during the summer months of 1992 we witnessed 400 people being buried daily."

By August 1992, the phrase "the walking skeletons" was referred to the Somalis. World Televisions showed young armed bandits motoring through Mogadishu, dying daily people for bullet wounds, hunger, and hunger-related diseases.

The families of the warlords were living outside Somalia and were safe from the disaster. Mr. Sahnoun reminded the Somali warlords that for those who turn their backs on their own people when they are needed most, would regret a day in which they cannot rewind the tape. He finally convinced Aideed, the most critical of foreign troops in Somalia to allow limited UN troops (Losing Mogadishu: 24). Though not enough, some foods were reaching certain drought-stricken places at that time.

First UN Troops to Somalia

The first armed 500 Pakistanis of the UN arrived at Mogadishu on September 28, 1992, just to secure the port, safeguard the food shipments to and from the airports, and escort food convoys from the port to the destinations. General Shaheen, the head of the Pakistan contingent and next to the Envoy, quickly learned how to deal with the elders, young thugs, warlords, and the general public as well.

The top agenda of Mr. Sahnoun was to get closer to the political factions. Here are some reasons for the ambassador's substantial success.

He convinced the international donors to increase their relief contributions mainly food supply and medicine. Mr. Sahnoun rallied warlords to perform their obligations to ease the suffering of their own. The Envoy listened to the concerns of the intellectuals who advised him to weigh on political reconciliations more than anything else.

But while the agent was performing the much-needed task for the less fortunate nation on behalf of the world, the UN bureaucracy in New York was on his back, meddling with the internal politics of the country. He did not appreciate hearing unfair accusations against his employer, but neither was free of suspicion. Sahnoun was not ready for a worse than he was in about southern Somalia, but according to Somalia: The Missed Opportunities by Mohamed Sahnoun himself, p39, one Unmarked planeload of newly printed Somali shilling worth more than $20 million dollars with military hardware landed at the airfield of Ali Mahdi in the north of the city on October 1992.

After a short period, other Unmarked planes with suspicious cargoes showed up at the same airfield. The Envoy became infuriated with the UN bureaucracy in New York and openly criticized its policy about Somalia. Such condemnations annoyed his bosses in New York.

In addition, he also felt that he was not getting the needed backup from the UN to stabilize Somalia's political chaos. Still, all those distractions did not handicap him to perform his duties.

At the end of October 1992 with the help of the Swedish Institute of Life and Peace, the Envoy had held a conference with a group of Somali intellectuals from all over the country in Seychelles, an Island in the Indian ocean. The group offered some excellent suggestions on how to resolve the political problems of their country according to Sahnoun.

Though he had his bosses' approval, the motion agitated the UN leaders in New York. The head office immediately advised him to refrain from criticizing UN actions in Somalia (Sahnoun p39). Though during the assignment of Sahnoun things improved somewhat, at that time, the death rate in Baidao (Baydhabo) was the highest in the nation.

Relief supplies were going to Somalia but either the gunmen looted on the route or were still on the deck. Rakiya Omaar of Africa Watch in London called Mogadishu a very dangerous place. She also characterized its port as one of the most dangerous ports in the world. One French aid worker said, "It was not the distress alone that made Somalia's extraordinary, but the distress and craziness."

Snipers killings of the NGOs never stopped either. Armed bandits murdered UNICEF workers in Baardheere (Bardera), Kismayo, and ICRC workers in Baidoa and Mogadishu. The bad boys (young gunmen) resented anybody whom they thought would take away their freedom of looting, raping and killing.

The egalitarian, nomadic, poet, cunning society which clan fighting over minor things and quick conflict resolutions by clan elders are not strange to it, got no mercy from the famine.

Somalia became one of the most discussed topics in the world. However, as an author, and Somali ethnic born and raised in Somalia, I fail to see why the Somalis are cunning people— unless someone is saying that they are cunning people for themselves for wrong reasons.

The Arab League, the Organization of African Unity, the Organization of the Islamic Conference had not done anything significant about Somalia's crisis. The peace reconciliation they organized with the UN in New York in January 1992, collapsed before almost it began.

Though Kenya had accepted at least 300,000 refugees in its country, its security forces badly roughed Somalis up which they do all the times. Somalia became an easy pick for most comedians.

The attitude and the jokes of many of those were somewhat offensive and unprofessional. But for sure, there is no question that the final blame of the chaos belongs to the Somalis. Dr. Philip Johnston, the author of Somalia Diary, quoted one United States official that the entire country should be paved over and turned into a parking lot.

Once you fail yourself, I believe the bad things people say about you are good candidates. The ruthless individuals who sent away their families into safety, and on the other murdered innocent people deserved demeaning statements.

Since Somalia failed itself and it made headlines in the international arena, force-feeding was one option thought over by many world leaders.

Yugoslavia was another hot spot which severe ethnic cleansing was taking place. Many western countries would have liked to settle the crisis in the Balkans before anyone else. The news aired by the media from both locations was something of an urgent need. The case of Yugoslavia had something to do with different religion and land, while in Somalia the case is different.

Somalia is one of the most homogenous societies in the world. Just bad administration, unrestrained and lately polarized ethnic rivalries escalated the whole trouble.

Different religious sects which get formed one after the other during the chaos added to the chaos. Their incriminate and mass killings, and redefining the religion other than as peace and loving faith further alienate the ordinary Somalis. People will not remember the extremists as Islamists who fought either for Islam or for the country.

Whoever was blamed for the plight of Somalia, the world was becoming restless and tilted to intervene. Somalia was on the first pages of major Newspapers; magazines and the broadcasting companies were showing horrendous pictures. The graphic pictures shown on the TV made the talking. ABC World News aired, "Dead people being carted away in wagons."

PBS (Public Broadcasting Service, in the US) said, "The worst story in the world, the one in Somalia, that the African nation where people are dying in numbers and in a way hard for most people to imagine."

The behavior of those who wanted to pursue a technique of ethnic cleansing through starvation and bullets seemed unacceptable to the international communities. But they did not act properly early enough either and the "Why" may never be known in full context.

The interests of the international NGOs and the media sometimes coincide. Both elite groups need a disaster to report and help at the same time. I do not term that they lack a moral compass or anything like that, but in the sense that a disaster of human tragedy was taking place to report.

Primarily, each relief organization in southern Somalia wired its worst pictures to his TV/radio station and then aired. Newspapers and Magazines did the same thing. Somalia was a real prey which it made itself. The areas where there were no clan fighting and famine were safe from sometimes certain self-served media coverage.

Central, northwestern and northeastern regions were pure examples. Undeniably, the crisis in southern Somalia was real but also exaggerated. As one put on Time magazine at a UNICEF feeding center in Bardera/Baardheere:

9:35 A.M. a boy of five with red bracelet (color the feeding center used for those on the verge of death) passed out in the crowd. Two workers rush over, hoist him by his spindly limbs and lay him down beneath a shade tree on the far side of the courtyard. He is suffering from severe dehydration, and the nurse hastily inserted an intervenors tube, hooking the bottle to a branch. It is too late as the boy's eyes roll back beneath fluttering eyelids; an older woman gently presses them shut. The boy came from the village of Malweyn, 55 km away, where both parents and eight of his brothers and sisters succumbed to starvation in the past six months. Four days ago, he set for Bardera with his last sibling an older brother, who now rocks quietly weeping by his side.

As one put on Time magazine at a UNICEF feeding center in Bardera/Baardheere:

9:35 A.M. a boy of five with red bracelet (color the feeding center used for those on the verge of death) passed out in the crowd. Two workers rush over, hoist him by his spindly limbs and lay him down beneath a shade tree on the far side of the courtyard. He is suffering from severe dehydration, and the nurse hastily inserted an intervenors tube, hooking the bottle to a branch. It is too late as the boy's eyes roll back beneath fluttering eyelids; an older woman gently presses them shut. The boy came from the village of Malweyn, 55 km away, where both parents and eight of his brothers and sisters succumbed to starvation in the past six months. Four days ago, he set for Baardheere/Bardera with his last sibling an older brother, who now rocks quietly weeping by his side.

"The unfortunate thing about Africa is that you have to have a certain body count before people really care." The media played the most important role to electrify the outside opinion. Western Relief Organizations which in 1992 put more money into the third world countries than the world bank selected the worst cases for journalism.

Dr. Yeron of UNICEF said, "I have been in the refugee camps during the Ethiopian famine, and I have never seen such a catastrophe as we have in Somalia (Somalia Diary: Viii)." Daniel Miller of the U.S. Centers for Disease Control and Prevention said, "The mortality is higher than that of the Irish Potato Famine. It is the worst nightmare you could think of."

These were true disasters in Somalia but exaggerated in a bit in reporting. The thousands of selected news clips reaching the international media were their main weapons. They showed in ways too painful for the citizens of the developed nations to watch certain pictures.

Colin Powell said in his book (My American Journey, 565), "This is some of the times when the privacy of the western citizens is invaded. The media brings horrible news to the bedrooms of the people regardless of their lifestyles in society."

The Somalis failed to feed their own and therefore could not protect their privacies. When mothers tore their pots from starving children to feed their own, Somali leaders were vying for power.

In certain places like Baardheere/Bardera, when things improved somewhat, the death rate was 40 a day mostly women and children. The titles of the periodical and the newspapers ranged from Landscape of Death, A Day in the Death of Somalia, Dilemma for the World, Starvation, The Pain Of waiting, Death chooses the young Beyond Hope, Beyond Life, a World of Dust, the Cry of a Dying People, Infrastructure Limits Food Relief, Exporting famine, the Mad War, the Offspring of Anarchy, Death and Life in a small town, Somalia Fights for its life, and many more.

If the situation of innocent human beings was extremely that bad, why did it take so long for the international communities to intervene?

Perhaps, the following Somali saying suits best. "A weak she-camel its owner holds down cannot get up" (Ruqo ninkii lahaa dabada hayaa ma kacdo)." Though it was exaggerated, according to Dr. Philip of CARE (Seattle Post Intelligencer, August 8, 1992), wrote, "In September, in southern Somalia especially in the inter-riverine areas, in total, 300 people were dying daily Baidao (Baydhabo) had been the worst."

(Christian Science Monitor, 6 September 1992), speaking to reporters in Nairobi, the UN'S humanitarian coordinator for Somalia, Mark Bowden said:

The only way to reduce the anticipated number of famine related deaths would be a massive influx of international aid. The international communities must also "Refocus" its aid efforts on southern Somalia, the epicenter of a drought related crisis affecting the entire Horn of Africa." "refocus" its aid efforts on southern Somalia, the epicenter of a drought related crisis affecting the entire Horn of Africa.

The warlords in southern Somalia did not feel ashamed at using starvation as their weapon. From Hiiraan up to the Kenyan border, there were two strong warlords and some juniors.

While the journalists and the leaders of the relief organizations were pushing for military involvement in Somalia, aid workers on the field were divided over whether the military' involvement would smooth the food shipments and neutralize the political situation or ignite further chaos.

In mid-1993, there were about 50 foreign NGOs in Mogadishu alone, and they had a right to worry. They were unarmed and many times within the public. Others did not care about the unfortunate crisis in the Horn as one U.S. citizen put it, "there is no national interest at stake."

When the military regime was massacring northwestern of Somalia population with their own fighter-planes taking off from Hargeysa airport, bombing Hargeysa itself and coming back to the same airport United States did not intervene because "When it comes to looking after the American goal and objectives, human rights of other citizens are not counted that much. 80% of the buildings in Hargeysa were destroyed. And because the U.S. vital interests were on the line, the Reagan administration has pretended blindfolded from the massacre in the north." Perhaps for not pretending to be blindfolded, Sahnoun could not remain as an ambassador.

The Resignation of Sahnoun

On October 27, 1992, a rumor that Sahnoun was resigning circulated around Mogadishu. And two days after, he announced his resignation. It shocked the humanitarian relief agencies, the NGOs and the Somalis. General Shaheen of Pakistani contingent who was second to Sahnoun became the acting Special Envoy of UNOSOM.

The UN was formed at the end of the WORLD WAR TWO at the Opera House in San Francisco in 1945 with 50 countries. Africa had only four independent signatories: Liberia, Ethiopia, South Africa, and Egypt. Asia east had had three: China, partly self-ruled India and the Philippines. Since then, the organization had supervised more than 41 peacekeeping missions which still 16 of them were under operation.

The current (2019) 193-member body and 5.4 billion budgets, in 1992, there were 185 member-states and a combined budget of around $4.5 billion. When Professor Boutros-Boutros Ghali of Egypt was elected to become the first African Secretary-General of the World body in 1991, the organization was in debt. Over three billion U.S. dollars were owed by the various nations which the United States alone owed more than a billion.

The collapse of the Soviet Union, a new world order was new. With all those crises, the UN wanted to set an example of being an effective world body. But it is a well-known fact the veto-powered nations run the UN, especially the United States. When these big powers are in agreement, it performs well, and when they are in disagreement, it is incapacitated. Due to these, Somalia was a litmus test for the world powers, UN in particular. It lobbied for military involvement, for a country which was already in chaos.

From the Somali perspective, the idea of sending foreign troops to their country has never sunk into the minds of many, but neither were in a position to be consulted nor could they stop the world.

Culturally, Somalis are very informative people and too sensitive whenever foreigners are on their soil. They accept death rather willingly when their dignity is hurt than to negotiate.

History reveals that they do not even leave their dead when they have to retreat. It is not something new to know that Somalis are desert warriors. They dare to face the danger instead of being humiliated. All those characteristics have not been weighed.

Warriors: The Life and Death among the Somalis by Gerald Hanley, a Captain in the British army WORLD WAR TWO, good and bad, talked about the Somalis as they are, and he did not hide their sickness clannism and constant violence. Even the other African men in the fight with them used to say, "Somalis are no good. Each man is his own Sultan (Roy Irons, p.225)."

Also, Jardine said, "The Somali is largely an individualist." James Fergusson also adds, "The Somalis by character are too independent-minded to follow any foreign ideology for long that each is a prima donna." Many others who encountered with the Somali termed him as a pragmatist, and If there is an ideology to which he is in full trust, is most of his own.

Going along with the failures and successes of the Operation Restore Hope, in comparison to Bosnia, another troubled country where its ethnic cleansing cannot be compared to the Horn, the world saw Somalia as a piece of cake in terms of the manpower required. But the UN which never had a military of its own relied on the military of the other nations, the U.S. in particular.

But how dignity and bravery are defined? Being proud while you are starving your own people to death, killing, raping and looting, anything good you are said before does not count.

The United States, on the other hand, saw itself as the only superpower left, and it did not hesitate to flex its muscle for policing the world. It was telling to the world, the purpose of the Somalia mission was to save the starving children, women and the elderly in the inter-riverine area of southern Somalia. And That was also what the American media was conveying to the rest of the world.

Waves of media even suggested that the UN should take over the administration of the country until it stands on its own feet. Though Somalia failed to function in the best interest of its citizens, the country exists as a sovereign state and has a spot on the world. But a dying person for starvation or otherwise does not care who rules but who helps him. The mooryaan (bandits) outnumbered and outgunned the 500 Pakistanis.

Somali bandits ambushed and looted a convoy of 34 trucks carrying wheat to the starving. They also killed CARE (The largest or one of the largest Relief

Organizations in the world) workers and wounded five, all Somalis on 11 November 1992. A single truck reached the destination while the famine starved over 300,000 at that time. finally, the media coverage of the tragedy helped shape American policy towards Somalia, and the top decision-makers were ultimately convinced to exercise the U.S. Might.

Military Involvement Foundation Laid out

On November 21, 1992, the outgoing president of the United States, George Bush called Colin Powel, the Chairman of the American Joint Chiefs of Staff, the Secretary of Defense Dick Cheney, and a couple of top senior aides for a meeting (My American Journey of Colin L. Powell, 564). They told him that the operation would be done with minimum casualties and at a low cost.

November 25, Thanksgiving Eve, a holiday in the United States, the Bush administration which long considered Bosnia militarily untouchable, offered the UN the use of up to 30,000 troops to save Somalia. The president added that the military would be out of Somalia by Late January of 1993.

Whether the president wanted the troops to be out by the end of January (My American Journey, 565) and he believed "Simple people, simple problems and simple solutions," phrases I will talk them later, or he wanted to defend American interests, the administration made a timetable with wishful thinking. But the military intervention was also what Boutros-Ghali was lobbying for since he took office, especially after Sahnoun resigned.

The UN lobbied very hard to send a military force to Somalia but it had another agenda in mind too. It wanted that the warlords be disarmed to form a puppet government, or one credited to it. That goal itself was in conflict with the goals of the United States.

The UN works only when a veto privilege is not exercised against the Security Council. Fortunately, none of the other four veto powered states, Russia, France, UK and China voted against the motion while the United States was the one offered the 30,000 men of its own.

But not that all the U.S. politicians were for the U.S. military involvement in Somalia. The American Ambassador to Kenya in 1989-1993, Smith Hempstone (1929-2006) who visited some refugee camps in Kenya in July of 1992 did not hesitate to state his position.

Before he was nominated to ambassadorial-ship, he was a journalist and an author. He did not hide his displeasure of military involvement in Somalia. On December 1, the ambassador sent an urgent cable to the State Department. He said, "Think once, twice and three times before you embrace the Somali tar baby." Excerpts of his cable (Rutherford, 80 and *US News and World Report, December 14, 1992*):

I fail to see where any vital U.S. interest is involved. Somalis, as the Italians and British discovered to their discomfiture, are natural-born guerillas. They will mine the roads. They will lay ambushes. They will launch hit and run attacks. They will not be able to stop the convoys from getting through. But they will inflict--and take- casualties.

.. If you liked Beirut, you will love Mogadishu. To what end? To keep tens of thousands of Somali kids from starving to death in 1993 who, in all probability, will starve to death in
1994 (unless we are prepared to remain through 1994)? The Somali is a treacherous. The
Somali is a killer The Somali is as touch as his county, and just as unforgiving. The one "beneficial" effect a major American intrusion into Somalia is likely to have maybe to reunite the Somali Nation: Against us, the invaders, the outsiders, the kaffir (unbeliever) who may have fed their children but also have killed their young men. In the old days, the Somalis raided for camels, women and slaves. Today they raid for camels, women, slaves and food. Encourage the Somalis who want peace. Leave them alone, in short, to work out their own destiny, brutal it may be.

      The United States made available 28,000 U.S. troops for Somalia and tons of equipment shipped in from Diego Garcia, an American base in the Indian Ocean. United Nations Security Council which was delighted to drag Uncle Sam (U.S.) into the game and which also can hardly turn down an American proposal because the U.S. pays most of its bills, voted unanimously to support the motion.
      On the next day, President Bush went on the national TV to announce and justified what was named the Operation Restore Hope. The U.S. went into a new role as a military force.
      When the Somali armed bandits learned that Americans were coming, they went into the outskirts, hid their weapons and came back to the city to observe how things will turn out. They were well aware that they could not challenge the big guns.
      More than half of the U.S. troops were amphibious Marines who would land on the shores of Mogadishu to secure the airport and harbor for the United Nations Task forces.
      Once again, the African Continent had failed itself. Though Ethiopia is an exception whether it is how they treat displaced Somalis in their country, or it is the role which it had played to mediate Somali leaders, only the following nations such as Botswana, Zimbabwe, Nigeria, Morocco (1400), Tunisia (small contingent) had militarily contributed.

Sudan had one-time donated food to Somalia's crisis. In Sudan, the public criticized that move claiming that it was inappropriate to send food to a foreign country while some of the people (South Sudan) in the country were starving? Yoweri Museveni of Uganda met Aideed one time and offered mediation, and the situation showed that nothing good came out of it.

In any case, with or without them, Operation Restore Hope, an American-led UN operation was underway at the first week of December 1992.

Chapter sixteen referenced notes

Understanding the Somalia conflagration, 19
The Economist, March 4, 1995
The Missed Opportunities by Sahnoun, Vii
Boutros-Ghali "Quotation."   Somalia Diary, 4
Sahnoun p39-40
Dr. Yeron of UNICEF 1992
Somalia Diary: Viii
My American Journey, Colin Powell, 564-5
Dr. Philip of CARE (Seattle Post-Intelligencer, 8 August 1992
Christian   Science Monitor, September 6, 1992
UN Formation 1945
Roy Irons, p.225
US News and World Report, December 14, 1992

CHAPTER SEVENTEEN (Dec. 1992 - Apr.1996)

The intervention of Southern Somalia

Those who do not educate their children are doomed to be failed nations and will stay under the mercy of the developed ones.

In the last quarter of 1992, around 350,000 perished for starvation, and for whatever other intentions attached by the Western countries, the world could not watch any more.
Politicians always find a way to justify their decisions. The American led UN peacekeepers bombed any place suspected as a hideout of General Aideed, and thousands of Somalis get killed through the process. A good intention turned ugly.
And as a result, hundreds of thousands experienced daily nightmares. Images represent beliefs, norms values, ideas, and impressions. As I was one of the hundreds of thousands if not millions watching on TV, the night of December 9 (night in Somalia), 1992, is very well known in Somalia.
Somalia was invaded without any authorization from its people because anarchy ruled and they could not help themselves. 25,000 American troops went ashore at night at Somalia's capital, Mogadishu (My American Journey, 565).
The American amphibious Marines landed in Somalia. The only resistance they, the American Navy Seals encountered was from about 75 or so reporters and

camera crews beaming spotlights on them, determined to broadcast a military operation life.

The Somali gunmen who had already hidden their heavy guns in the countryside, and came back as spectators plus the rest of the public had never seen such manpower with such sophisticated pieces of equipment. That made them so surprised as the reporters and millions of others who were watching on the TVs.

The American Amphibious Marines easily secured the International Airport with no loss of lives and paved the way for the other troops.

The northern and central regions of Somalia were not on the priority list, but Baidao (Baydhabo), Kismaayo, Baardheere, Ballidoogle, Jalalaqsi, Marka, Beledweyn and Huddur (Xuddur), all in southern Somalia were the next targeted cities. Some reporters were asked to report from the northern regions, and they hesitated to "hang around Mogadishu to see another US soldier killed to make news, since the success stories in north could not" "Kenneth Rutherford, 2008:93).

The western media which usually influence the foreign policies of their countries jumped on the wagons to evaluate the "Operation Restore Hope." They immediately reported it as a success story.

As stated earlier, some international communities would have liked that the world would deal with the Yugoslavia crisis. The government of the Netherlands did not hide its displeasure with military intervention in Somalia instead of Yugoslavia. Time Magazine, 9 December 1992, quoted Former Dutch Prime Minister, Mr. Ruud Lubbers. He said to his parliament, "It is downright scandalous that there is an intervention in Somalia but not in Yugoslavia."

The operation in Somalia was more feasible both financially and militarily than for a similar one in Yugoslavia. Western countries believed that the cost of intervention in Yugoslavia was too great. Many White House officials breathed that "Bush and Joint Chiefs Chairman Colin Powell would never accept the Somali Mission if they did not believe it could be done quickly and at comparatively low cost."

In an article on the U.S. News and World Report on December 21, 1992, Tim Zimmerman, the author said, "The crisis in Yugoslavia is too tough to tackle." The media headlines were "Saving Somalia is easier than stopping Serbia, Feeding the Hungry in Somalia may be the easy part for America: Getting out may be tougher, Doing Harm by Doing Good, When Taming is Inflaming, The Price of Charity, Death by Looting."

The interests of European nations in one angle, Russia on the Serbia side, Islamic states with Bosnia, the United States as a World Police (US), and the UN as a new identity searcher contradicted. Also, Yugoslavia was not a pushover.

When the Americans landed on the Mogadishu shores, moved to the nearby international airport and other important airports, they ordered the curious

Somalis on the dock to lie face down, and then detained them. People quickly translated that as put down.

Although the southern Somalis are too sensitive when foreigners are on their soil because it reminds them of the fascist rule of Italy, the Mooryaan (young thugs or gunmen) and Aideed loyalists resented it further when the Americans overpowered them and stole their show. U.S. troops received welcome mainly from women and children.

Men were too anxious evaluating how the invasion would turn out. Generally, many peace-loving Somalis expected that foreign troops on their soil would help them get freed from rival warlords and the armed thugs.

Before the helping relationship between the public and the troops wounded, Fadumo Mohamed, 32, a mother of seven was one of the many Somalis who admitted enjoying the presence of the U.S. troops. When asked about the foreign troops in her country, she said, "I would like the U.S. troops to stay here for life."

Though men always make war and women and the children suffer the most, an ant Boutros Ghali demonstrator, Sadiyo Mohamed Warsame said, "We don't need foreign soldiers on our soil US and World Report, January 18, 1993."

But there were no questions that the majority of the public hated the warlords and their mooryaan more than anyone else.

No one could blame a terrorized mother of seven (Fadumo Mohamed) who did not sleep peacefully with her children perhaps since president Barre fled the capital. She lived in the city when the civil war was at its worst, and interpreted the foreign intervention as a way out of the lawlessness. Fadumo was 11 years old when the military toppled the civilian administration of her country in 1969. From that period on, the regime was committing some basic human rights violations, and thugs and warlords took away whatever left for Fadumo and many others.

The ordeals of the fighting, the famine, and ambushing the relief convoys were far from over when the international peacekeepers landed in Mogadishu. But in some drought-stricken areas, however, the rains had already partially made a difference. Some of the urban refugees went back to their places though still needed help and there is one more thing.

The heavily-armed U.S. troops plus more from other nations such as 1,500 soldiers from Belgium, 750 Egyptians and some others came to Somalia on a mercy mission, but there is an American saying of "There is no such thing as a free lunch." The Somalia intervention was also politically motivated, and the United States first had to defend its vital interests. In that angle, the mission succeeded militarily. The report card of the aggressive style of US army went back urgently. It said, "We subdued Mogadishu shores without losing American lives, mission accomplished."

It was true that the US army subdued Mogadishu shores, but it was far from saying "Mission accomplished." The United States is never immune to misconceptions. Americans translated their first assessments as "Simple people, simple problems and simple solutions." Americans did not learn much from Vietnam. From that to Beirut, and to Somalia, the U. S. made the same mistakes again and again.

The United States could accomplish more than easing starvation in Somalia with a minimum loss of lives. But naive psychological operations, aggressive-style of its military, quick and poor intelligence damaged the good perceptions that Somalis had about the Americans.

As Jill Smolowe of Time magazine said, "Between the objective of opening a food pipeline to feed the starving, and the dream of doing the job superbly, and go home safely, lies much room for disappointment and misunderstanding."

Where did things get out of control?

The two words "disappointment" and "misunderstanding" reversed on the line took place in reality. Here is another quote which points out to understand how the human rights of the most Somalis were initially neglected. Robert Oakley said, "When Somalis are fighting Somalis, we do nothing. They can do whatever they want to each other." `

Robert Oakley never had a good humanitarian record. Since at the age of 22, he was in many hot spots for his country. During the Eisenhower administration, he was involved in some kind of covert operation in Russia. He was in Vietnam to relive the ill-fated French operation in 1954 in Saigon, South Vietnam from 1965-1967, and in Lebanon during the civil war. He was also an Ambassador to Zaire where president Mobutu Sesse Seko nearly kicked him out.

As an American ambassador to Somalia, he had a bad relationship with the regime. In Pakistan as an ambassador, he was not good either. All those countries disliked him. Most likely for his country's ultimate goal, instabilities took place in all those nations either during his presence or shortly afterward. Hence, in that regard, Oakley's statements "When Somalis are fighting Somalis, we do nothing: they can do whatever they want to each other" are in contradiction with the objective of Operation Restore Hope.

Newsweek quoted Oakley on February 22, 1993. He said, "We are not going to be the meat in their sandwich, thank you very much." After all, his track record and his words go together. Also, President Bush insisted from the beginning that "Operation Restore Hope" was strictly a humanitarian mission (US News and World Report, December 14 1992), a term which is mostly designed to create or sustain a dependency.

As he was supposed to, the President did not mention the most underlining goal of the United States, Containing Islamic Fundamentalism, and oil interests in the region. About containing the Islamic Fundamentalism, Christian organizations had previously failed to recruit Somalis while Kenya is a Christian state closely watched and protected by the west.

Increasing western paranoia about Islamic Fundamentalism, Sudan became an Islamic state. Ethiopia, a traditionally governed by Christian minority state while about half or more of its population are Muslims, was in a volatile stage at the moment.

Perhaps, all those combined, until Ethiopia becomes strong enough to crush any religious opposition as it had done in 1994 and 1995, the United States decided to sit back and let Somalia disintegrate. And when intervened, Somalia's political problems have been treated with a military solution and called the operation Humanitarian.

Despite the universal coverage, as quickly as the next day of the "Operation Restore Hope" in Somalia, less than 24 hours, Thursday December 10, 1992, Americans and French troops whom most of them were not even France citizens but mercenaries and so on fired at a Somali van as it raced through a control point, innocently ignored orders to stop. The vehicle crashed into a wall. Two people lost their lives, and seven wounded. First, it was reported as an armed technical but later turned out to be an unarmed regular van. The journalists rushed to the scene and enquired if the use of the fire was justified.

Colonel Fred Beck, a spokesman for the United States, recalled the 1983 suicide bombing that took the lives of 241 United States troops. He said, "We don't have to recall to you what happened in Beirut. We acted in what we thought was an appropriate fashion."

There were Somali bystanders watching the whole thing, witnessed a different story and became very agitated of how the foreign soldiers handled the situation. Public minds clicked to reevaluate the behaviors of outside troops who came to help. Many American politicians quickly questioned the possibility of late January exit from Somalia. In parallel to that, foreigners define the Somalis as: "Merciless, proud, curious, volatile, independent and sensitive."

Another one says, "The Somalis are paranoid, insular, and unforgiving." I can add, The Somalis are suspicious of anything, irrespective to each other, impatient, discriminative and give not much care of a life.

According to their folklore tales, fighting is sometimes a sport for them. Killing the civilians which the militias never refrained from reenergized. The peacekeeping also turned into a peace-forcing.

And that was different than what most Somalis and many others in the world had in mind. The young gunmen disliked the intimidating style of the troops. They felt despised and ignored. And as a result, they picked ambushing foreign personnel and carjacking from where they paused—further starving and killing of their own.

Before leaving to Somalia, United States troops were not fully oriented about the culture of the people they were going to help. They got few tips such as not drinking beer and liquor, porno pictures which had been widely used anyway, but not about the values, norms and their national views of the nation. "Get down on your knees!" and "spread your arms" were some of the instructions which Americans are accustomed.

Somalis despise such acts and feel humiliated while it is normal in States when apprehending suspects and criminals.

However, the Somali thugs had ignored that they made humiliations when they raped, looted women, and halted the existence of innocent people of their own. Though the public suffered most either side, the Somali thugs received doses of their medicine from the foreign troops.

Puntites used to fight over water holes for centuries and though minimum during the rainy seasons or the good times, but still exists. In the Somali society, rape used to create clan war-fares if the family of the perpetrator did not come with remorse and appropriate compensations.

Customarily, good or bad, what is acceptable in American, French, Italian, Pakistan, Belgium, or Nigerian cultures are not necessarily acceptable in Somalia. The Euphoria of first-hand learning of how the Americans would behave quickly evaporated and resentment of foreign troops in their country relived.

New tensions started immediately. Rutgers University Professor, Somali born, Said S. Samatar (not alive now) had been quoted as (US News & World Report, December 14, 1992:29):

There are not men (referring warlords) who have supreme commands over a horde of followers and can deliver them to the field of battle, or a negotiating table. Their power depends on the dynamics of war, and when deprive them of the capacity to rape and loot, their supporters will slip away. The UN will have to base any new Somali consensus on local clan leaders, the traditional indigenous leadership that has been badly weakened by two decades of dictatorship. The United States and the UN could help legitimize these leaders by using them to help distribute food.

The Special Envoy of the UN, Mr. Sahnoun took advantage of the indigenous leadership for the time he had been in Somalia. General Shaheen, the chairman of the Pakistani Contingent followed in his footsteps. When the troops landed in Somalia, General was one of the insiders that foreign NGOs had relied on his advice. He gave the UN his perception of the Somali gunmen. "The young Somali gunman is brave and proud and not afraid of getting killed," said Shaheen. Also, Gerald Hanley, a British WORLD WAR TWO veteran, Captain in rank in 1941, who led a Somali battalion for the Burma campaign, showing both pride and prejudice wrote:

When the Somali battalion sailed for the Burma campaign, they demanded Indian scale rations, and uniforms with collars on them, like Indian troops. They did not want to dress like the Bantu troops. Who wore collarless khaki blouses, men, the Somali battalion, after a shattering artillery bombardment from the Japanese guns, finally attacked with the bayonet, they went headlong and their officers could not keep up with them? One of them was decorated for bravery in that battle, a Degoodiya (a Somali tribe) from the Northern Frontier of Somali Kenya, told me (Hanley) that he had enjoyed it, and that he admired the way the Japanese infantry liked to stand and fight it out.

Let me tell a bit about the author, Gerald Hanley. I read the "Warriors: The Death Among the Somalis (originally: Warriors and Strangers)" in 1993 in Toronto Canada and would have liked to see the author himself if I could learn more about the Somali character from him. But he passed away in 1992.

Having lived outside Somalia for more than 16 years, I went back to Somalia in 1996. I enquired if anyone (men of 80 and above years old) could remember anything about him. Without giving him any details, I said to my father, "Aabbo, can you remember a British officer in Somalia in WORLD WAR TWO who was a camel milk lover, tough and friendly with the Somalis?" "Aabbo, I cannot remember if he was not Effendi," my father said.

Effendi was the name that the Somalis used to call him. My father was an Italian-Somaliland soldier in WORLD WAR TWO. When the British defeated Italy in the Horn of Africa, my father became a Prisoner of War for the British and spent more than a year in an Addis Ababa jail. After more inquiries, I met a gentleman in Gaalkacyo whose father, Hersi Daallin met Hanley in mid-1941 in Nugaal countryside.

After that much said about Gerald Hanley and his working and friendship relationships with the Somalis, both the UN and the United States did not take Shaheen's advice either.

Still, the United States-led leadership did not realize that Somalia's problems were more complicated than how they approached. A country which had been run by warlords and armed thugs since 1990 badly needed military muscle, but the military had either ignored or lacked the tools to work with the public (the warlords, traditional indigenous clan chieftains and the concerned intellectuals).

Also, the behavior of the foreign troops on the field which acted like that they could perform a surgical operation on a chaos-run country made things worse.

Even before the troops arrived, some Somalis were accusing the United Nations team already in the country of either partial or inadequate. Another important factor increased the uneasiness of the Somalis towards the foreign forces. Although nobody can realize what hunger and lawlessness are like unlike one had experienced them, the famine was still taking its toll. In some areas, it was in its worst stage.

An article on Time Magazine, "Starvation - it takes more than food to cure" by Michael D. Lemonick; it stated:

An alarming night greeted American health officials visiting the town of Huddur (Xuddur) in Somalia. Relief workers had distributed unmilled wheat to starving villagers, and scores of living skeletons were pounding the wheat by hand to make an edible mush. To the casual witness, the rhythmic thuds might have seemed the music of deliverance, but to those familiar with the grim calculus of starvation, they formed a dirge. The energy expended in grinding the wheat vastly exceeded the nutritional benefit of the mush. Relief supplies were killing the starving.

Peace forcing in The Name of Peacekeeping

After more than 60,000 foreigners were stationed in Somalia, and of which more than 40,000 of them were well trained and equipped, most Somalis became skeptical of the presence of such force of such magnitude on their soil. Having been briefed about the national concerns of the people, President Bush reaffirmed that America had "no intentions of dictating of political outcomes."

On the other side of the White House, other U.S. politicians including President-elect Bill Clinton tied the withdrawal of American troops to the political stability of Somalia. 'An artificial timetable cannot be imposed on the troops' mission," Bill Clinton. The foreign policy of the House was contradicting.

Since the Somalis who always stay informed themselves around the world, heard the contradicting political statements, they became suspicious. Could the troops install peace? Extremely hard. Only Somalis can make peace among themselves. Still searching in2020, for whatever reasons they might be, they failed to reconcile letting their country once was the media center in Africa in the worst sense in the 1990s.

Some of the most famous reporters of the world were in Mogadishu. To get a piece of the reporting pie, the powerful forces in the country could not silence the journalists for good. Whenever there was friction between the UN forces and the Somalis, the safety of the civilians, UN personnel, the aid workers of humanitarian relief agencies and the journalists got worse, and the media used to report quickly.

The press is always quick to complain that the freedom of the press is under attack while some things they cover are self-serving lies and exaggerated news. George Bain (1920-2006), a Canadian journalist once said, "Those of us in the news business are quick to cry that freedom of the press is being attacked, and a lot of what we say is self-serving rubbish."

However, in many ways, western journalists in southern Somalia fed the world. Scenes from selected parts of the operation were getting into rooms of the world policy-makers who then grasped the moments to set objectives for their long-range interests. If one politician had the power and the will to make a global decision, then in his favor, politics has no moral.

Now, in this technologically advanced world, journalists know how to ignite the minds of the international decisionmakers. Somalia was a pure example.

The famine which was the direct result of the fighting in southern Somalia and the delay of rains did not slowdown in some remote areas. It was documented as one of the worst droughts ever happened in the world.

In certain places where it rained heavily, people were too weak to cultivate or animals to produce milk and meat.

Contributing more to the chaos, some of the peacekeepers were narrow-mindedly satisfying their egos at the cost of innocent human beings. And because of all those combined, hundreds of Somalis had been crossing their fingers waiting for good outcomes. I have to repeat and repeat that if I cannot take care of my family, even the good and the moralistic people always put your interests second.

Regardless of how Somali intellectuals previously failed their citizens when they had a government, from the time the civil war broke out, they knew what was at stake. Taking arms and killing other Somalis was not their choice.

As a result, they became the least respected and one of the most displaced groups. The warlords at least knew what they were fighting for, power and they used the thugs with the guns.

But despite its faults, the intervention had reduced the death rate and slowed down the banditry in much of southern Somalia. Equally, the UN had never been impartial of Somalia's volatile and unpredictable warlords. Aideed was always against foreign intervention. He had no ambition of less than to sit on the chair of the one he ousted.

And in that case, the UN had been siding with the interim President, Mr. Mahdi. And when got the opportunity, it naively went ahead to enforce peace without proper consultation with the most concerned national leaders.

The European countries previously locked the African continent from America. Uncle Sam (US) somewhat wanted to change his foreign policy towards Africa. But the mission of Somalia was orchestrated before Clinton took office.

Though the international communities sometimes characterize the foreign policy of the Democratic Party of the United States as secondary compared to the Republican party, Bill Clinton, the president of the U.S. (1993-2001), inherited unresolved foreign policy from his predecessor, George Bush.

When Clinton took office in late January 1993, Operation Restore Hope was already two months in business. Concentrating heavily on domestic affairs, a quick political review of the mission in Somalia was not on his priority list.

The United Nations, on the other hand, had already put its long-sought agenda on the table. The UN wanted the bandits disarmed having in mind that military might will do the job.

Somali leaders, on the other hand, were also restless to put their country back together. But every time it seemed that Somalia was coming to its sense of reconciliation, new clan warfare was erupting somewhere. The law of banditry, looting and rape have become the driving forces and could not be contained. The Somali warlords were running the county in their own ways while each kept an eye on the top chair. They were selfishly in a loop while the country was bleeding, and nothing has changed even today, 2020—it seems "my way or no way."

Looking back.

Other than stating what happened in chronological order, what the nation could do differently?

The corruptive democratic administration was in a position that a civil war was a candidate. In clannish alliances, some tribes took the government as theirs while some were in a marginalized status. The government was not very transparent about the balance and checks, nor the public had the education to ask for transparency.

However, both the freedom of the press and the freedom of movement were not under duress. Those who could be able to go anywhere and the press could able to publish the views of the public. Perhaps, it would not explode as 1990s. The nation needed a rescue from corruption but not a military takeover.

In the case of the Supreme Revolutionary Council (SRC) Council, the education of the armed forces was limited to the officers. And most of the officers did not have the opportunity to further their fields of education. SRCs immediately perceived the Freedom of the Press as an enemy. That restricted the debates for the common good. The regime weighed loyalty for its existence above education, honesty, and the ability to serve.

When the power got into one hand, and the ideology became "My way is the sole right," the public and the elite views did not count anymore, which resulted in more than three decades of 'Tiih (Meehanaw (Jaahwareer))"—chaos in loops.

Chapter seventeen referenced notes

My American Journey, 565
Time Magazine, December 21, 199
U.S. News and World Report on December, 14, 21, 1992
Newsweek, February 22, 1993

Warriors by Hanley
I interviewed my father in Gaalkacyo in December, 1996
How 6000 refugees Transform an American town by Cynthia Anderson From Tyranny to Anarch: The Somali Experience by Hussein M. Adam

CHAPTER EIGHTEEN (Jan. 1993- April 1996)

Consequences of Undefined Objectives

Four weeks of the Operation Restore Hope, in the first week of January 1993, a foreign aid worker was assassinated in Mogadishu. Then in the same month, snipers fired on an American convoy. There is a well-known training slogan of the American security forces. It says, "Be the killer instead of being the killed."

In retaliation of the snipers, U.S. Marines fired on a crowd in a Mogadishu street. They killed eight Sammies (skinny Somalis) as Americans used to call them. From there on, both sides defined the mission differently.

The relief operation changed from defense to offense, and the new policy-shift did not make the situation easy for anybody. The offensive strategy of the military put all foreign agencies in the country in a very risk safety situation.

In Somalia, the word of mouth quickly reaches beyond the intentions in minutes. The news of the incident spread with misinterpretations, and the intimidating style of the American forces immediately became the talk of the city. The clan fighting in the capital ceased temporarily.

On March 4, 1993, the U.S. handed over the control of the Operation Restore Hope to the United Nations. UNOSOM One which some warlords such as Aideed previously accused it of siding with a local warlord, Ali Mahdi became UNOSOM Two. Another Political Reconciliation Conference, Addis Ababa One had been tried and held in Addis Ababa, the capital of Ethiopia. It was March 15-27, 1993. The major points were (a) Disarmament and security, (b) rehabilitation and reconstruction, (c) restoration of property and settlement of disputes, (d) transitional mechanisms and (e) conclusions. But the bottom line of the Addis Ababa agreements was (a) to form an Interim Integration Council immediately, and (b) to form an Interim Government to hold democratic elections within two years.

Agreements reached in Addis Ababa had not materialized. There were too many hands in it, and the Somali leaders could not escape from them. They failed their citizens again. Operation Restore Hope eased the starvation and somewhat banditry, and one thing left was political stability.

The food was getting to the destinations, and farmers were put to work expecting a good harvest. But those who had the guns and were determined to use them refused to be forced unemployed. Somali gunmen killed two Italian journalists on March 20 of 1993.

Whether the killing was politically motivated or not, the UNOSOM got a valid reason to enforce peace from that day. While still, the reconciliation conference was taking place in Ethiopia, without consulting with the Somali leaders, the UN approved a new resolution.

The bureaucracy in New York which portrayed Aideed as a threat to peace and security capitalized on the situation. It proposed to neutralize Aideed's militia. The UN Security Council passed Resolution #794 on December 3, 1993 and said, "Establish as soon as possible a secure environment for humanitarian relief operations in Somalia."

On June 5, a Sunday, the Pakistani UN peacekeepers attacked the National Radio Station of Somalia without warning, which the Somali National Alliance of Aideed controlled in Mogadishu. During the shootout between the loyal forces of Aideed and the UN Pakistani forces, 24 Pakistani soldiers and some relief workers lost their lives, Somalis, close to hundred.

Later in May 1994, high UN officers conducted an investigation of the incident and published an article published in The New York Times confirmed that the UN forces started the provocation.

The report showed that the UN erred the situation since it violated its mandate to survey the radio station of the SNA. The UN and the US leaders in Mogadishu decided to silence the SNA radio without full approval from New York.

Most probably, the UN would claim a victory if the attack would have been successful. After the Bay of Pigs invasion of 1961 when America failed with that operation, and finger-pointing could not stop, president JFK said, "Victory has thousands, defeat is orphan." General Thomas Montgomery, an American officer who was then the acting chairman of the United Nations force, had without telling the Pakistani commander of the Somali reaction, sent Pakistani troops on June 5 to inspect an Aideed weapons storage site in the same building.

Previously, the chairman of SNA, General Farah warned that any attempt to inspect his weapons storage would lead to war. The SNA had a good reason to refuse inspection. The disarmament was not fair that its bottom line was to weaken Aideed's militia. After the deadly clash without proper investigation and appropriate consultation with the concerned parties, they blamed SNA for the killing.

The Pakistanis who had long enjoyed peace with the Somalis lost their buddies and got angry. American Central Intelligence Agency (CIA) which initially firmly advised against the involvement fed the operation leaders that Aideed was the only threat to peace in Somalia. For sure, he was a threat to peace but not the only one.

On June 11, 1993, American warplanes indiscriminately started bombing on locations suspected of weapons dumps and other sites that warlord Aideed controlled. The raid continued for a couple of days. President Clinton declared it a complete success. The U.S.-led UN leaders authorized the punishment of the Somali factions blamed for the death of the Pakistanis. More than 65 Somalis lost their lives plus four UN personnel.

The public peacefully took to the streets on June 13, 1993, complaining about the offensive actions. Angry Pakistani soldiers fired on the crowd of mostly women and children killing 20 Somalis and wounding more than 50. The Pakistanis took the law into their own hands. Foreign journalists witnessed and confirmed that Pakistani soldiers opened fire first without warning from a sandbagged fortress. the Pakistanis claimed that they acted on self-defense.

This is how on Tuesday, June 15 depending where you live, The New York Times stated "Gunmen, an obviously rattled group of Pakistani peacekeepers opened fire on the Somali civilians. It was precisely the wrong target; women, children, and civilian demonstrators are not the enemies in Mogadishu.

The Pakistanis' grievous error handed a propaganda windfall to the Mogadishu Warlord, Mohamed Farah Aideed."

After the Pakistanis fired on the demonstrators, and finger pointing escalated. Then, General Hassan of Pakistani Contingent said, "His soldiers were authorized to shoot at armed gunmen even if they were in a crowd." UNOSOM decided to disarm the mass and launched a door-to door search of weapons.

Though killing the Somalis and then justifying it became a trend, reacting to the searches, the Somali gunmen killed three Italians through the process. The temporary peace was disturbed.

The UN defined Aideed as the only challenger and the peace spoiler. He was the only one on the way of the UNOSOM in Mogadishu at that time.

Putting Tag on General Aideed

The United Nations took one step further. Having decided to test the military capability of General Aideed, the UN urgently passed another resolution. "Arrest and detention for prosecution" of "those responsible for killing the Pakistanis" and "the disarmament of all the Somalia parties," said resolution #837. The accused, the strongest Somali Warlord, General Mohamed Farah Aideed was the target. The UN directly declared war with the SNA of Aideed.

Knowing that their country was behind them, American leaders in Mogadishu deeply got involved with the hunting of the General. The objectives of using necessary force to protect humanitarian operations and waging war against a particular warlord got mixed.

U.S. Policy in Somalia: Hearing Before the Committee on Foreign Relations, United States Senate, One Hundred Third Congress, First Session, 29 July 1993, Vol.1 (www.forgottenbooks.org), page 10, Peter Tarnoff, Under Secretary of State:

Some of the questions which are being looked at is to have him (General Mohamed Farah Aideed) tried under Somalia law. The Somali code of Justice could be fairly applied, given the current situation in Somalia. One of the alternatives is to see whether the international system, the U.N. in particular, could authorize a tribunal to be established.

Senator Kassebaum, page 3:

I strongly agree with Admiral Howe that the U. N. must move to apprehend General Aideed. He is someone who has continually tested the U.N. He is in many ways, a thug in how he has handled his role in trying to restore stability to his own country. The sooner he is brought to justice, I think, the better the entire U. N. operation will succeed and the country will be more quickly restore.

Some of what said of General Farah were true, but he was not in custody. Just capturing him was foreseen as granted. On behalf of the United Nations, Howe told reporters that they wanted to capture Aideed alive and put him on trial.

The retired general, UN Envoy, Mr. Howe said, "We have a clan leader who had declared war on the UN operation, and is trying to obstruct our mandate."

Without serious discussions with among senior U.S. policy-makers over the expanding of the Somalia operation from peace-keeping to hunting down Mohamed Farah Aideed, Admiral Jonathan Howe also put $25,000 reward on the head of general Aideed (My American Journey, 583). Aideed announced $100,000 for the capture of the American General as a counteroffer. It was a cat-and mouse game.

The Somalis who lost everything except their violent minds were no longer afraid of anything gathered their resources to support their warlord. The countries of the coalition forces had different peacekeeping policies where some juniors were trying sabotage the Superpower, or the Un.

Though the UNOSOM put all the available resources together to apprehend Mohamed Farah Aideed, the operation ran its own courses. Mr. Farah firmly defied the coalition forces and gained overwhelming public support.

Even those who previously hated him finally supported him for what he stood for. For sure, some stood with him for fun of war. There is an Arab idiom: "My brother and I fight against our cousin, I and my brother and my cousins against the world."

General Howe dreamed of capturing Aideed, and there was not a math formula to accomplish. In the same token, the chairman of SNA, General Aideed had an opposing objective. He was determined to kick the coalition forces out of his country. None of the two generals knew an easy solution to the problem, but the game favored the Somali General. He was running all the operations from the underground. During the crisis, general Aideed never left Mogadishu.

A very reliable political insider told me that Aideed was sometimes among the demonstrators, cross-dressed. UNOSOM leaders, on the other hand, relied on American military muscle, which imposed a Rambo (An American movie made in 1982 of Vietnam war which Silvester Stallone was the actor) approach on the nation.

As a final preparation, Howe, the retired American General, Turkish Lieutenant General Ceric Bir, the UN commander and the American commander Major General Thomas Montgomery asked for extra precision weapons.

America provided AC-130 strike planes to attack the strongholds of General Mohamed Farah Aideed. The Secretary of Defense, Les Aspin delayed approving the request, but about 400 U.S. commandos arrived in Mogadishu in early August.

The media was ahead of everybody and the journalists started to analyze where and how the UN will try General Aideed. They speculated that six African judges on a ship would try him. The American Airborne units increased their searches for General Farah.

American Naval Destroyers were sailing at the Indian Ocean shores of Mogadishu and their loaded Helicopters circled above the capital and pounded the strongholds of General Farah on June 17, 1993. Many toilets in Mogadishu are open at the top, and as a result, the Somali women were very shy to use their own toilets.

On the ground, the UN troops stormed Aideed's compounds. The casualties were 4 UN peacekeepers and more than 70 Sammies dead, and over a hundred wounded.

Most of the Somali casualties were women and children. There is a different version in this. Somalis at the place during the raid confirmed over 100 killed and 200+ wounded.

As mentioned earlier, te term "Human Rights" has a couple of meanings in the American White House. During the Gulf war, U.S. fighter planes intentionally bombed civilian bunker in Baghdad to assassinate Saddam Hussein. They bombed Libya in 1986 where women and children lost their lives.

Noriega, the ruler of Panama in 1983-1989, signaled for not renewing the lease of the Panama Canal. They attacked Panama, captured the leader, tried him and kept him in prison for many years. It is a widely known American policy that when American interests are on the line, Human Rights of other than Americans are secondary.

During the hunting down General Mohamed Farah Aideed, American led UN forces killed Somali civilians. They carried the attacks knowing that the civilian casualties would be high. Perhaps, forgetting that the Somalis are speech analysts, General Montgomery said, "The strike had been planned carefully. We knew precisely where every piece of equipment was." "The assault was essential," Clinton added.

The Somalis were well aware that at that moment, the ultimate goal of the U.S. was to get General Farah. And though still at large, he was a heavily armed warlord vying for power in a civil war devastated the country after the overthrow of General Mohamed Siyad Barre.

The public, mostly those loyal to the cause of Aideed was willing to fight until the last drop of blood. Howe and his Generals were obsessed to kill or capture the Somali warlord. They knew that finding Aideed in the streets and houses of Mogadishu was a very remote chance. They cared less who would be killed during the process.

In general, Somalis are not very secretive people. More than 30 Somali informers were on the payroll of UNOSOM. Bombing any place tipped as a hideout of General Farah became a norm.

American forces attacked SNA compounds having tipped that weapons were inside on July 12, 1993. More than 40 Somalis and 4 photographers lost their lives with 200 Sammies wounded.

High-ranking officers of Italy, Saudi Arabia, and U.A.E expressed their anger about the attack, but Uncle Sam downplayed it. From June 5, 1993, up to July 12, the number of UN soldiers killed raised to 35 and 137 wounded.

Somalia crisis made headlines on the first pages again. It became a political arena for all foreign countries which thought they could have a shot influencing the political outcomes of that African nation.

On August 8, a mine blast killed 4 American soldiers. They were the first U.S. combat deaths since the UN took over of the peacekeeping operations in May. That also raised the number of U.S. troops killed in Somalia to 12. American citizens started questioning the policy of Clinton in Somalia. They became angry at their servicemen killed and wanted to be justified.

Somali leaders spoke up for their civilians killed as well. Because they were divided and had not yelled loud enough earlier, and they were the ones starving and bulleting their own people, western media had no ears for them.

Speaking of Americans killed, the U.S. media which knocks on any door to get to the minds of the politicians did not let President Clinton have a quiet Sunday on August 9. They forced him to give a signal.

"We will do everything we can to find out who was responsible and take appropriate action," he told reporters on his way to the Church. His advisers about the mission told him that killing or capturing General Aideed was the only way out of this crisis.

Then, hunting down Mohamed Farah Aideed became global. Both the UN and the U.S. saw General Aideed as the only one in their way. But General Aideed was the one who forced Mohamed Siyad Barre to leave Mogadishu. He was not in any way, whatsoever, planning to leave his country for the U.S., the UN or anyone else. He saw himself as the one who should replace Barre.

Regardless of more than 30,000 deaths during his campaign, two-thirds of that in the capital, to his followers, he was a Somali nationalist.

To be a nationalist, the love of your nation has to come first and to achieve that goal you have to accept humiliation, defeat and swallow a major portion of your pride. Few Somali leaders reached that stage like Michael Mariano, Abdullahi Isse, Aden Abdulle Osman, the pilot who landed at DiJabuuti instead of bombing Hargeysa and Burco. General Mohamed Farah Aideed was a Somali who cannot be named with that group.

When the Hunting Down of Aideed was going on, in Mogadishu, there were at least ten more political factions—most of them branched from USC (Kenneth:133). We cannot call them nationalists either. Somali nationalists are mostly unknown.

A Somali informer tipped the U.S. army where he thought Aideed was hiding on August 30, 1993. American forces raided the place capturing Somalis and UN employees. The tip was a hoax. Some of the tips that informers intentionally relayed to the UNOSOM leaders were setup.

Seven Nigerian UN forces were killed on September 6, 1993. Before the fighting, Somali elders at the Pasta factory told the Nigerian troops to leave. But whoever they got the order from, Nigerians provoked. Some rumors said that Italians set the incident being pushed out of the main arena by the superpower. There were rumors that Italians were selling weapons to Aideed and other warlords as well.

At the beginning of the operation, Italy portrayed itself as a junior superpower in the Somalia affairs and wanted broader participation. But the real superpower (America) told it to behave. There were a couple of reasons why Italy wanted to have a more say in the Somalia affairs.

First, other than being a former colonizer of the region giving them an edge of how to deal with the Somalis, Italy was the main consumer of the Somali banana which later became a war of itself between Dole, an American owned company and Italian farmers where the casualties of both sides were Somalis.

Second, the Italian Ambassador to Somalia, Enrico Augelli, was the only, or one of the foreign diplomats remained in Mogadishu on January 27, 1991, the last day of Barre's rule which is also known as The Last Day of Modern Somali State.

Third, Italy always preferred to weigh more on the reconciliatory approach than military might.

Fourth, until the incident of June 5, General Mohamed Farah Aideed whom after the clash of June 5, the UN defined him as a war criminal, terrorist and the Saddam Hussein of Africa was a close friend of the White House in Somalia.

Before June 5, Robert Godsend, the American Diplomat who replaced Oakley whom we talked about him earlier had a message from the White House to Mogadishu. "Give Aideed whatever he wants." But regardless of how Rome felt, Italian troops in Somalia of about 2600 were forced to move from the UN peacekeeping troops in Mogadishu to a none important location. Some of them have been stationed in Aadan Yabaal, a town near Mogadishu where their mission in there was another very ill-fated operation worse than what Canadians have done in Beledweyne.

Which leads to the point of why an American dead body was dragged on Mogadishu streets, on 9 September 9, 1993, U.S. Cobra helicopter fired into a crowd and killed more than 100 Sammies. One of the peacekeepers was killed and four wounded which raised the total number to 48 and the Somalis in the neighborhood of thousands.

During that raid, the Somali gunmen ambushed U.S. combat engineers, Pakistani forces and blew up a Pakistani M-48 tank when it tried to come to the rescue. Southern Mogadishu became a war zone.

The contract of Howe was up for renewal at the end of October, and he did not want to be replaced as a scapegoat. With bad intelligence and perhaps underestimation of Aideed, the U.S.-directed UN forces got into an ugly course with the most powerful warlord in Somalia and showed him as an outlaw.

In 1993, Aideed did see himself as the only future president of Somalia. Losing Mogadishu by Jonathan Stevenson, 79 writes, "He (Aideed) had not any interest in reconciliation except within his own clan, the Hawiye. He (Aideed, "There is no comparison between Ali Mahdi's forces and mine. I control 11 of the 18 regions in Somalia." The General counted out all other warlords except Egal in Somaliland." That was delusional that General Farah could bend other power-hungry clan leaders to his agenda. In his calculation, Hawiye and Isaaq were only in business.

Since the political viability of Somalia existed as such at that time, Sahnoun cleverly avoided any incident like that during his UN leadership in Somalia.

That time, the UNOSOM leadership was deeply preoccupied with capturing Aideed, but the goals of the involved nations collided. The name was a UN operation, but the operation became a pure American show. Clinton's foreign policy became under fire in the Congress, and from the allies as well. The four hundred Rangers and Delta-Force commandos which arrived in early August have launched a massive manhunt.

"America has no intentions of dictating of Somalia's political outcomes" by Former President Bush passed its limits. American army showed the intimidating style.

The informers were tracking the whereabouts of the General Farah. Although the perception of the American troops of "simple people, simple problems and simple solutions" faded away, they did not change their attitude towards the Somalis. Hunting down the general united the public against Uncle Sam. In reality, the UN easily dragged the U.S. army further into the mud, the manhunt.

The UN wanted disarmament while the US preferred negotiations. There were claims that in some occasions Aideed used women and children as human shields to divert attacks against his militia.

American military training is an intimidation. Corporal James Moore (losing Mogadishu: 59) said, "In a normal combat environment, you dehumanize the enemy—that is your job: to eliminate him."

On September 14, 1993, again, UNOSOM leaders received a tip that General Aideed was having a meeting at the Olympic Hotel. The Un forces raided the hotel. One U.S. Cobra was shot down killing three American soldiers.

Then, two days after, on September 16, two Italian peacekeepers were shot dead while jogging. UN Generals were pressured to do something about the situation. For Aideed, hunting him down, boosted his political and military positions. After all, it was Aideed's game, typical Somali guerrilla warfare.

Again, on September 25, 1993, three U.S. peacekeepers lost their lives when an army Blackhawk helicopter on normal patrol was hit by a rocket-propelled grenade and crashed. The pressure on both sides was insurmountable.

When the crisis peaked, the White House thought to move away from the hunting General Aideed and isolate him from the Somali political arena. But that would have been explained as a submission and could not be done either.

The Deadly Tip

The confrontation between the SNA of General Aideed and the UNOSOM reached its boiling point. June 5, 1993, was a Sunday. October 23, 1983, America lost 241 Marines in Beirut, Lebanon was a Sunday too (US News and World Report, October 8, 1993). Finally, on Sunday, October 3, 1993, the deadly tip came through. The American Rangers and the U.S. Delta Force ran head-to-head into a stiff firefight in Somalia with Aideed's SNAs. Two cobras were downed killing 18 Americans, wounding 77 and a helicopter pilot captured.

The battle was going on in excess of fifteen hours. Over 500 (Kenneth:160) Somalis lost their lives and 700 wounded. Most of them were women and children.

The Somalis kept fighting just to show the Americans that they can fight regardless of the firepower against them.

We will see some American quotations of the number of Somalis killed during the operation. U.S. forces had videotaped the operation. Movies were made, and many books published. The names of the Somalis killed, who they were counted for!

In the United States, later, when the media requested the videotapes, the defense department rejected to release them claiming that the technology used to make the film is too sensitive to reveal. The scenes included two U.S. range helicopters crashing, two members of a sniper team dropping from a helicopter to protect their survivors of one crash until the snipper, in turn, run out of ammunition, and another small helicopter making a daring landing in the middle of a street to rescue wounded troops.

While the American pilot was in the hands of SNA, dead body of an American serviceman was dragged on the streets of Mogadishu. The American public was horrified by the incident and the death of their servicemen. "Once again, TV images were shaping American foreign policy."

In the Somali side, "Somalis who lost everything no longer feared anything." President Clinton quickly reviewed the American foreign policy in Somalia which resulted to announce the withdrawal from the Horn of Africa on March 31, 1994. Around that time, not more than dozen international NGOs stayed in Mogadishu,

But the policy review did not end without a cost. As mentioned earlier, Les Aspin, the secretary of defense, and other top aides were forced to resign. As a private citizen, Aspin died in 1995. He was 56 years old. While negotiating for the release of the pilot looking for someone to blame for his foreign policy's failure, President Clinton accused the UN of assigning American troops the police function of finding people responsible for the killings of the Pakistani soldiers.

The Americans went to Somalia perhaps with a wrong perception, and misunderstanding and for sure left it with disappointment.

When it was badly needed, the UN did not fully consult with the humanitarian organizations which had been in the country longer than anyone else except the indigenous. Before the UN decided to intervene, the international NGOs learned how to go around in terms of to whom to talk. For that reason and so on, perhaps the UN did not like that the Somalis identified more with others other than itself.

The New Yorker, March 20, 1995 writes "There were more than 1000 local NGOs (Somali NGOs) in Mogadishu alone to channel foreign funds into mostly fake projects for personal gain. They are in different magnitudes and with different backings, but it is a known fact that Political tensions always bring big relief operations." Somalis made Somalia a prey all kinds of predators invited themselves. December 2010, international NGOs claimed that there was a famine in Mogadishu. Former prime minister of Somalia, Abdiweli Mohamed Ali (*War Crimes of Rasna*

Warah, 81) rejected that notion and said, "Aid Agencies became an entrenched interest group and they say all kinds of things they want to say. They are Lords of poverty. I do not believe there is a famine in Mogadishu. Absolutely not."

The NGOs, on the other hand, felt that the UN leadership in New York did not give much consideration to their safety. Both the UN and the United States acted as authoritarians than mediators. The first special envoy, Mohamed Sahnoun was not there anymore and a new person in his position, Ismat Kitani, an Iraqi Kurd, who was new to the people and the area as well, took a long time to learn the ropes.

All the Envoys after Sahnoun lacked his extensive knowledge of the area and the people, charisma, tirelessness, conviction of understanding of the Somali mind which was an important key to solving problems. He always wanted the consent of the warlords and proposed the limited deployment of arms at selected points. He was familiar with the Somalis' fear of foreign occupation. Since UNOSOM Two took over, hundreds of UN officers lost their lives for lack of thorn-picking in advance.

Without the massive airlifts of relief supplies, especially the most needed food and medicine to remote areas by the U.S. Air Force, the German Air Force, the Royal Canadian, and many others, the number of people died for starvation would have been much higher than it was when the operation ended.

About the Operation Restore Hope, America lost 44 servicemen in Somalia. The original justification for sending foreign troops to Somalia was easy and appropriate, and the exit was quick with disappointment. The UN failed Somalia politically when it took sides in the internal power struggles, but without a doubt, Operation Restore Hope saved so many lives.

On October 17, 1993, the UN Security Council unanimously voted to formally call off (Resolution 885) the hunt for General Aideed because of the pressure from the United States. "Human rights violations" is one of the excuses that Western countries use when they want to meddle with the internal politics of disobedient nations.

And when it comes to looking after the American goals and objectives, human rights of other citizens are not counted. Geneva convention is another fundamental rule as written to be respected.

But let us see some American actions which for sure some Americans might feel good about how their enemies were eliminated. The Battle of Mogadishu: 116-117:

I remember seeing a woman who kept running into the alleyway in front of us and directing fire for RPG (rocket propelled Grenade) gunners positioned in front of us. We had to determine whether she was an innocent caught in the crossfire, and so the first couple of times she came out we let it go because we were not really sure what she doing. But it quickly became apparent that she was acting as a spotter, or a forward observer, for the Somali gunners, and she was counting on the fact that we would not shoot her. We were all busy shooting at the targets (Somalis), though at one point I remember asking captain C., our team leader, what we should do, and he gave the order that we should take her out.

On page 184: Whether he had been hit by Pringle or not, I don't know. It looked like he (Somali man) was hurt; he had a grimace on his face. I shot him first, two rounds in the chest. I drew a bead on the guy next to him and shot him in the chest with two more rounds in rapid succession.

On page 205: After Durante's release we were going home. We lost eighteen guys on Somali soil, killed hundreds of Somalis, and took down half of Aideed's leadership. We broke one of the cardinal rules."

When Siyad Barre was forced out of Villa Somalia (presidential complex), many people whom he exiled, imprisoned, bombarded and shot their loved ones on the name of his administration felt good. But for sure, what came after him is beyond their imagination. However, in the eyes of the other people, you are a Somali.

I do not tell you where and when in Somalia, but I have to tell this piece. There was a meeting between a UN delegation and some Somali leaders. I was there and was to make some interpretations. A white man of the UN delegation said, "What happened between U.S. Rangers and Aideed militia put off many western countries to help Somalia."

A Somali leader said, "Those who killed the Americans are not us." I felt bad, and I did not say that in English. The Somali man was also fluent in English. So, when I declined to put his words into English, he said to me in Somali, "You should interpret the words in the way they are said, or you should not be in this business from the beginning."

The UN head of the delegation who was a Canadian was referring to the world politics, specially the one of United States. Humanitarianism under fire by Kenneth Rutherford, 167, "After the international communities departed, Somalia disappeared from the most diplomatic and media radars until a few years after the September 11, 2002, terrorist attacks, when Osama Bin Laden declared Somalia the third front, after Afghanistan and Iraq, on the global Islamic war against the United States."

Finally, most Somalis hated Aideed, but they had been proud of how he challenged the Americans. According to the Somali culture, death is a very acceptable outcome when it comes to despising and humiliating.

Perhaps, Americans did not bother to know more about the cultures and the customs of the people. The New York Times of October 7, 1993, said, "Operation Restore Hope started with pictures and ended with pictures." And at the same time, none of the pictures looked good.

Many nations took part in the Operation Restore Hope and saved thousands of lives.

But an article "Who Needs Tears, December 27, 1993 which quoted The New York Times of December 8, 1993, General Anthony Zinni, a U.S. director of military during the Restore Hope Operation was quoted as "between June 5 and October 3 there were anywhere from 6,000 to 10,000 Somali casualties (dead and wounded), of whom maybe two thirds were women and children of Aideed's clan, who 'Felt they were on the edge of clan eradication,' bore the brunt."

When American forces subdued Mogadishu shores in December of 1992 and early 1993, Operation Restore Hope looked easy for many. Staff Sgt. Richard Roberts, 29 of St. Louis (Somalia Diary: 109), "We came to help people here and we succeeded. If America goes home now, who can do the job? If we go home, the UN mission will probably fall and Somalia will probably go back to where it was, or even worse."

Chapter eighteen referenced notes

UN Resolution #794, 837
My American Journey, 583
Kenneth Rutherford, 133, 160, 167
Losing Mogadishu by Jonathan Stevenson, 79
US News and World Report, October 8, 1993
The New Yorker, March 20, 1995
UN Resolution 885
The Battle of Mogadishu: 116-117, 184, 205
The New York Times of October 7, 1993
The Nation of December 27, 1993
War Crimes: How Warlords, Politicians, Foreign Governments and Aid Agencies Conspired to Create a Failed State in Somalia, Paperback, 2014 by Rasna Warah

CHAPTER NINETEEN

Canadian Role of Operation Restore Hope

There is no question that Canada is one of the best countries to live in and be proud to be a citizen of it. It was a member of the coalition of Restore Hope. However, some men of the Canadian Airborne Regiment which the government disbanded in January 1995 were a bunch of racists. And when it did find out, the government respected the law of the land. Heads rolled and the whole units were dismantled.

On the night of March 16, 1993, Shidane Abukar Arone, a 16 years old, Somali prisoner, was tortured and beaten to death by Clayton Matchee, a master corporal serving with the Canadian Airborne Regiment Battle Group in Somalia. This crime sparked the biggest peacetime scandal in the history of the Canadian Armed Forces [Significant Incident: Canada's Army, the Airborne, and the murder in Somalia by David Bercuson: Cover].

Regardless of who (Somalis) were clapping when southern Somalia was inundated with forces, today, any one of them can hardly look if they can find the pictures of the Somali teenage whom the Canadian peacekeepers tortured to death.

During the Restore Hope Operation of 1992, the Airborne Regiment of Canada was stationed in Beledweyne of Somalia. Young Somali men started stealing weapons, radio parts, personal effects, and army rations anything of value they could carry out of their vehicles and the camp perimeter. Those actions made the Airborne Regiment very angry and decided to answer. That resulted from the torture to death of Somali men.

Though Clayton Matchee, a master corporal served with the Canadian Airborne Regiment Battle Group in Somalia was convicted for it, Shidane Abuukar Arone

(Shidane Abuukar Caroon), a Somali man of 16 was beaten to death knowingly by a group of Canadian troops from March 16, 1993, to the 17th. Not only he was killed, but for four hours, Canadians soldiers tortured him, even when he was already dead.

By the time the United Nations was lobbying for military involvement in Somalia, Canada, one of the yes-nations when a global decision had to be made by the United States had decided to contribute troops for Operation Restore Hope, an American-led UN operation.

During the preparation of the Somalia mission, the Canadian senior military officers knew well in advance that there were longstanding disciplinary problems within 180-man of 2 units commando including a self-styled "Rebels" faction. The two commando-unit adopted the U.S. Confederate flag as its symbol and had a reputation for heavy drinking and creating troubles for themselves, especially those who don't follow their self-designed guidelines. Mr. Mackenzie who did not leave behind a good reputation when Bosnians are concerned was informed about the problems with the unit as a superior general.

Furthermore, the high-rank military officers were also well aware that the Canadian Airborne Regiment harbored soldiers with ties to hate groups and therefore, something was very wrong with the culture of the institution. The federal government had been informed but turned a blind eye.

Canada sent 1,200 troops to Somalia for a peacekeeping mission with racist soldiers in it. The media was airing the good side of the Airborne and the operation from the Canadian perspective.

Shortly after they were dispatched to Beledweyne, abusing the natives started. The commander of the Airborne battle group, Colonel Serge Labbe said to his soldiers, "I am looking forward to my first dead Somali" and "A case of champagne (beer) to the first person who gets or kills a Somali? " One officer, Mark Boland, was one time chastised by another officer for not killing an intruder.

Initial Military Coverup

Until someone blew the whistle, and the media aired certain embarrassing violent acts of the Canadian troops in Somalia, the Airborne had the support of the whole country. But many innocent Somalis whom some we may never know their ordeals disappeared.

In parallel to this, from the head office of the Airborne in Beledweyne, beginning from December 1992 to July 1993, the soldiers were ordered to destroy photos and other evidence as part of an effort to conceal repeated acts of violence in the ugliest terms.

Documents later obtained through to The Access to Information Act, confirmed that in October 1992, some soldiers of the Airborne set fire to a sergeant's car,

Lieutenant-Colonel, Paul Montreal, the commanding officer of the Airborne as it prepared to go to Somalia. He urged his immediate superior, a Brig. General, Ernest Bono, not to send the 2commando unit to Somalia. The officer, Col. Paul told his boss that the unit did not meet the standards of a peacekeeping mission.

He also proposed to delay the commando unit until it was dealt with. But instead of looking into the matter in its merit, the General replaced the Lieutenant-Colonel with a Colonel who later faced a court martial for the Regiment's involvement in the torture and murder of Shidane.

Despite the inadequate training and the misconduct of the self-styled rebel faction units, the Generals deliberately allowed their soldiers to do many bad things to the Somali society.

On January 27, 1993, five Somalis were photographed and put on public display with signs saying "Thieves around their neck." Another soldier while beating a Somali said, "Shut up, fucking nigger, go ahead, pray to Allah." On January 28, 1993, a senior officer ordered the destruction of photos taken on the 27th (Toronto Star, November 11, 1995).

Abuses did not stop until at last, one high moral Canadian officer came forward and broke the silence.

The information became widely known on April of 1993 after a reporter from Pembroke of Ontario, Canada, 150 KM northwest of Ottawa, wrote about the death For the Pembroke Observer (Magazine/Newspaper). The reporter had previously heard about the violent actions of the soldiers while being in Beledweyne to report the activities of the soldiers from Petawawa, the original base of the units, near Pembroke. The released information to the media and later learned by the public raised serious questions, not only the discipline, accountability and the failure of leadership among the units' senior officers but also how much information of the case the federal government knowingly withheld to stop the further embarrassment.

The Chief of the Defense Staff (Rav Castelli) of the then Prime Minister learned about the death only hours after it took place. The prime minister herself, Ms. Campbell later admitted that she was briefed about the death on the 17th.

Then on April 28, 1993, the Prime Minister contradicted herself and told the Canadian House of Commons that she was informed of the incident on March 31 of 1993, when military police returned from Somalia.

In this world of the information highway, it was hard to accept that the top policy-maker and the Defense Minister did not learn about the incident shortly after it reached the Chief of the Defense Staff.

Neither the Prime Minister nor the minister of defense also spoke to the public when they got the news. The federal election was coming which the Prime Minister was campaigning to be elected for the job as the Conservative Party leader.

The Liberal party leaders who later the Somalia scandal dragged them into political hot spots were at that time blaming the Conservative of Campbell for a coverup. Finally, when the story became public, the country learned more details of the mission and the fate of the Airborne.

More of The Agony

During the court hearings, soldiers and officers alike confirmed that the beating death of Shidane was not an isolated incident. Most of the details of the ugly mistreatment against those they supposed to help did not come out as they were learned. Agonizing some of the natives began as soon as the Canadians have replaced the Americans in Beledweyne.

March 4, 1993, almost two weeks before the death of Arone, Ahmed Afrah Aruush was shot in the back while fleeing the members of the Airborne. Aruush 29, was killed and his friend Abdi Hunde Beir Sabrie was wounded unarmed at the outside of the Canadian military compound.

When the press got involved, more important pieces of evidence disappeared, some for good. Before the media learned the death of Shidane Arone, a military investigation was delayed for five weeks which in that period, the chain of command had plenty of time to destroy relevant information and be prepared to sell their side of the story.

And until certain gruesome videotapes were obtained, in any part of the government, neither the federal nor the defense or the military, there was no urgency whatsoever to the new inquiry. Ottawa never completely addressed the root of the affair until late 1994, and we may never get to the bottom of it.

Some officers admitted in the military court that senior officers tolerated killing, raping and torturing the Somalis. Officers charged in the incident said in front of the military court that not only the officers allowed any kind of abuse against the Somalis, but ordered to the prisoners for whatever.

One officer, Mr. Boland (Maclean's March 28, 1994) writes, "Thieves have slipped through the wire on two previous occasions and I deemed it necessary to put a stop on those infiltrations. I said I want the prisoners to be captured. I did not care if they abused them." "I want the prisoners to be captured."

Does that mean that all the people in Beledweyne were prisoners, and it did not matter who they would capture? Or was he talking about those already in captivity? Not only the racism was in the military, but even the media was until later covering the scandal as for the defense of the military.

From 9 PM until midnight of March 16, 1993 (next day actually), Shidane was being abused and finally, in tribulation, beaten to death (Maclean's, March 28, 1994). The ordeal took more than four hours. They had beaten him with a wooden riot baton and a metal pipe. Shidane was crying 'Canada! Canada! Canada!" during the torture. As soon as they caught him, they handcuffed, blindfolded and bound him by ropes. At least 16 Canadians heard him crying or witnessed during the captivity, and none bothered to stop the tribulation.

The Canadian government was ever trying to cover up the murder, and the other abuses. The night of the Shidane's torture, officer Boland, the one who was reprimanded for not killing Somalis said to his fellow soldiers, "I don't care what you do, just do not kill him." A Major called Tony Seward, one of the commanding officers who ordered his troops to "abuse" prisoners had been in the bunker and fully participated in the torture. The torture of Shidane took more than four hours. The following is how the man had been tortured minute by minute. From 8:40 P.M. to 9:20 P.M.:

Shidane was captured at March 16, 1993. He was immediately' detained while soldiers started kicking and punching him. His arms were bound behind his back and handcuffed, then turned over to a 2 Commando platoon leader. Captain Michael Sox. The platoon leader. Mr. Sox placed a riot baton between the Shidane's arms and his (Shidane) body. Another Canadian by the name of Brown joined Sox. They took Arone to a nearby bunker made of sandbags used as a holding cell. A third soldier joined the two and beer drinking started.

From 10:00 to 11:500 PM:

Some of the soldiers became drunk. They increased their actions. Kicking him went on for several minutes. Then something very alarming happened. Amazingly, they washed him up and told him to relax. For what reason one may ask. Most probably, since some of them were drunk, the for sexual abuse. however, Arone could not hold and fell asleep. KIC ng him regardless of where on his body was going on intermittently. The amusement and the torturing of the Somali on his soil passed into a second stage.

For later entertainment, they got cameras and took four shots. At that point, they thought he may not survive. And as a result, they started worrying of how to keep the incident out of reaching the media, but the torture increased and some even competed for better torturing. 12 more photographs were taken. Arone was still semiconscious. Some of them made phone calls to their families in Canada. It was clear for some of them that Shidane would not survive from the tribulation. Though they were still hitting him with riot baton, using his feet as ashtrays and each one was making fun out of the agonized man, he could not make any more screams.

It was too late. He was dead. From 11:500 to 1:00 AM. Finally, they realized that he was dead. Hence, he was rushed to a Canadian Field Hospital in Beledweyne where he was pronounced dead. The medical officer of the Canadian troops in Beledweyne placed the time of death at between midnight and 12:15 AM of March 17, 1993.

Videotapes were released to the public later and one broadcasted by the CBC (Canadian Broadcasting Corporation) on January 15, 1995, further explained many things about the circumstance and the history of the Airborne. It showed several members of the unit making racial slurs.

Matt McKay (Corporal) who was a chief master of the nasty group was a member of the Ku Klux Klan, a notorious hate group which promotes white supremacy to claim superiority over any other race.

The military confirmed that he used to be a member of a white supremacist group known as Aryan Nation Group, also called Church of Jesus Christ Christian, prominent Christian Identity—base Hate Group founded in the United States in the 1970s.

In addition to that, the video showed that Matt McKay who was photographed in Winnipeg in a Hitler T-shirt giving a Nazi salute was complaining that he did not kill enough niggers (Maclean's, March 28, 1994). Still, the information passed to the public was just the tip of an iceberg. About 50,000 documents related to the Somalia case, were put together during the first quarter of 1996.

When it became public, at least two walls of a cover-up of the soldiers, the junior officers and of the high-ranking officers including the minister of defense began building up. While in Beledweyne, the soldiers had confidence that if they abuse the natives, they could get away with it, and also knew that if they go down, court-martialed, many senior officers would be dragged into the crime. Officer Brown who was also one of the commanders who approved the torture admitted he was at the bunker (The Toronto Star, 11 November 1995).

When the story broke out in March 1993, because of the federal election, all the relevant information which the government knew were withheld. Another video made in Somalia in 1992 just before the beating death of Shidane but released to the press in 1995, a soldier called PTE. David Brocklebank was shown waving a loaded machine gun and talking about getting niggers. This case became a public outrage because it was caught red-handed by the doctor who blew the whistle.

The scandal made then aware of what was going on in the military's backyard while in Beledweyne and even after the case went public. During the trials, it came out that four more Somalis were killed. Women were also raped. However, of those reported, until later, only Shidane was identified.

The Coverup in The Federal Level

When the military court-martial became inevitable, the different walls of defense to protect each other from punishment further safeguarded. Ten pictures of Shidane's torture became public, but many others were destroyed or concealed at the head office of the Defense Department.

From the top down up, in all levels of the military and civilians alike, many collaborated on concealing, rewriting, and falsifying documents. Even when the case reached the military court, there was a miscarriage of justice.

Some documents showed that the military trial judge erred in instructing the five-officer panel hearing at the trial. One soldier, Mark Boland was re-assigned to another position as a military employed civilian and given 90 days in jail, but later in 1996, the appeal judges increased the jail term to one year and out of the army. A Lieutenant, Michael Sox was lowered in rank to and severely reprimanded (Maclean's, January 30, 1995, Cover).

The nucleus of The Scandal

Despite all, the Somalia case made a U-turn in the last quarter of 1995. Especially in the West, when there is a scandal, as usual, weaker ones first get punished. Though at last in 1996, the prosecutor asked for a more severe sentence for Mr. Seward, Major in rank who was convicted in 1994 of negligent of performance duty over his actions in Somalia and given a severe reprimand, Shidane A. Arone, Ahmed A. Aruush and some others are dead now, and they cannot testify and tell their side of the story.

The government rejected to give visas to many others who were tortured and raped to come to Canada to tell their experiences. In Canada, humanity has a meaning, and people demand it all the times, and they watch the law of the land.

Going back to the story of the Canadian Airborne Regiment, the convictions of the crimes committed, soldiers, junior and middle officers were lightly punished. As the case dragged and as much as the media wanted to dig down, in early 1996, it went on up to the minister of defense. Esprit De Corps, a military Magazine obtained extensive documents. The documents showed that on March 5, 1993, the defense department stopped a military police inquiry in the shooting death of a Somali man.

It is not known yet whether that man was Aruush or not. Vice-Admiral Larry Murray stopped the investigation into March 4 of 1993 (Toronto Sun, December 15, 1995).

This further confirmed that the right from the beginning, the Canadian government, and military superiors, in particular, were aware that the Somalia mission was in deep trouble, and when Armstrong blew the whistle, instead of releasing all they knew, they installed coverups one over the other.

In the military, a Canadian Major, Vincenti Buonamici was the lead investigator of the Somalia case. When his seniors saw him doing the job the way it should be, they intervened. He was advised to keep quiet. Then for not taking the orders, many dirty tricks designed were being played against him. The Major also confirmed that the defense department obtrusively attempted to discredit Major Barry Armstrong, the military surgeon who blew the whistle.

During the investigation, most senior military officers seized the files of Buonamici and threatened him to be kicked out of the military. The generals who interfered the investigation events of Buonamici in Somalia were forced to go early. Taking early retirement in a situation like that had an especial ramification. If later these Generals go to trial and get convicted, they may lose their pension. For that main reason and perhaps more, they decided not to take risks. The last of them had to leave mid-July of 1996. But that was not all.

On January 22, 1996, the prosecutors of the case also asked the military court that Maj. Tony Seward who headed the Regiments 2 commando to Somalia and authorized his men to abuse Somalis while in Beledweyne should be dismissed from the Canadian forces with disgrace. Still, the brunt of the blame was laid on the soldiers and junior officers. Earlier in 1993, the minister of defense David Collenette, said that the RCMP looked into the matter and concluded that there was no evidence of criminal wrongdoing. That was not true.

Since media always run an extra mile for news coverage, it learned that the RCMP, the Royal Canadian Mounties Police did not investigate the case when the minister claimed they did. RCMP was not asked to investigate.

In another time, the minister said in front of the Canadian House of Commons that he was misled by his military staff (Toronto Sun, January 24, 1996). Shifting the scandal away from his boss, the Liberal Prime Minister, that was an unsuccessful attempt of making the case as a dealt with the matter.

Lieutenant-General Jean Boyle, who took over as Chief of Defense Staff effective January 1, 1996, was one of the senior officers who were responsible for the defense of the investigation to the torture of the military scandal of the defense department. They were entrusted with the responsibility of getting to the bottom of the case once and for all.

However, they participated in falsification and rewriting the documents related to the case. CBC obtained some documents with the help of The Access to Information Act with the signature of General Boyle who earlier denied that he did anything wrong.

In Late January of 1996, a lawyer representing General Ernest Beno, the general who replaced the Lieutenant Colonel Paul Montreault in October 1992 when told him that the unit did not suit to be peacekeepers fiercely cross-examined Mr. Montreault, but stuck to his original position (Toronto Sun, December 21, 1995). General Beno had been shown pictures of Somalis being abused in 1993 but did not take any action which shows that as far as it did not reach the press, his troops were nice guys.

When he saw the pictures, he wrote to a Colonel under his direction, Serge

Labbe. He said, "If such photographs were shown to the press, it could disturb the Canadian population (Toronto Sun, October 6, 1995)."

At the end of March 1996, an insider from the public affair office of the military tipped the media that three senior military officers from the defense department destroyed and faked official documents relating to the Somalia affairs.

The insider also leaked the names, and Colonel Geof Haswell who was one of them came forward. He accused the department of trying to make him the scapegoat in the latest Defense debacle involving the deliberate destruction and falsification of the documents.

The Somalia case already passed its expectations. Haswell said, "General Boyle, the Chief of The Defense Staff, had full knowledge of a plan devised in the public affairs office to rename a class of documents relating to the case and then destroyed them routinely." The documents were rewritten erasing highly sensitive and embarrassing pieces of information and then allowed the press to see the rewritten version.

No one can go into the minds of the soldiers and their bosses who ordered the torture against the Somalis. It will take forever to get to the bottom of this case since it is a dealt issue right now.

Nevertheless, the point here in this book is not any more to prove that there were at least three layers of coverups or the magnitude of the scandal, but for the Somali public to educate itself, and for the Somali nationalists regardless where in the society to go beyond this.

Canada is a moral society, and there is no question that it is one of the best countries to live in and be its citizen. The rules of the land are the guiding principles.

Chapter nineteen referenced notes

Significant Incident by David Bercuson: Cover
Toronto Star, November 11, 1995
Toronto Star, November 11, 1995
Pembroke Observer (Magazine/Newspaper)
Maclean's March 28, 1994
Same article, Maclean's, March 28, 1994
CBC Videotapes, January 15, 1995
Maclean's, March 28, 1994
The Toronto Star, November 11, 1995
Maclean's, January 30, 1995, Cover
Esprit De Corps, a military Magazine, March 5, 1993
Toronto Sun, December 15, 1995

Toronto Sun, January 24, 1996
Toronto Sun, December 21, 1995
Toronto Sun, October 6, 1995

Chapter TWENTY

What it takes to Negotiate

"We are not preaching hatred, but we are not going to forget the massacred people."
_Suad (Sucaad Odawaa) of Somaliland at the Somali Heritage Debate in Jibouti, December 14-18/2018.

That statement of Suad reminded me "Si kasta oo aan u goobnay ma aannaan helin qoraal Soomaaliyeed oo si hubsan u qoraya tiradii dadkii Tsunaamigu ka diley Soomaalida iyo magacyadoodii," (no matter how hard we tried, we could not find the exact, or even close, the number of people perished and wounded, and their names of the 2004 Tsunami (Baadisooc by Ali Abdigir, 294)).

Hargeysa

The real question that the Somalis have to ask themselves si: Did the Somali Government bombed its citizens with their planes? If it is yes, then there is no reason not to be angry and talk about it. "It is not a matter of preaching hatred but not to forget about it (Sucaad Carmiye))." Any Somali killed without due process needs a remembrance.

To the records of modern governance, the Somali was neither good enough to govern himself nor comfortable to be governed by another. The Somali must realize one thing before anything, the value of life. It is not an insult to sat that the Somalis are opportunists, fanatics without following the real principles of the religion, always suspicious and vindictive.

It is worth to repeat what the Somali intellectuals said in 1959. The question asked was: Are the Somalis mature enough to govern themselves? The answer was:

No. We cannot manage alone either economically or politically. The day the Europeans leave, we shall start fighting. We shall assemble with our arrows and bows, spears, revolvers, rifles; and the result will be that every little village will try to win mastery over its immediate neighborhood. Everybody will want to rule everybody else; and nobody will want to let him be ruled. Everybody will want to be a king or a president.

…. If it comes to civil war, then the Ethiopians will come and annex us. …. If there should be unrest in my country, as I fear there will be, and if we cannot find enough strong men to keep the country together—we never manage a democracy—then we shal have shown that we are not ready to govern ourselves.

Remember that John Buchholzer quoted an intelligent Somali District Commissioner in 1959.

That does not mean that the Somalis are incapable of building a viable administration, but they do not try hard enough for the sake of the common good. The clan egos overweigh the necessary sacrifices. The Somaliland model which also Puntland had adopted is an example which others can exercise. You have to settle peace among the residents of your region or district. Your brothers who achieved that are ready to help you with the knowhow if you ask.

In the previous chapters, we stated in details how the Somalis neglected their national responsibilities. From the late 1980s, Somalis were on the move in diverging views, forming tribe-based insurgents and taking interests in events beyond their frontiers. The public neglected its rights and responsibilities. We reminded you how the lion killed the three bulls which he could not face them together. All those combined, finally costed the whole nation.

The blow to the national pride,

There is a blow to the aspirations of the Somalis and their dream of greater Somalia but never accepted to be looked down. Listening to their voices, Somalis will prevail ultimately. It is said thousands of times, and we repeat it. The stars of the Horn of Africa (Xiddigaha Geeska) always compose very moving nationalistic songs. I love listening them.

The Somalis can achieve a lasting peace only when the majority of them democratically choose the road ahead. *35th president of the United States of America, John F. Kennedy said, "A man may die, nations may rise and fall, but an idea lives on. Children are the world's most valuable resources and its best hope for the future."*

Many Somalis became familiar with guns, bullets, and their effects. Behavioral disorders, such as hyperactive disorders, diabetes, low self-esteem, and new communicable and dangerous diseases were taking their tolls.

In the democratic systems, however, political authority is divided among autonomous sets of governments, mainly one national and the others subnational, all of which operate directly upon the people.

In Somalia, each warlord wanted to sit on the top chair alone and a part of the public lined behind him. What came of that is the civil war which still goes on. When others decide to help you to stand on your own feet, you have to remember that "There is no such thing as a free lunch."

For sure, some developed countries give aid in one hand and take away with the other with self-serving policies. You recall "I fail to see where any vital U.S. interest is involved," said the former U.S. Ambassador to Kenya when American-led

UN forces were being sent to Somalia" in December 1992, [US News and World Report, an Ambassador's warning, December 14, 1992, page 30].

Another U.S. State Department official said, "We do not have a strategic interest in Somalia, and we do in an unstable Balkan (US News & World Report, December 14, 1992)."

Americans killed thousands of Somalis and at the same, the President of the United States negotiated with Mohamed Farah Aideed for the release of an American hostage, Michael Durant. The point is not that an American is better than a Somali, but it is that patriotism is to put the welfare of your citizen first.

There are so many Somali administrations hoping to come together as one state right now, but still waiting for honest, brave and visionaries to lead. The situation in Somalia is in the Holy Koran: "Verily never will God change the condition of a nation until they change it themselves," [13:11].

Negotiation Tools.

Somalis are in a 'Tiih (loop)' right now. In most cases, they do not impress each other, and unless they overcome that self-put-down, they stay confused waiting help from others. Those who see their interests in helping the Somalis may give some money or do other little things. Many of those who can help, the Western developed nations believe that you cannot help yourselves.

All European Union members do not love each other. They are united to compete for their own survival against giant developed countries such as the United States, China, Russia, Japan and India. When people depart from the right ways of reconciliations and swallowing some of your pride for your existence as a nation, stumbling and falling are a guaranteed outcome. The old games of dividing the people into clans, sub-clans, and sub-subclans killed communities. People have to go back to painful and ongoing reconciliation processes. No ways around.

Any move of power needs a move of conciliation. An imposed outcome is always unstable, and therefore, you have to give someone your way for the sake of peace. Some examples:

- Put forward of what is possible but not what is impossible.
- Put emphasis on the commonalities but not on the differences.
- Reframe from who was wrong in the past and focus on what can be done about the problem now.

The Somalis had many peace talks both inside and outside the country, but not many under a tree, Xeer Somali: the most Somali traditional way of conflict resolutions. The Boorama and Garowe Accords which each took more than four months worked. Somalia ranks among the world's most corrupt countries. Corrupt government officials tolerate illegal activities, and the judicial system is very unstable and easily corruptible in all administrations of Somalia. We spoke this phenomenon extensively in the book which no administration proved otherwise.

The police are ineffective to fight crime. Companies usually arm themselves against threats. Fair and trusted system is almost absent, and the only places where tax is enforced is at the ports and airports. Bribery is common when clearing goods through the ports. Trade is wide open at any border. Public funds are found to be frequently diverted and misappropriated. Freedoms of speech and press are the least protected.

Somalia ranks among the most dangerous countries in the world for journalists. There is a young generation who try to make honest reporting and investigations. They meet assassinations routinely.

According to 'Be a woman': Remembering Canadian-Somali journalist Hodan Nalayeh's legacy By Ebyan Abdigir, The Toronto Star, Sunday, 21 July 2019, "Since 1992, over 66 journalists have died violently, according to the Committee to Protect Journalists (CPJ)." Hodan Nalayeh of 1976 to July 12, 2019, was a Somali-Canadian Media Executive, marketing consultant, social activist and entrepreneur.

Nalayeh was the president of the Cultural Integration Agency and vice president of sale and programming Development of Camera works productional International. Hodan and her husband were killed during a terrorist attack in Hotel Asasey (Somali: Cascasay), Kismayo Somalia, July 12, 2019. Al-Shabaab claimed the responsibility for the attack.

Somaliland

Lasting peace can only be reached by involving the elites, traditional elders, religious groups, business sectors and the bulk of the public. That is how it worked for Somaliland and Puntland state during the formation. Somaliland has sought international recognition as an independent state since 1991. No foreign government recognizes its sovereignty, but many effectively acknowledge the region as separate from Somalia. Some, such as France, the United Kingdom, and United States, as well as the European Union, sent a delegation to observe Somaliland's 2017 presidential election.

The region had held its own democratic elections since 2003, and every time, the transition of power was smooth. Even, some of the public believe that Ahmed Mohamed Mohamud (Siilaanyo), who was a one term president and refused to run for a second term was the victorious of the term before him.

A recorded statement with the BBC Somali, after he lost may be of fraudulent balloting as he claimed said, "We are not going to pick up weapons and fight for the president-ship like Mogadishu, but we trust our judicial system." Somaliland started hating the centralization of power in the capital immediately after the formation of Somali Republic until the collapse of the military administration, but Hizbia Digil Mirifle was campaigning for that even the independence.

The Organization of Islamic Conference (OIC), the African Union and the Arab League fear that formal recognition of Somaliland as an independent state would give a legitimacy other secessionist movement on the continent, such as Nigeria's Biafra or Morocco's Western Sahara.

Since the creation of a continental bloc in 1963 (African Union), there have only been two widely recognized border changes in Africa: Eritrea's split from Ethiopia in 1993 and South Sudan's independence in 2011. Many countries have encouraged the state elections and economic development of the breakaway Somali region, but respected other rightful subjects.

The fair and the free elections and the peacefulness are trends of good governance. The Somalilanders are predominantly from the Isaaq clan and the main obstacle for the lack of recognition of Somaliland is within. Isaaqs are the cradle of Somali nationalism and Somalism is in their bones and blood.

However, they are sick and tired of what is going on in Mogadishu, and the lack of real visionaries to deal with. There are also other major clans that are not very comfortable to deal with the Isaaqs alone, for fear of domination.

The city of Hargeisa had always been the second capital and the second largest city of Somalia. Today, it is the most stable and the most beautiful city in Somalia. Unless Mogadishu sees that, Hargeysa keeps attracting many more Somalis. To recognize it as the capital of Somalia in the near future is not remote. That is if it plays the real and fair game.

People go and establish life where there is a peace. If Somaliland is ever recognized as an independent state, other autonomous administrations may also demand the same.

The Somaliland leaders are not smart enough helping Hargeysa to be the capital of Somalia. As far as certain groups of people shun other groups to be a part of the development (leaders, residents, business) of the city, then it remains a tribal city. There are many flaws in its constitution. Who can be a citizen of Somaliland is far from reality?

In any administration, the main ingredients of stability are to abide by the law and respect each other. Somali administrations either autonomous, or regional once looked like some kind of building blocks. But none has dared yet to follow its drafted constitution.

The public elected the current members of the parliament of Somaliland in 2005. What seemed promising did not materialize. Extension after extension, still, the same members sit on the chairs.

Having travelled in May and June 2019, from Hargeysa to Boorama, from

Hargeysa to Berbera through Sheekh and Burco to Galdogob, Gaalkacyo and Garowe and back, the Somaliland public has some control of the peace and is committed to keep it that way. One of my days in Hargeysa, a man flowed me for about 30 minutes just for security reasons because of my questions of certain places. Other than that, most people welcome you as a Somali, or as a peaceful citizen of the world. They are as open as they used to be. They are proud to be Somalis.

They commonly raise a question I could not answer. To rejoin the south, who should we talk to since Mogadishu sees itself untouchable, and it is a killing field? But as far as you are putting journalists like Cabdimaalik Coldoon in jails just stating the facts as a reported, then, you remain a paranoid and clan administration. If Somaliland wants to secede from Somalia, I believe that the only viable and right option is a fair referendum when the time is ripe.

Back in the days Xamar became the pearl of the Indian Ocean at the expense of the rest of the country. It does not see itself yet that it will never be the same. An Edmontonian (Canada) good friend of mine who was born in Beledweyne and grew up and raised in Xamar decided to give a visit Mogadishu, Kismaayo, Gaalkacyo, Garoowe, Boosaaso, Hargeysa and Berbera in early of 2019. He went to Gaalkacyo and built a house.

Before his departure, I told him that he will be very disappointed in Mogadishu, will feel better in Gaalkacyo, happy in Garowe and Boosaaso and very happy in Hargeysa. He did not buy my prediction of what his state of feelings will be. He started his landing in Mogadishu. He was there for ten days and tried to advance his flight from the capital. In Mogadishu, for two days, he could not get out of the house.

In Gaalkacyo, he could not believe the stability better than what I told him about it, compared to Mogadishu, and he calls Garoowe a real capital. He could not go to Hargeysa, but he learned that Hargeysa is beyond his imagination.

Puntland

Puntland (Somali: Buntilaandi), officially the Puntland State of Somalia, Centered on the city of Garoowe in the Nugaal province. The name "Puntland" is derived from the Land of Punt mentioned in ancient Egyptian sources, although the exact location of the fabled territory is coming to the present-day Somalia. Like Somaliland, the political elites, traditional elders (Isims), members of the business community, civil society representatives, and some international partners held a constitutional conference in Garoowe in 1998 over a period of almost four months. They founded Puntland where Abdullahi Yusuf Ahmed who was a major figure in the establishment of the administration became the first president.

As stipulated in Article 1 of the Transitional Federal Charter of the Somali Republic, Puntland is a part of the Federal State of Somalia. As such, the region seeks the unity of the Somalis and adheres to a federal system of government. Unlike the secessionist region of Somaliland to its west, Puntland is not trying to obtain international recognition as a separate nation.

Both regions (Somaliland and Puntland) have one thing in common: they base their support upon clan elders and their organizational structure along lines based on clan relationships and kinship. Since 1998, Puntland has also been in territorial disputes with Somaliland over the Sool and Sanaag regions—just those regions play the same card to each administration.

A Buuhoodlian (a politician from Buuhoodle) told in Garowe in 2000 that Sool and Buuhoodle play the same card to both Hargeysa and Garoowe until a national government comes. The agony of the Somaliland-Puntland an ongoing border dispute is that just Somali people get killed for nothing, so-called territorial defenses.

Though relatively peaceful, Puntland briefly experienced political unrest in 2001 when then President of Puntland, Abdullahi Yusuf Ahmed, one of the founding fathers of the Puntland State and its first president, wanted his term extended. Ahmed and Jama Ali Jama fought for control of the region, with Ahmed emerging victorious the following year.

Ahmed served his second term as president until October 2004, when he was elected President of Somalia. He was succeeded in office by Mohamed Abdi Hashi, who served until January 2005 when he lost a reelection bid in parliament to General Mohamud Muse Hersi.

Puntland State administration has not established a one-man one-vote system like Somaliland, and it is unfortunate and a weakness. 66 members whom the Isims nominate every five years—a system that cannot be free of corruption choose the president.

Regardless of the intellectuals, the youth and wise elders, kinship is the basis for selection of the member of the parliament and other high government posts. After the power struggle of Abdullahi Yusuf and Jama Ali Jama, the transfer of power has been smooth sometimes one or two votes in between. Like Isaaqs in Somaliland, the population is predominantly Harti clan, and fairness is the only condition that others can ask.

Puntland gets a new leader every 5 years, and none have shown yet good leadership. The incumbent is always out-spent within the 66 representatives of the state. If you are a notable figure, you cannot be in touch with the general public without a security concern in any major city of Puntland—Gaalkacyo being the worst. Al Shabaab has a good presence in major cities of Puntland State of Somalia. The administration is rooted with corruption where personal gains always outweigh the public service.

The way Puntland behaves to the federalism is not up to its claims. No president of Puntland handed over the administration without blood in his hands. Perhaps, Mohamed Abdi Hashi is the sole who did not commit gross violations. Puntland Administration shores are the gateway of arms and weaponry for the rest of the Somali inhabitants. Though it cannot control the flow of the illegal products coming to its shores, there is also a window of unwillingness.

When the public entrusts you with the highest office of the land or the administration, you are judged with the highest moral standards. Hence, you have to be aware that the integrity and the responsibility of the office are more important than your ego.

The crimes that Abdirahman Faroole committed before he became the head of the Puntland state of Somalia, and during his administrations just for the lust of power are very insulting to the region and to the Somalis as well. A leader should feel good when his people feel good about his rule. The leader can get close to that stage when he swallows his egos for the sake of the common good.

Humans are far from being perfect creations and claim to be efficient. Originally, the system of governance came into existence to take advantage of the others. Those being taken of advantages challenged the system and demanded improvements. The improvements still go on, and the best process so far is by the legal voice of the general public—fair democratic elections.

Though time will tell what comes after that, Said Deni started his administration with a scandal and blood. On another page, according to Ilyas Aden, the father of Asha, and the Somalia media, Puntland president, Mr. Deni permitted the execution of two of the three men who raped and killed Asha Ilyas Adan (Caasha Ilyaas Aadan in Somali) on 11 February 2020. That decision of the execution of the murders created one golden page for himself and his administration in the history books.

Galmudug

This is another autonomous state within Somalia established in 2006. The leaders of southern Mudug region founded this federal state. The name is derived from a conflation of Galguduud and Mudug regions. It does not have a strong administrative system yet, and there are unfinished political and tribal frictions between Mudug and Galguduud districts or clans, especially where should be the center of administration. It claims to have a population of 1.3 million.

South West Administration

The leaders from Bay and Bakool regions established this administration in 2002. It was dissolved in 2005 and then reestablished in 2009. This federal state of Somalia claims to have a population of about 2 million. The region has arable land and rich in livestock, but Al-Shabab has a very visible presence. The people in this region do not identify themselves with bloodlines but on peaceful coexistence and on traditional laws.

Jubbaland

Jubbaland proclaimed its existence since 2011 but became an official federal state of Somalia in mid-2013. Originally, Jubbaland was a part of the Northern Provinces of the Somali regions in Kenya. British gave Italy in 1925-1926 as a reward for the Italians joining the Allies in World War One. The transfer of Jubbaland to Italy was completed on the Treaty of London, January 29, 1925.

Jubbaland claims to be responsible of one million citizens. Kenya has a military presence in this region to keep an eye on Alshabaab. It is rich in marine resources, livestock, and farming. Since 1991, it has been one of the least stable regions in Somalia.

Hirshabeelle

This is another federal state of Somalia. It has yet to develop a peaceful and viable administration. Hiiraan and Middle Shabelle leaders with the help of Hassan Sheikh federal government established it as a federal state in 2016. It claims an estimated population of 1.8 million people.

Al-Shabab remains capable of carrying out massive attacks in this region and most of the southern Somalia despite a long-running African Union offensive against the Islamist group.

One of the central issues of any peace process is the willingness of leaving a room for the participants to save face for an acceptable offer. The best approaches which turned out to be fruitless were no one accepted humiliation for the sake of national integrity.

The relative stability achieved by Puntland State administration and Somaliland, especially Somaliland is something to be proud of. Then, why not they are praised and ask how they achieved? "A credit delayed is a credit denied." It just puts off the good faith of the negotiation.

The ultimate goal of a negotiation is to settle a dispute in good faith. One must not show how difficult he can make the situation for the other but as a win win situation. Another essential variable in the process of negotiations is how the parties define the issues. The following are examples of common choices in the

demands of one party. To accept agreements on the available terms that is to say upon the terms the originator proposed;
To attempt to improve the available terms by bargaining
To break off the negotiations because neither of the previous choices is acceptable.

The last, "To break off the negotiations" should always be avoided because it is just a scapegoat. We learned in school that a problem understood is a problem half-solved. Therefore, how the parties define the issues can neutralize the situation and defuse tensions. When one party does smoothly clarify the agenda, and other parties are convinced because so much of thorn-picking was already done, then the process can proceed.

For the sake of a joint agreement, each of the participants must thrust himself into painful and uncertain negotiations and be prepared to swallow a part of his pride.

Conflict management is an ongoing process. You cannot stop and get overwhelmed. You have to take each challenge as it appears. Lastly, in principle, unless conciliatory approaches are applied, just what any negotiator hopes to accomplish is unclear.

In Somalia, the outcome shows that neither many good conciliatory techniques were applied nor the central issues were clearly defined. Or, nor many leaders swallowed some of their pride for the common good.

Perhaps, the things that ate in all Somali reconciliations are lack of necessary reconciliation skills and experiences for a very complicated and highly polarized political situation of a nation. Somalis can succeed if they realize that they always fail unless they listen to each other, understand each other and be respectful of each other's concerns.

Realization of What is at Stake

In a democracy, every citizen, regardless of his interest in politics, "holds an office"; every one of us is in a position of responsibility.
__ John F. Kennedy

Because of what the chaos subjected them to, surprisingly, many Somalis regardless of their clans would like the return of the corrupted elected administration while others would like the return of the military system. That is not for the fond of the rulers, but for the love of a government that just maintains law and order—and then the public can go from there.

Though corrupted, during the nine years of the elected administration, the importance of kinship was not growing. Just people hated the corruption and the ineffectiveness. And there is no doubt that when Somalis formulate an agreeable Federal or Confederal government or whatever, as it must be one day, the public will give a good thought for any new governmental changes. Confederal or federal administration maybe the best possible one.

I have viewed some of the world's Federal and Confederal Constitutions. If these two articles are guaranteed, future conflicts can be solved.

We repeat this quotation you have seen earlier, "*Their bright intelligence, their courage and their confidence will be of value to the new Africa shaping now (during World War II), if only because they never for a moment felt inferior to any white man, and were never tiresome about being black, or about you being white.*"

Today, 2020, for many of those who grew in the Western countries are struggling with such proudness.

In Canada, I do remember that a Somali-Canadian said to me, "Why am I so dark!" That was not being curious about why humans have different skin colors, but she would have loved to be a white lady. Then, "…. they never for a moment felt inferior to any white man, and were never tiresome about being black, or about you being white" hit me like a rock. During the 1940s, not even 10% of the Somalis could read, or write, but let us see what Gerald Hanley quoted from an elder:

It was the oldest of the chiefs who, when the drafts of the laborers for the plantations came in, said to me what I had always known I felt, but had never heard spoken by one of the subject's race. 'We are lending you the laborer's' he told me. 'But only because you are living with us here on the river, and because you have spoken well, and not because we recognize this new government which replaced the Italians. We do not want to be ruled by any strangers any more. They beat us with cannon, but every inch of this land is ours. Ours. It can never belong to any strangers. Men cannot live under strangers who taken their lands. Never. If I had a spear and you had nothing and I came and I took your house from you, and made you work in your own garden for me, you would not like that. This is what they have done, these governments (British, Italians or any other European). And it must come to an end now (Hanley, 91).

Division of Powers:

A Government is a group of people that have a power to rule in a territory, according to the law. The most important part of the definition is "*according to the law.*" What law you can ask? The one they drafted and agreed to abide by.

Division of powers between the central government on the one hand and the state/unit governments on the other is an absolutely essential condition of a federation. In it, one part of the authority and power of the state is vested with the central government and the rest is vested with the state governments.

Each works within a definite and defined sphere of functions. As such the mode of division of powers can be different but it has to be essentially affected in every federal state. It is the signpost of a federation.

For sure, the Somalis in Somalia do not have that. In some places, there is a sense of relative peace. The months of May and June of 2019, I have traveled in the northern regions of Somalia, Hargeysa, Berbera, Sheekh, Burco, Buuhoodle, Galdogob, Gaalkacyo, Burtinle and Growe. I put my findings into a book *"Travels in Northern Somalia in 80 days."*

The effects of the Somali civil war are very much alive. People are still in a mood of ambiguity in life. Some of the youth are graduates of local universities, from neighboring countries, India, Pakistan, Malaysia, the Philippines, and some other places, and still not happy with the future of the mother land. If they see an opportunity of going to Europe, North America, Oceania (Australia and New Zealand), they do not even blink.

About the cities I have visited, a would-be couple does not have the luxury of going to a nice restaurant or even walk on the streets with confidence. Hargeysa is the only city I did see that young couples can go to affordable restaurants without reservations of their safety.

Oriental Hotel built 1953 is a two-story building in the amenity of Hargeysa—in the middle of four main streets. About 20 rooms are for the public. Five or more of the daily occupants are non-Somalis—not as a quota but many foreigners like to come because of its location, price and tourism services. The most of all is the stability in the region.

You always see pairs of opposite sex eating in, sometimes families of three and four during the dinner times. Baadisooc by Ali Abdigir, page 344 (available at www.amazon.com and all other amazon websites), quote from an unknown Somali:

All people know of Somalis is current day Somalia, but there was a time when Somalis were happy (well some) and life was good and people dressed well, had parties, went to the beach, worked hard. Somali women had a lot more freedom than any of the women in the Arab/Muslim world and beyond Africa as well. They could go to school, work, drive, wear whatever they wanted. They were not oppressed. They had culture. Somalia was very cosmopolitan once. Sad to see what it has become today.

Supremacy of the Constitution

In a federation, the constitution is the supreme law of the land. Both the central government and the state governments derive their powers from the constitution. They always work within their own spheres as demarcated by the constitution. No one can violate the provisions of the constitution.

Each Somali administration writes a nice constitution but does not respect it, and that is where the conflicts always emerge. I wrote a book (available at www.amazon.com) about Puntland State administration (Hortii Ma La Iska Baandheeyey (Has it been Shuffled (screened) First? (back cover))) in 1999. Diakonia of Sweden, UNESCO and UNICEF had big offices in Garowe. They read the manuscript and declined to take part in the publishing because of how I predicted the situation of the administration after the transitional period which was three years.

I was not a magician but studied the draft (constitution) and looked at the culture of the administration which I was a part. People started asking about the book when Abdullahi Yusuf Ahmed and Jama Ali Jama fought for the leadership.

We briefly spoke of five Federal member states, the federal government and the breakaway one, Somaliland.

Somaliland is the most stable one but share the corruptive culture with the rest. None of the rest including the federal has complete control of the area it claims. Mogadishu is called the capital of Somalia, and since 1991, it has been the mother of anarchy and suicide bombings.

Some will be agitated when they read the two above sentences, but can they challenge the truth? When it comes to clan resentment and hatreds, Somali societies do not want to talk about them because they are not ready to talk about the truth. I believe that when the Somalis start telling their rooted religious and cultural mistakes, or myths, they are ready to heal and go forward.

There are always conflicts of interests between the politicians and the public interests. Since both options cannot prevail, the choice must be what is at stake.

John F. Kennedy was right to said, "In a democracy, every citizen, regardless of his interest in politics, "holds an office"; every one of us is in a position of responsibility."

If the Somalis want to be a proud nation again, nobody is on their way but themselves. Many people claim that there are many foreign hands in rebuilding Somalia. It is so true, but every nation on earth gets some kinds of imported ideologies. Religion, kingdom, and democracy are examples. It is your role to harmonize those imported ideologies into your way of life and systems.

Damages beyond death

Wars destroy communities and disrupt the development of all kinds. Having created huge inflex of refugees, long-term negative effects, violence as a status-quo, less self-esteem, stress, Cannibalism of the infrastructure, other social, economic and political damages are beyond the deaths. Even, within close communities, trust within each other is lost.

Many who are born during the civil war, life is as a status-quo. Hundreds of proto-states get created, and there is no love between the public and the so-called leaders. Violence becomes way of life and guns are sold in open markets. Traditional leaders are driven by personal gain, while the business society becomes ruthless profiteering entities. The Somali Civil War did not discriminate. From Mooryaan to a child who was born after, in one way or the other, sooner or later, in the final analysis, it is an equalizer.

After more than four decades of killing each other, cannibalizing the naturals resources and the infrastructure, still, Somalis tend to blame the international community.

Rape as a new phenomenon.

Do we know that many people are still traumatized by the civil war without even knowing it? They have tremendous mental problems and think they are just fine. Perhaps, the tribal administrations do not even think of formulating a healing policy of the Civil War Post Traumatic Stress Disorder.

I was born and raised in Somalia, and I can state that rape had not been a big deal in the Somali communities. Women never had a big say under the tree — the traditional way of settling issues. Nada.

If a man rapes an unmarried woman, the public puts a stigma on her, the victim, and worse if she bears a baby because of the rape. The elders of both sides discuss the matter, and not long ago, they used to agree upon the man marrying the woman he raped—because of so-called shame, or the connotation that may bring. Right now, in 2020, less than 40% can read in which only 26% of the female are literate. For more than 30 years, the legal institutions were non-existence in Somalia, and worse made everything.

Asaruur (back cover) by this author available through www.amazon.com, covers four stories of agony that happened during the Somali Civil War. Three of the four are in the international media.

Thursday, January 14, 1993, 5 women who were accused and convicted of adultery, in Hargeysa, Somalia, were publicly stoned to death by cheerful villagers. UN people were present and tried to intervene, but they could not help and feared for themselves.

NAIROBI, Kenya - The United Nations said Tuesday that a Somali stoned to death by Islamist militants after she had been accused of adultery was a 13-year-old girl, Asha Ibrahim Duhulow (Caasha Ibraahim Dhuxulow in Somali) who had been raped while visiting her grandmother. She was placed in a hole and stoned to death on Oct. 28, 2008, in a rebel-held port city, Kismaayo, in front of a crowd, after local leaders said she was guilty under Shariah, the legal code of Islam based on the Koran. Witnesses said at the time that the victim had been a 23-year-old woman. "Reports indicate that she had been raped by three men while traveling on foot to visit her grandmother in the war-torn capital, Mogadishu," UNICEF, the United Nations children's agency, said in a statement. "Following the assault, she sought protection from the authorities, who then accused her of adultery and sentenced her to death," UNICEF added. "A child was victimized twice — first by the perpetrators of the rape and then by those responsible for administering justice."

Hargeysa 2014: Muna Mohamed Abdullahi and at least two of her mature children killed her business partner, Rukiya Said Ayanle. Not only that. Muna called Rukiya to repay an earlier loan. When she came, they killed her and buried in the house she was called to collect the money on February 24, 2014. Muna and her eldest son were executed on January 17, 2016.

In December 2016, six young men took two girls to the countryside of Galdogob, raped, videotaped, and put into youtube.com. The men did not meet the deserved conviction. The habit spread and took place in Guriceel, Garowe, and some other places.

In February 2019, three men of her neighbors raped, wanted to bury Asha Ilyas Aden alive, and finally died. Though two of the three were convicted and executed on 11 February 2020 according to her father, Ilyaas Aadan ant the Somali media, raping girls continue.

April 5, 2020, according to www.bbc.com 'Somali outrage at the rape of girls aged three and four,' were seized by men who took them and assaulted them while walking home from school, in Afgooye, Somalia. Violence and clan-warfare used to be deeply rooted in the Somali culture, and not much has changed since then.

12 September 2020, according to the police of Somalia in Mogadishu, Xamdi Maxamed Faarax—a 19 years old recently graduated from high School was raped and then thrown off the roof of a several-storey building in Mogadishu's Waaberi District.
September 2020, to www.somaliaffairs.com "A few days ago, a mentally unsound 16-year old girl was kidnapped, raped and tortured for several hours before she was found tied up in the Puntland capital Garoowe.

Hanley (Afterword:225) said, "One may recoil in disgust from Somalis for the cruelty and suffering upon each other and catastrophes bring themselves, yet tend to blame on others." *Warriors by Gerald Hanley originally was warriors and Strangers) page 9:*

I once told a chief that I would kill him myself if he let his warriors go killing again (something he was planning to do). He liked that. He smiled, after studying my face. Afterall he could understand that more easily than the kind of government he thought I represented. He knew I meant because I had come to hate him as much as he hated me. Even so, he started laughing, I laughed with him at the absurdity of our situation in the wilderness. "What if I cannot stop the warriors?" he said. "Do you want to stop them?" I asked him. He laughed. "I will be honest," he said. "I do want them to kill their enemies. But I will and stop them. You are not allowed by the government to kill me, are you?" he asked me, serious and calm.

That conversation had been between a British Officer (Gerald Hanley (of Irish parents)) and a Somali elder (Nabaddoon) in Somalia in 1941. In 79 years, did that nomadic culture change? The irony of the Somalis about nationhood is that most people cannot free themselves from clan mentality. They paint even their bad clan leaders with green and the rest with whatever color they feel comfortable.

How much is a human life worth in the Somali societies? *T*o the modern records of governance, the Somali was neither good enough to govern himself nor comfortable to be governed by another. The Somali must realize one thing before anything, the value of life. The Somali fighter plane monument in Hargeysa is not for teaching hatred, but to keep remembering the lives lost is a national obligation and humane.

Whether they can see and not daring to say, or they may not dream of getting out of the Tiih or Meehanaw (chaotic loop), or most accepted the tiih as a Status Pro Quo, there is a naked truth.

Somali leaders, whether traditional or otherwise, do not give much consideration to the effects that their words may create. It is unfortunate and irresponsible that they many times say unhealthy and unacceptable statements that stir or revive old wounds. We have to be very careful and better educated about those kinds of talks which may do more harm than good. How and what you say always matter. *The East Africa Protectorate (1905, 121-122) by Sir Charles Eliot:*

It is certainly to be desired that we should utilize the Somalis. There can be no doubt that they are the most intelligent race in the Protectorate, though it may be urged with some justice that they are also proud, treacherous, fanatical and vindictive. Too much stress, I think, is often laid on these bad qualities, and it is certain that the average Englishman has little sympathy for the Somali. He tolerates a black man who admits his inferiority, and even those who show a good fight and give in; but he cannot tolerate dark colour combined with an intelligence in any way equal to his own. This is the secret of almost universal dislike of Babu, it reappears in the unpopularity of the Somali among East African officials. The Somali are not willing to agree to the simple plan of having a fair fight and then shaking hands when defeated., but constantly indicate that they think themselves are equals or superior, and unfrequently prove it. But meanwhile I think we had better let the Somalis alone, and avoid these conflicts between a lion and swallow.

Though the European characterization of the African race in general is a racist authorship, as a reader, and probably as a Somali, you may ask yourself why I put on almost half a page of a colonialist Englishman, Sir Charles Eliot. "Independent, alert and proudness" are traits of admiration. It is absurd, however, that Europeans illusioned themselves with a superior mentality. It is also an irony that colonialists occupied Somaliland and demand forgiveness, loyalty from the Somalis; and, when the Somalis reject the subjugation, then they were called "treacherous and vindictive.

The point we raise about Eliot's statements is not only that he was a racist colonizer, but also that the Somali readers may be misled to feel good and think that the Englishman praised them—while the real point is: Charles Eliot carried a notion that because Europeans developed weapons to conquer weakly and be less-educated nations illusioned him to be biologically superior to other races.

Having said that, equally, if the Somalis are whom they are said to be, after the Europeans left them alone to govern themselves, why are they treacherous and vindictive to each other? Somalis do not need regular and average people to lead. They badly need extra-ordinary, highly visionary, risk-takers, none-vindictive and none-treacherous, honesty and not-ego-lovers to lead this nation out of the Tiih (meehanaw). You have to keep in mind one thing. There is a big difference between a politician and a nationalist politician.

On these words you have read, I rest the draft of *The Genesis of Somalia's Anarchy: A footprint in The Past."*

Chapter twenty referenced notes

Heritage Debate in Jibouti, December 14-18/2018.
Baadisooc by Ali Abdigir, 2018
US News and World Report, an Ambassador's warning, December 14, 1992,
Warriors: Life and Death Among the Somalis by Gerald Hanley
The East Africa Protectorate,1905 by Sir Charles Eliot

War Crimes: How Warlords, Politicians, Foreign Governments and Aid Agencies Conspired to Create a Failed State in Somalia, Paperback, 2014 by Rasna Warah

Appendix A

Sequential Dates

The Horn of Africa has been home to Somalis as long as there was a life on earth.
King Mernera, a pharaoh of the sixth Dynasty ordered Harkhuf, a nobleman of
the kingdom to make expeditions into Nubia and further to the Land of Punt
1490 BC or 1493 BC -Pharaoh Hatshepsut made an expedition to the Land of Punt,
Early First century AD-Periplus, Greek merchant visited Somalia coast
Arab scholars such as Al Masudi (935), Al Bakri (1067), Al-Idris (1154), Al-istakhri (960), Ibn Hawqal (977), Al-Burruni (1030), Al-Bakhri (1067), Al-Idrisi (1154), all wrote about the Gulf of Berbera and the Somalis.
1285AD-1415AD, Ifat-Adal kingdom existed
1331, Ibn Battuta visited Saylac, a location in Raas Casayr (unknown yet) and Mogadishu.
1346, Ibn Battuta, a Moroccan traveler met Abdul-Aziz Al- Maqdashawi (From Mogadishu) as a ruler of one of the Maldives Islands
1567AD Adal Sultanate with Ahmed Gurey met its final defeat by the Ethiopians and De-existed
13th-17th centuries - Ajuran Sultanate dominates much of the Horn of Africa before collapsing into rival regional sultanates.
1839-1861-Xaaji Sharmaarke Cali Saalax ruled Saylac
1862-France purchased port of Obock
26 March 1885-Issa Chiefs and France government signed an agreement at Obock (Obokh),
1875 - Egypt occupies towns on Somali coast and parts of the interior.
April 18-19, 1885, William Stroyan, a British explorer was killed in Berbera, and John Speke, another British explorer was seriously wounded   **1887** - Britain proclaims protectorate over Somaliland.
1888 - Anglo-French agreement defines boundary between Somali possessions of the two countries. It took place on February 9, 1888.
9 February 1888, France and Britain concluded the Treaty of Saylac
1889 - Italy sets up a protectorate in central Somalia, later consolidated with territory in the south ceded by the sultan of Zanzibar.
1895-Sayid Mohamed Abdulle Hassan landed at the Berbera port

1896-British Government completed protection treaties with the following Somali tribes: Gudabursi (1884), Issa (1885), Habar Toljecla (1884), Habar-Gerhajis (1885), Habar-Awal (1884), Warsangeli (1886) and Ogadeen (1896).

March 25, 1909, Britain reached a point of complete withdrawal from the interior of Somaliland for the fear of Daraawiish raids.

January to February of 1920-Britain used fighter planes against the Daraawiish of Sayid Mohamed Abdulle Hassan

The old port: Historic heart of Mogadishu Emerged as Arab settlement in 10th century, bought by Italy in 1905

Mogadishu became the Capital of independent Somalia from 1960 Estimated population: 1 million

1925 - Territory east of the Jubba river detached from Kenya to become the westernmost part of the Italian protectorate.

1936 - Italian-Somaliland combined with Somali-speaking parts of Ethiopia to form a province of Italian East Africa.

1940 - Italians occupy British-Somaliland.

1941 - British occupy Italian Somalia.

1950 - Italian-Somaliland becomes a UN trust territory under Italian control.

1956 - Italian-Somaliland renamed Somalia and granted internal autonomy.

1960 - British and Italian parts of Somalia become independent, merge and form the United Republic of Somalia; Aden Abdullah Osman Daar elected president.

1963 - Border dispute with Kenya; diplomatic relations with Britain broken until 1968.

1964 - Border dispute with Ethiopia erupts into hostilities.

1967 - Abdi Rashid Ali Sharmaarke beats Aden Abdullah Osman Daar in elections for president and chose Egal as a prime minister

1969 October- Muhammad Siad Barre assumes power in coup after Sharmaarke is assassinated.

1970 - Barre declares Somalia a socialist state and nationalizes most of the economy.

1974 - Somalia joins the Arab League.

1974-75 - Severe drought causes widespread starvation.

1977 - Somalia invades the Somali-inhabited Ogadeen region of Ethiopia.

1978 - Somali forces were pushed out of Ogadeen with the help of Soviet advisers and Cuban troops. Barre expels Soviet advisers and gains support of United States.

1981 - Opposition to Barre's regime begins to emerge after he excludes members of the Majeerteen and Isaaq clans from government positions, which are filled with people from his own Marehan clan.

1988 - Peace accord with Ethiopia and the government of Somalia bombed its northern regions, Hargeysa and Burco in particular.

1991 - Mohamed Siyaad Barre is ousted. Power struggle between clan warlords kills or wounds thousands of civilians.

1991 - Former British protectorate of Somaliland declares unilateral independence.

1992 - US Marines land near Mogadishu ahead of a UN peacekeeping force sent to restore order and safeguard relief supplies.

1993 - US Army Rangers are killed when Somali militias shoot down two US helicopters in Mogadishu and a battle ensues. Hundreds of Somalis died. US mission formally ends in March 1994.

1995 January- Ex-President Mohamed Siyad Barre, died in Nigeria

1996 1995 - UN peacekeepers leave, having failed to achieve their mission.

1997 August - Warlord Mohamed Farah Aideed died of wounds and is succeeded by his son, Hussein.

1998 - Puntland region declares autonomy.

2000 August – After 13 failed attempts at making peace, clan leaders and senior figures meeting in Djibouti elect Abdulkassim Salat Hassan president of Somalia.

2000 October - Hassan and his newly-appointed prime minister, Ali Khalif Gallaydh, arrived in Mogadishu to heroes' welcomes. Gallaydh announces his government, the first in the country since 1991.

2001 April - Somali warlords, backed by Ethiopia tried to make Arta government to be inclusive.

2004 August - In 14th attempt since 1991 to restore central government, a new transitional parliament inaugurated at ceremony in Kenya. In October the body elects Abdullahi Yusuf as president.

2004 December - Tsunami off Indonesia displaces 10,000s on Somali coast.

2005 February-June - Somali government begins returning home from exile in Kenya, but there were bitter divisions over where in Somalia the new parliament should sit.

2005 November - Prime Minister Ali Mohammed Ghedi survives an assassination attempt in Mogadishu.

2006 February - Transitional parliament meets in central town of Baidoa for the first time since it was formed in 2004.

2006 March-May - Scores of people are killed and hundreds are injured during fierce fighting between rival militias in Mogadishu, worst violence in almost a decade.

2006 June-July - Militias loyal to the Union of Islamic Courts took Mogadishu and other parts of south after defeating clan warlords.

2006 July-August - Mogadishu's air and seaports are re-opened for the first time since 1995.

2006 September - Transitional government and Islamic Courts begin peace talks in Khartoum and failed. Somalia's first known suicide bombing targets President Yusuf outside parliament

December - Ethiopian and transitional government put Islamists to flight, capturing Mogadishu. Ethiopian troops, government forces routed the Islamic Courts,
Union's militias, Timeline: Ethiopia and Somalia

January - Islamists abandon their last stronghold, the southern port of Kismayo.

President Abdullahi Yusuf enters Mogadishu for the first time since taking office in 2004. Air strikes in south against al-Qaeda figures are first direct US military intervention in Somalia since 1993.

March - African Union troops landed in Mogadishu amid pitched battles between
Islamist insurgents and government forces backed by Ethiopian troops, after UN Security Council authorized six-month peacekeeping mission. Pirates operating out of Somalia make key international.

May 2007 - The UN Security Council allows countries to send warships to Somalia's territorial waters to tackle pirates.

January 2007- Ethiopia completes withdrawal of troops, announced the previous year, and Al-Shabab capture Baidoa, formerly a key government stronghold.

Meeting in Djibouti 2007, parliament elects moderate Islamist Sheikh Sharif Sheikh Ahmed president, extends transitional government's mandate for another two years.

2009 May - Islamist insurgents launch onslaught on Mogadishu and advance in the south.

2009 October - Al-Shabab recaptures the southern port of Kismayo after defeating the rival Hizbul-Islam militia.

Formed as a radical offshoot of the Union of Islamic Courts in 2006

Include foreign jihadists Has launched cross-border raids into Kenya, Uganda estimated to have 7,000 to 9,000 fighters, announced merger with al-Qaeda in 2012, Somalia's al-Shabab join al-Qaeda Alshabaab highpoint

2010-12 - Famine kills almost 260,000, the UN says.

2010 January - UN World Food Programmed withdraws from Al-Shabab areas of southern Somalia after threats to lives of its staff.

2010 February - Al-Shabab formally declares alliance with al-Qaeda, begins to concentrate troops for a major offensive to capture the capital.

2011 January - Pirate attacks on ships worldwide hit seven-year high in 2010, with Somali pirates accounting for 49 of 52 ships seized.

2011 July - UN formally declares famine in three regions of Somalia. Al-Shabab partially lifts ban on foreign aid agencies in south, and UN airlifts its first aid consignment in five years to Mogadishu. Al-Shabab pulls out of Mogadishu in what it calls "tactical move".

2012 2011 October - Kenyan troops enter Somalia to attack rebels they accuse of being behind several kidnappings of foreigners on Kenyan soil. American military begins flying drone aircraft from a base in Ethiopia, Ethiopian troops return to central town of Guriel (Guriceel).

October 2011 Kenya entered Somalia in to curb al-Shabab Islamist militants Airforce hits al-Shabab bases. Navy blockades Kismayo into surrender A lot to lose - Kenya's Somali gambit

2013 February-May - Al-Shabab loses key towns of Baidoa and Afgooye to Kenyan, African Union and Somali government forces.

2012 August - Somalia's first formal parliament in more than 20 years wa sworn in at Mogadishu airport, ending eight-year transitional period. Pro-government forces capture the port of Marca (Marka) south of Mogadishu from Al-Shabab.

2012 September - MPs in Mogadishu elect academic and civic activist Hassan Sheikh Mohamud president over the incumbent Sharif Sheikh Ahmed. First presidential election in Somalia since 1967.

2012 October - African Union and government forces recapture Kismayo, the last major city held by Al-Shabab and the country's second-largest port, and the town of Walloweyn town, northwest of Mogadishu.

2013 January - US recognizes Somalia's government for the first time since 1991.

2013 June - Veteran Al-Shabab leader Sheikh Hassan Daahir Aweys is taken into custody by government troops after he is ousted by more extreme Al-Shabab figure Ahmed Abdi Godane. Spike in violence with various attacks by Al-Shabab, including on presidential palace and UN compound in Mogadishu.

2013 September - International donors promise 2.4 billion dollars in reconstruction aid in three-year "New Deal".

2013 September - Al-Shabab seize shopping Centre and kill 60 people in Kenyan capital Nairobi, saying it is retaliation for Kenya's military involvement in Somalia.

2014 May - Al-Shabab says it carried out a bomb attack on a restaurant in Djibouti, saying the country is used as a launch pad to strike Muslims.

2014 June - Al-Shabab claims two attacks on the Kenyan coast which killed more than 60, saying operations against Kenya would continue.

2014 September - Al-Shabab leader Ahmed Abdi Godane killed in US drone strike. Government offers 2-million-dollar bounty for his successor, Ahmad Omar.

2015 **2014 November** - Government launches country's first postal service in more than two decades. Mogadishu's first ever cash withdrawal machine installed in a hotel. **2014 November**-December - Al Shabab carry out mass killings in north-east Kenya, including on a bus and a camp of quarry workers.

2016 April - Al-Shabab claim responsibility for killing 148 people, mainly Christian students, at Garissa University College in northern Kenya.

2015 May - US Secretary of State John Kerry pays brief visit to Mogadishu, the first officeholder to do so, a few weeks after Alshabaab raid government quarter of the city and kill 17 people.

2016 February - African Union leaders agree on need for more funding and support for their military presence in Somalia after weeks of increased Al-Shabab attacks on public spaces and progovernment troops. Government and African Union troops recapture southern port of Marca that Al-Shabab briefly seized.

2016 November - Leaders of two Somali regions, Puntland and Galmudug, agree to respect a ceasefire in the disputed city of Gaalkacyo. Fighting in the city reportedly displaced 90,000.

2017 February - Parliament elects former prime minister Mohamed Abdullahi Mohamed, known as Farmajo, as president. Al-Shabab threatens to target anyone collaborating with him.

2017 March - Pirates seize tanker off coast of Puntland in the first hijacking of a large vessel in the region since 2012.

2017 May - President Mohamed at London conference calls for lifting of arms embargo to help defeat al-Shabab. UN Secretary General Antonio Guterres says conditions are now in place in Somalia for it to become a success story.

2017 October - Double truck bombing kills 350 people in Mogadishu. Al-Shabaab is prime suspect.

Index

A

Abdullahi Ahmed Abdulle (Azhari), 8, 134, 148

Abdiweli Mohamed Ali, Former prime minister of Somalia, 237

African Union, 14, 140, 152, 157, 254, 258, 269-0

Ahmed Gurey, 31-2, 49, 77, 79, 266

Ahmed Ibrahim Awale 8, 23, 28, 31, 41, 77

Ahmed Mohamed Mohamud (Siilaanyo), 192-3, 254

Ahmed Omar Jees-SPM militia, 179, 181, 194

Ajuuraan Sultanate 12, 45-6, 57

Aadan Yabaal, 234

Ali Garad, minister of education, 135, 138

Ali Hassan Booni (deputy prime minister), 135

Al-Ittihad, 155, 188

Abdelaziz Farah, 201

Algeria, 49, 52, 204

Abdi Hunde Beir Sabrie, 243

Ali Mahdi Mohamed, 191-2, 194, 196-7, 199, 201, 204, 207, 228, 235

Abdiqasim Salad Hassan, ex- minister, also TNG president 1997—2000, 194

Allan Gibb (British officer killed in Burco in 1922), D.S.O., D.C.M., British officer, 93-4, 99

Al-Shabab, 135, 258, 269-0

American Central Intelligence Agency (CIA), 229

American Peace Corps, 149, 161

Abdirashid Ali Sharmaarke, 38, 61, 129, 135, 143-6

Arabian Sea, 51, 81, 125

Abdirazak H. Hussein, 132-3, 139

Abdurahman Sharif (Author), 54, 76, 139

Artificial boundaries, 157

Abdullahi Isse, 13, 116, 121, 135
Abdullahi SuldanTima-Cadde, 127
Afgooye, 190, 194, 198, 264, 269
Ahmed H. Duale, minister of Agriculture, 135
Assap (city Eritrea), 87
Abdurahman Sheikh Nuur, 38
Australia and New Zealand 44, 47, 261
Addis Ababa,17-8, 21, 30, 42, 45, 52, 54, 74, 113, 157, 167, 185, 204, 223
Awdal, 23, 39
Aden (Yemen), 18, 27, 51-2, 57, 63-4, 69, 71, 74, 80-1, 87, 91-4, 99, 104, 115, 120, 126, 129, 141-2, 156, 174
Aden Abdulle Osman, 129, 134, 138, 233, 267

B

Ballidoogle, 217
Bamburi Memorandum of understanding, 137, 142
Bardera (Baardheere), 40, 205, 208-211
Bay and Bakool, 38, 129, 192, 258
Baydhabo (Baidao), 40, 127, 198, 202, 205-7, 211, 217
BBC Somali, 141, 254
Beira (city in Mozambique), 33, 58
Beirut, Lebanon, 214, 210, 221, 236
Belgium, 219, 222
Berbers, 23, 27, 49, 51-2, 57, 72
Berbera, 12, 17-8, 22-7, 33-4, 39, 43, 45-6, 48, 50-2, 6-2, 65, 68-70, 73-4, 7780, 85-90, 93-4, 99, 103-4, 112, 115, 125, 127, 130, 135, 151, 159, 168, 184-6, 195, 250, 256
Beyra (38 km, north of Gaalkacyo), 81
Bill Clinton,214-6, 229, 232-6
Black-market, 164-6
Bombay (India), 61, 92
Boorama, 38, 127, 138, 191, 253, 255
Boosaaso, 74, 115, 127, 130, 138, 145, 201, 255
Botswana, 62, 215
British government (Great Britain, Britain), 13, 21, 26, 60-2, 64-6, 69, 71-2, 77, 79-80, 88, 90-1, 99, 103, 114, 116, 118-121, 123, 126, 130, 136, 138-0
British Military Administration, 37, 74, 115-6, 119-21, 122-3, 147

British Military Aviation, 97
British National Museum, 23
British-Somaliland, 13, 47, 63-5, 88, 91-2, 94, 97-9, 103-111, 114-5, 117, 119, 122-3, 127, 130-2, 135, 137-8, 140, 147, 154, 159, 199
Boutros-Ghali, 204-5, 214-5
Brussels General Act, 85
Buchholzer, John (Author), 36, 68, 71, 122-3, 131, 159, 251

C

Cadale, 38
Canada, 41, 44, 71, 84, 95, 139, 223, 240-2, 244-5, 247, 249, 255
Canadian Airborne Regiment, 240-1, 247
Captain Cawil Cadnaan Burhaan (hijacked Somali airline plane), 167
Caynabo town, 154
Ceylon (Sri Lanka now), 50
China, 53, 81, 100, 132, 212, 214, 253
Christopher and Vasco Da Gama, 32, 47
Sir Charles Eliot (author), 15-6, 32, 35, 42, 63, 76, 144, 166-7
Church, 33, 125, 233, 245
Churchill, Winston 89, 91-3, 96, 99, 142
Clayton Matchee (court-marshalled Canadian officer), 240
Colin Powell, 210, 216, 218
Columbia University, 141
Colonel Dheel, 150
Colonel Geof Haswell, 248
Colonel Salaad Gabayre Kediye, 38, 150
Cuba (Cuban forces), 157-8, 160, 267

D

Daraawiish, Dervish,54, 59, 70, 73, 76-92, 94-7, 100-4, 106-8, 128, 181, 262-3
Daaroods or Daarood, 73, 190-1, 193-9, 202-3
David Collenette, 248
De Gaulle, 140-1
Dick Cheney, 213
District of Columbia, 166
Djibouti, 16, 18-9, 27, 34, 39, 46, 72, 77, 110-1, 120, 122, 128, 135, 150, 152, 158, 160, 165, 167, 189, 190-1, 196, 264-6

273

Douglas Hall (last governor of British Somaliland), 127
Dr. Hassan Hashi Fiqi, 194
Dr. Hussein Bood, 183, 194
Dr. Abdirahman Sh. Hassan (Isfiilito), 194
Dr. Phillip Johnston, 208, 211, 216
Dr. Neville, Chittick, 16, 22, 30
Dr. Yusuf Abdi, 8, 82
Dr. Abikar, 8
Dr. Baadiyow
Dr. Yeron of UNICEF
Dromedary camel, 54-5
Dhudub, 81
Dulmadoobe (40 KM, southeast of Burco) Battle, 92, 94-5, 99, 102-3

E

Ebyan Abdigir 253
Egyptian, 12, 16, 18-9, 22-3, 25-37, 49-51,54-5, 62, 69, 158, 219, 256
Eritrea, 18-19, 30, 46, 49, 63-4, 87, 114-5, 123, 147, 158, 168
Europe, 12-3, 16, 18, 37, 44-7, 50, 56, 5960, 64-6, 68, 70-1, 76-9, 83-7, 89-0, 94, 96, 103, 117, 123, 125-6, 135, 137, 160, 210, 217, 245, 247-8, 255-6
Eyl, 28, 57, 75, 80

F

Family Code of 1975, 154, 159
Farah Mohamed Jama "Farah Awl," 194
Farah Mohamud Mohamed, 8, 35, 73, 76, 78, 132, 167, 169, 177, 194
127, 161-22, 170
Former Finance Minister, Mohamed Sh. Osman, 194
France, 12-3, 16, 33-4, 48, 65-8, 70, 73, 84, 86-7, 100, 103, 115-6, 118, 123, 130, 140-1, 147, 155-6, 176, 214, 221, 254, 266-7
French Ambassador, Mr. Gueury, 155
Fergusson, James (author), 36, 40, 62, 68,76, 213

G

Galdogob, 127, 167, 255, 261
Galguduud, 167, 258
Gaalkacyo, 5, 15, 39, 53, 81, 115, 127, 130, 138, 150, 179, 183, 195, 200, 223, 227, 255-7, 261, 270
Galmudug Administration, 258, 270
Gallaaddi, 81, 98
Garbahaarrey, 127, 188
Garoowe, 127, 130, 133, 202, 255-6, 264
Gebiley, 127, 163, 174
Gedo, 180, 187-8, 195, 198
General Anthony Zinni, 239
General Alihashi, 194
General Galaal, 194
General Mohamed Abdi, 194
General Shaheen, 198, 203, 213-4
General Egerton, 80, 100
George Bush, 78, 205, 213-5, 220, 224, 226, 235
Geoffrey Archer (governor of British Somaliland 1913—1922), 47, 66, 69, 93, 98-9, 104, 106-8, 111
Gerald Hanley, 21, 35-6, 69, 76, 160, 176, 206, 212, 223, 260, 264-5
Germans (Germany), 33, 37, 47, 61-2, 130, 133, 146, 150
Gudabursi, 38, 56, 66, 87, 267
Gulf of Berbera (see Berbera)
Gulf of Tojorrah (also Tojorrah), 52, 65, 86-7

H

Habar-Gidir, 191, 195, 201-2
Habar-Awal, 65, 75, 87, 108, 267
Habar-Yoonis, 108, 193
Habar-Gerhajis, 66, 87, 267
Habar-Toljeclo, 66, 87, 108, 193
Hargeysa, 5, 11, 23, 39, 74, 105, 117, 127, 132, 136, 138, 158, 172-3, 191, 197, 200, 201, 211-2, 233, 255-2, 256, 261, 2635
Harold Macmillan (UK prime minister 1957 to 1963), 90, 127
Hassan Gouled Abtidoon, 199
Hatshepsut, 18-9, 24-5, 266
Hawiye or Hawiye clan, 5, 143, 194-5, 197-8, 202-3
Hiiraan region, 5, 41, 135-6, 222, 258
Hirshabeelle Administration, 258
Hitler, 114, 245
Hobyo, 12, 62-4, 139, 154, 183
Admiral Howe, 2
Huddur, 209, 215

274

Hussein Hassan, ex-director of Foreign affairs, 194
Hussein Kulmiye Afrah, 194, 199
Hussein Sheikh Ahmed Kaddare, 38

I
ICRC, 208
Ifat, Adal, 12, 31-2, 38, 45-8, 57, 266
Ilig (town near Eyl), 28, 75, 80, 91
India, Indian as a country and people
Indian rupees, 18, 23, 33, 43, 47, 49-2, 56-7, 59, 62, 71, 74, 80-2, 86-7, 98-101, 105, 111, 117-8, 125-9, 133, 164, 174, 202-3, 201, 212, 215, 223, 232, 253, 255, 261
Island or Rabshiga mountain, 126
Issa tribe, 142
Italian (Italy as a country and people),13, 34, 37,47, 49-50, 62-5, 69, 72, 79 83-5, 99, 114-122, 128, 130-1, 176, 181-2, 191-2, 210, 214, 225-6, 253
Italian Bishop, 176
Italian ambassador, 156, 234

J
Jalalaqsi, 217
Jama Ali Jama, 256-7, 262
Jama Qorshel, 38, 143
Jamal-adin, Sabra-adin, 48
Jubbaland Administration and Jubbaland,63, 115, 127, 258
Jardine, Douglas (author), 21, 28, 30, 68, 75-6, 81, 83, 96, 99-100, 106-7, 113, 213

K
Kaambooni, 18, 134
Kenya, 16, 18, 34, 43, 52, 63, 73-6, 112, 114-5,122-7, 133, 141-7, 156-8, 165, 188, 190, 194-7, 208, 211, 214, 220, 223, 252, 258, 263, 267-70
Khedive, 62, 69
King Amda Seyon, 46, 48
King Haile Selassie, 48, 68, 86, 93, 119, 122-3, 139, 141

L
Laas-Caanood, 38, 127, 145
Laas-geel, 11, 23
Laas Qoray, 12, 45, 72, 88
Larry Murray (Vice-admiral),247
Leelkase, 181, 183
Lieutenant-General Jean Boyle, 248

Leyden University, 53
Libyan Embassy, 165

M
Madagascar, 51, 112
Mahdi of Sudan, 62, 80
Majeerteen, 5, 61, 64-5, 110, 131, 139, 162-3, 183, 193-5
Malao (Present-day Berbera), 50
Maydh, 23, 126
Maldives Island, 51, 266
Marka (Somali city), 38, 46, 73, 85, 127, 129, 217, 269
Maryland, 164, 166, 169
Massachusetts, 166
Matt McKay (Corporal), 245
Mediterranean, 49, 51
Menelik, 66, 74, 79, 80, 85-7, 93, 120
Mengistu Haile Mariam, 156, 158, 167, 185, 188
Michael J. Durant, 21, 40, 252
Michael Mariano and his party, NUF, 119, 122, 134-5, 233
Michael Sox, 244, 246
Military Security Agency, 162-3, 165, 173, 182
Mobile military court (MMC), 165
Mobutu Sesse Seko, 220
Mogadishu Friday Massacre, 175
Mohamed Ali Hamud (author), 34, 42, 113, 158, 167, 188
Mohamed Abdi Hashi (Puntland president), 57, 256-7
Mohamed Aynanshe, 38, 150
Mohamed Farah Aideed, 41, 76, 149, 187, 191, 193, 195-9, 201-7, 215, 1217=8, 225, 228-239, 252, 268
Mohamed I. Egal, 37, 134-5, 138, 143-5, 192, 197, 235, 267
Mohamed Osman Omar (The author of Road to Zero), 14, 119, 123, 143, 145, 152, 164
Mohamed Sahnoun, 162, 168, 196-9, 203, 206-7, 214, 227-9
Mohamed Said Hersi (Morgan), 198, 205
Mohammedan Amir Abdullahi, 66, 103

275

Mohamed Urdoh, 142, 172, 178, 180
Mohamud Muse Hersi of (Puntland president), 256
Mombasa,34, 120
Moscow, 156
Mr. E. De Holte Castello, 120
Mr. Mackenzie, 241
Mr. Manuel Escudero, 120
Mr. McCorder (British officer against Daraawiish), 92
Ms. Campbell, Prime minister, 242
Mudug, 64-5, 115, 132, 150, 154, 163, 167, 183, 195, 258
Muslims, 32, 35, 44, 54-5, 70, 127, 221, 270

N

National university, 136, 138, 145, 154, 166
National Assembly, 120, 129, 136, 140, 143-4
National Geographic magazine/Society, 71, 76
National Radio, 133, 179, 229
National Security Courts (NSC), 150
National Security Service (NSS), 1450, 162
National United Front (NUF of Michael Mariano)), 122, 134
New York, 41 147, 155, 159, 181, 205, 207, 229-230, 237
Nigerian brigade (also Nigerian), 114-5, 222, 234
North Frontier District (provinces), 118
Northern Massacre, 172, 191, 196
Nova Sofala of Mozambique, 34

O

Obock (Obokh), 65, 87, 266
Ogadeen, 63, 66, 68, 74, 110, 118-120, 139-0, 146, 156-7, 192, 267
Oman (country), 12, 16, 23, 45, 48, 55, 59, 61-2, 71, 126
Omar Arteh Ghalib, 197
Organization of Islamic Conference, 254
Osman Ato (caato), 202-3
Osman Yusuf Keenadiid, 38-9 Ottawa, 242-3
Oxford Atlas, 16, 21, 56

P

Pakistanis (Pakistan), 206, 212-3, 220, 229-0. 243, 236, 261
Paleolithic period, 23
Pan-Africanism, 141, 179
Peacekeepers, 217, 225, 229-0, 232, 234-5, 240, 248, 268
Pennsylvania, 166
Persian Gulf, 34, 43, 164, 174
Pharaoh, 12, 18-20, 24-7, 29, 53, 266
Political Reconciliations, 198, 205, 207

Portuguese, 21, 32-4, 47-8, 58, 69
Potsdam, 13, 116
Prime Minister David Lloyd, 89
Professor Mohamed Ibrahim Abyan, 194
Professor Abdi I. Samatar, 87, 134, 136, 147
Professor Said S. Samatar, 83, 88, 96,99, 179, 222
Puntland state (Administration), 18, 136, 138, 254, 256-8, 262

Q

Qaw (Bender Zeida), 74

R

Rasna Warah (author), 143, 237, 240, 268
R. H. Smith (Chief British military administrator of Italian-Somaliland after WW2), 74, 117, 120
Rahanweyn, 5, 38, 202-3
Rakiya Omaar (Africa Watch, London), 184, 207
Rangers (American Rangers), 5, 38, 198, 202-3, 235-6, 260, 264, 268
Rav Castelli (Canadian defense staff), 242
RCMP (Royal Canadian Mounties Police), 248
Red Sea, 18, 24, 43, 51, 61, 64, 67, 69-0, 72, 89, 107, 121-2, 135, 152
Red-hatted (Red Berets or military police (Somali: Koofiyadcas)), 163
Regional Security Council (RSC), 165
Richard Burton, 20, 68-70, 75
Robert Godsend (an American diplomat), 234
Robert Oakley, 220

276

Royal Airforce fighter planes (British fighter planes), 93
Russia, 13, 116, 123, 147, 156-7, 161, 214, 218, 220, 253
Roy irons (Author of Churchill and the Mad Mullah), 75, 89-0, 93, 96, 99, 101, 112, 213
Rutgers University, 82, 179, 222

S

Saad-adin, 20, 46
Sammies (skinny Somalis), 228, 232-4
San Francisco, California, 116, 212
Saudi Arabia, 55, 71, 85, 164, 184, 197-8, 203, 233
Sayid Mohamed Abdulle Hassan (Mad Mullah, widely covered in the book, at least 2 chapters in various names)
Saylac, saylac islands, 12, 23, 31-3, 45-6, 54, 56-7, 59, 61-2, 65-6, 69-0, 72, 74-5, 86-6, 125-7, 154,174, 266-7
Serbia, 218
Serge Labbe (Canadian colonel), 234, 241
Seychelles, 207
Shidane Abukar Arone, 240
Ship Mary Ann, 60-1
Shire Jama Ahmed (current Somali Alphabet inventor), 38
Showa/Shaba, 12, 46-7
Smith Hempstone (US ambassador), 214
SNA of USC, 197, 204, 229-0, 233, 236
Somali Airlines, 8, 133
Somali Heritage Debate in Jibouti, 250
Somali National Congress (SNC (during the democratic administration)), 138
Somali National Democratic Union (SNDU, formed in NY 1991), 181
Somali National Front (Mareexaan (SNF)), 197
Somali National League (SNL, in the north formed 1936)), 13, 38, 116, 122, 134, 138
Somali National Movement (SNM (formed in London, 1982)), 165, 168-9, 171-5, 180-2, 189, 192-201
Somali Salvation Front (SSF), 162-3, 165
Somali national museum, 22
Somali Youth Club (SYC), 37, 116

South African battalion see south Africa
South West Administration, 258
Soviet advisers (Soviet Union, soviets), 118-8, 149, 152-3, 157-8, 161, 212, 267
Somali Sea, 17-8, 27, 43, 51, 57, 81, 125, 127
Spain, 18, 47-8, 70
Stadium Massacre, 182   Stafford (British Brigadier general, the head of British delegation of the UN in Mogadishu in 1948), 117, 120
South African (battalion) and Rhodesian fighter planes (hunter planes), 72-3
Suad (Sucaad Odawa), 250
Sudan, 18-9, 49, 55, 62, 80, 86-7, 92, 114-5, 129, 164, 177, 215, 220, 254
Suez Canal, 74, 86, 92
Sultan (king) Osman Mohamoud, 12, 64 67
Sultan Yusuf Ali, 12, 62-5, 67
Sultan Ali Yusuf, 63-5
Supreme Revolutionary Council (SRC), 14, 38, 149, 156, 227

T

Taffeta (ship taffeta), 64   Tanzania, 21, 34-5
The Cape of Spices (Cape of Guardafui, Aromatifera corner, Raas Casayr), 17, 19, 22-3, 49-52, 57, 62, 69, 81, 115, 127, 266
The Tree-of-bad-Counsel, 85, 96, 111
Tigre, 168
Thomas Montgomery (American general), 229, 232
Thomas Fisher (American general), 111
Treaty of Peace with Italy (WORLD WAR TWO outcome), 121
Turkish Lieutenant General Ceric Bir, 232
Turks (turkey), 16, 33, 49, 61-2, 69, 92

U

U.S. Centers for Disease Control and Prevention, 210
Uganda, 176, 215,267
UNICEF, 208-210, 215, 262-3
United Arab Emirates, 71, 203
United Somali Congress (USC), 157, 179,

181, 185-6, 191-204, 234
UNOSOM, 204, 212, 228-237

V

Videotapes CBC (Canadian Broadcasting Corporation), 243, 245, 249
Videotapes (Mogadishu fight), 236
Vietnam, Saigon, 219-0, 232   Villa Somalia, 183, 189, 238

W

Walwaal, 81
Walloweyn town, 132, 269
Warsangeli, 12, 45-6, 57, 66, 72, 87, 134, 267
Warsheekh, 12, 65, 67
Western Somali Liberation Front (WSLF), 139, 156-7, 161
William Stroyan (British Explorer and officer killed in Berbera in April, 1855), 61, 70, 267
Wisil-Colguula Massacre, 183, 195
World War Two,13-4, 35, 69, 86,114-8, 128-9, 132, 146, 212, 223

X

Xaaji Cali Ciise (our slaves (other Somalis left)), 73
xabbadi-keentay (bullet-brought, 174
Xabbadi-sugtay (bullet waited), 174, 190
Xamar see Mogadishu   Xiis (His), 23
Xaafuun (Hafun), 23, 43, 51, 115, 134

Y

Yemen,18, 23, 27, 52, 55, 67, 68-9, 71, 156, 159, 161, 174
Yugoslavia, 208, 218

Z

Zambia, 61
Zanzibar, 12, 47-8, 64-5, 67, 86, 91, 267

Printed in Great Britain
by Amazon